Web Publishing
with Acrobat/PDF

Springer
Berlin
Heidelberg
New York
Barcelona
Budapest
Hong Kong
London
Milan
Paris
Santa Clara
Singapore
Tokyo

Thomas Merz

Web Publishing with Acrobat/PDF

With 92 Figures and a CD-ROM

 Springer

Thomas Merz
Tal 40
80331 München
Germany

Title of the Original German Edition:
Mit Acrobat ins World Wide Web
© Thomas Merz Verlag 1997

CIP-Data applied for

Die Deutsche Bibliothek – CIP-Einheitsaufnahme
Web Publishing with Acrobat, PDF / Thomas Merz. – Berlin ; Heidelberg ; New
York ; Barcelona ; Budapest ; Hong Kong ; London ; Milan ; Paris ; Santa Clara;
Singapore ; Tokyo : Springer.
Einheitssacht.: Mit Acrobat ins World Wide Web<dt>

Buch. – 1998
CD-ROM. – 1998

ISBN 3-540-63762-1 Springer-Verlag Berlin Heidelberg New York

Typesetting: Camera ready by author
Cover design and illustrations: Alessio Leonardi, leonardi.wollein, Berlin
Translated from German by Richard Hunt, Tadcaster, UK, and the author
SPIN 10726488 Printed on acid-free paper   33/3012 – 5 4 3 2 1

The Websurfer's Point of View

The Publisher's Point of View

The Webmaster's Point of View

Preface

What do the following organizations have in common: the IRS, IBM, anti-McDonalds protestors, the FBI, the Los Angeles Times, and the Institute for Crystal Growth? Right – they all publish Acrobat documents on the Internet. While working on this book, from time to time I heard remarks along the lines of "Acrobat on the Web – what's so special about it?" Naturally, it's not difficult to offer Adobe Acrobat PDF files on a Web server alongside HTML, text and multimedia files. There are many ways of integrating Acrobat with the World Wide Web, and that is what this book shows you how to do.

But there's more to the topic. In many areas it is very important whether the documents require extensive editing after conversion to PDF format, or whether hypertext elements, such as links, can be built in before the conversion is done. The pdfmark operator plays an important role here. This operator is explained, for the first time and with plenty of examples, in this book – without requiring an extensive programming background.

Another underestimated aspect of Acrobat is the extensive set of form features which appeared in Acrobat 3.0. Adobe put another layer of flexibility and usability into the form functions by integrating the JavaScript programming language in Acrobat. This hot new feature offers plenty of opportunities for streamlining Acrobat usage on the corporate intranet or the worldwide Internet.

Readership and structure of the book

The book spans a wide arc, and attempts to cover all current Web technologies which play a role in the integration of Acrobat. It's clear that I can't cover all languages and interfaces – CGI, JavaScript, VBScript, Active Server Pages, to name just a few – comprehensively. In these sections, the emphasis is on showing the beginner working examples and inspiring the experienced developer to further programming.

To make the material more accessible, the book is divided into three parts, each of which looks at the theme of "Acrobat and the Web" from a different perspective, assuming different levels of prior knowledge. I hope that this way of dividing the book, not according to technical or thematic criteria, but according to the reader's requirements, will make it easier to use the book.

The first part gives a Web surfer's view of PDF and HTML, compares the document formats, without going into details, and describes the combination of both formats.

The second part is concerned with generating PDF documents from a publisher's point of view. By "publisher" we mean anyone who prepares documents for publication – whether as an author, translator, technical editor, or graphics designer. Basic knowledge of modern DTP techniques is assumed, and the reader ought to have seen a Web browser more than once. Acrobat's basic functions are explained briefly, but comprehensively. The excursions into script programming will motivate some readers to find out more, and confirm others' view that programming is not much fun for them.

The third part tackles the theme from the perspective of the Webmaster, the person who is responsible for the operation of the Web server. Some topics from the second part are picked up again in more detail. The CGI interface, Active Server Pages implemenation, and C and script programming assume more prior knowledge, but should not be daunting for a Webmaster or Webmistress. It can also be useful for publishers to acquire at least an overview of the way things interact on the server.

Helper applications

Many heartfelt thanks to all the people who helped in one way or another during the writing of this book: Katja Karsunke always knows how to do things – from getting rid of typesetting errors to fixing broken ISDN installations, from looking after the plants on the balcony to software installation. Alessio Leonardi, who in spite of permanent overwork never lost patience and was always ready to listen to me, gets my thanks for his friendly cooperation (and for assistance on the topics of wine and pasta). Margrit Müller not only let me benefit from her production experience but is also a good person to talk with about important things like diving or travel.

My selfless and faithful proof readers, who never quit despite ridiculous deadlines, are responsible to a large degree for the quality of this book. The original German version was proofread by the following people: Detlev Droege (University of Koblenz), who knows the PDF format like the back of his hand; Alexander Gabriel, whose e-mailed corrections arrived with astonishing rapidity; Dieter Gust (Institute for Technical Literature, Munich), who despite tiring struggles with technical stuff (and the customers) always found time for specialist discussions; Michael Heinzel, who was not to be put off reading proofs, even in Cinqueterre; Tobias Höllrich (Adobe Systems, San Jose), who even carried on during his vacation at Lake Tahoe (sorry, Candice!); Peter Körner (Adobe Systems, Munich) for his personal involvement and support; Thomas Müller (Düsseldorf), who had to be content with old fashioned paper printouts; Frank Schumacher, the patent folder from Berlin, who despite diverse setbacks fought mightily with the material; Florian Süßl (CitySatz & Nagel, Berlin), whose attention had to be divided between his small daughter and the galley proofs.

Since the Web is evolving with astonishing speed, I had to rewrite and update several sections of the book for the English edition although it appeared only a few months after the German edition. Several people have helped in various ways to improve the text – each of them in a unique way. Nelson H. F. Beebe had a hard time explaining, among many other things, the finer details of the English language. He raised the level of mathematical rigor of the text to what I wanted, but failed to produce in a non-native language. D. P. Story initiated many fruitful discussions and edited all chapters with accuracy. Sebastian Rahtz contributed important corrections and new material, although he proofread the text in India despite being sick at the time. Mark DeVries and his family nearly missed the opening ceremonies of the Winter Olympics due to pdfmarks and related stuff. And no, don't call it nit-picking – your comments definitely improved the quality of the book!

Thomas Merz

The Websurfer's Point of View

1 HTML and PDF

Hypertext Markup Language (HTML) and Portable Document Format (PDF) are presentation formats: they describe documents which usually only need to be read and not changed or edited. This might seem rather strange for a file format, but corresponds to the age-old publishing model: a newspaper reader does not usually need to be able to alter the contents of his favorite paper. Publishing, the distribution of information to a small or large circle of readers is, for the most part, a one-way street. This does not exclude the possibility of interactive applications and the collaborative creation or editing of documents, but the operator of a Web site, not its readers or users, is the one responsible for its contents.

HTML and PDF are very different in the methods they use to present documents and in the different possibilities they offer when creating a publication. Before going into the practical use of the formats, here is a brief overview of the properties of HTML and PDF.

1.1 What is HTML?

HTML is a markup language for structuring documents. It contains powerful hypertext elements – digital added value in the form of links and other useful aids which are not possible on paper – and limited layout control. This dry description contains a fact which many people have ignored in the recent Web hype: HTML does not describe the layout of a document – that is, the appearance and positioning of the elements – but their arrangement into semantic units like heading, paragraph or listing. Additionally, there are hypertext elements (links), interactive elements like forms, and graphic enrichment using embedded pictures.

It is popularly believed that it is not possible today to build an attractive Web site using just these elements – users expect the same layout and typographical and multimedia bells and whistles as in local use. Because of this, HTML continually has new extensions tacked on which take it further away from its original concept, document content description, and tries, often using strange tricks, to give the document author more control over the visual appearance. However, by doing this one forgets that one of HTML's great advantages is that each browser can adapt the on-screen representation to the available resources. For example, screen size can vary from 13 inches, for a Notebook user, to as large as 21 inches. Anyone arguing that hardware is continually improving forgets that the Web is always expanding to new areas as well – only think of a mobile phone with its built-in Web browser. Such a device certainly doesn't support a screen resolution of 1024 x 768 pixels!

HTML has its roots in the powerful markup language SGML. Its basic idea is separation of structural and layout description. This means that the structure can be retained even if the document is printed or displayed under different conditions. In a similar manner, an HTML document should be able to get its message over when viewed with any browser on any computer platform. Designers who develop their HTML pages so that they only look good with one particular browser should think about whether they would design a magazine or poster so that it looked fantastic for 80% of readers, but just looked a mess to the rest.

The commercialization of the Web and the Internet's open culture brought with it a ruthless battle between manufacturers over formats and standards. Because of the competitive situation there is no unified HTML, but a series of extensions, add-ons, and manufacturer-specific features which build on the quasi-standard HTML 2.0 (version 3.2 is not fully supported by all browsers). While these extra functions may be very good and have their uses, they do hinder the unity and universal usability of Web documents. Although the World Wide Web Consortium (W3C) has been able to establish itself as a competent and respected body representing manufacturers and other interested parties, there is no standard to which all browser manufacturers must adhere. Deviations from the new HTML 4.0 version are already visible – think of the confusion surrounding dynamic HTML, layer technology, and the incompatible implementations of Cascading Style Sheets (CSS).

Without any doubt, one of HTML's big pluses is its simplicity. Documents consist of text and simple tags and can be created with any text editor. It is easier to use one of the widely available HTML editors which provide easy access to the various HTML functions, inserting the necessary tags automatically. Files created like this can be modified later by hand to insert special tags not supported by the editor.

When converting existing documents, the relationship to SGML and the importance of structure becomes clear: the more structured the document, the better the conversion to HTML goes. As the majority of the current generation of text and DTP programs don't generate structural information, one usually has to use workarounds involving paragraph styles or similar elements.

Cascading Style Sheets (CSS) are an attempt, in newer versions of HTML, to master its inadequate layout controls. However, in accordance with the basic philosophy of HTML, not only does the author of a document have the possibility of laying down formatting guidelines, but the user can define style sheets for his own requirements. This means that the final appearance of the document is not controlled by the originator, and in addition the layout cannot be controlled by CSS to the same extent as a designer is accustomed to expect from modern DTP software.

Regarding the further development of HTML, it is worthwhile – apart from the new versions with extra tags, which the Web community will certainly busy itself with extensively – to take a look at the new Extensible Markup Language (XML). This is a further derivative of SGML. Unlike HTML, which is already overloaded, XML is not restricted to one area of use, but can be expanded in a flexible manner and be adapted to new areas. HTML is one application of XML, ensuring compatibility. With XML, new functionality can be included which HTML could not previously cope with or which were at the limits of its capabilities. For example, there are XML implementations for chemical and mathematical equations. Unlike present browsers, no new implementations or extra plugins are required, but only a description (Document Type Definition, DTD) of the relevant application. XML also provides a solution for the problem that in many situations HTML data can not be re-used without further processing. For example, think of extracts from a database which HTML can only represent as text and not as a collection of fields with different data types.

If you are getting the impression that I am somewhat critical of the current route of HTML development, then you are right. A document format with many dialects which forces the designer to use transparent GIF images of single pixel width for formatting, or to squash text into tables to bring a semblance of order to the screen, has definitely exhausted its uses.

This does not mean that HTML is useless, however, or will shortly be replaced by a new format. HTML documents are excellent for the purpose for which they were designed. HTML, no matter how many extensions there are, will never be fully satisfactory for uses where the emphasis is on layout and not on structure.

1.2 What is PDF?

PDF (Portable Document Format) is a file format for saving documents which are graphically and typographically complex. PDF ensures that layout will be preserved both on screen and in print. All layout-related properties are a fixed component of a PDF file and do not allow any variation in its interpretation – the appearance of a PDF document is completely fixed.

PDF also has its roots in an older and very powerful predecessor, namely the PostScript page description language. Postscript – a cornerstone of the DTP era – not only deals with text, graphics, and pictures, it is also a powerful programming language. PDF uses the page description elements from PostScript (the so-called imaging model), but for the sake of simplicity does not use the programming constructs (for example, conditionals and loops). In addition, PDF uses many hypertext functions and interactive elements to enrich the document.

The powerful functionality of PDF takes its toll in the form of a complicated file format. The structure and content of a PDF file is rather opaque:

there are direct and indirect objects, tables with file positions, compression, and encryption. In order to read and understand a PDF file, you need to have programming experience, which is not necessary for reading HTML files. Creating a nontrivial PDF file by hand in a text editor is an exercise which will defeat even an experienced programmer – PDF can only really be created using software.

Such software is available from Adobe Systems and increasingly from other manufacturers. Adobe is the originator of PostScript and PDF, and is also the guardian of both standards. In the case of PDF, this word is really deserved as there are no variants or manufacturer-specific dialects. Since Adobe introduced Acrobat in 1993 with PDF 1.0, there have only been two major extensions of the file format to the current version, PDF 1.2, the basis of Acrobat 3.0.

Although some people regard file formats determined by a single manufacturer very skeptically, this situation has its advantages. First, with Acrobat, Adobe's developers showed that they could both develop and successfully bring to market a powerful format without locking out competitors. The widespread distribution and acceptance of Adobe applications in the graphics trade made it easier to gain acceptance for the new format, as it was made easy for this important group of users to adopt the new product. Free distribution of the viewer program Acrobat Reader via the Internet was also important (Adobe announced in summer 1997 that over 20 million copies of Acrobat Reader had been downloaded from their Web site). The current adoption of Acrobat by the printing industry and its integration into prepress, with large amounts of investment involved, is also a factor in favor of PDF's long-term stability and secure position.

To make it easier to use PDF with existing documents, Adobe offers two simple methods of creating PDF files. PDF documents can be created either on a Mac or in Windows by using the special PDF Writer printer driver (although this places some quality limitations on the output). If higher quality is required, or on other operating systems (such as Unix), Acrobat Distiller converts PostScript to PDF. As just about any major software package is capable of producing PostScript output, this program gives the potential for creating PDF to a huge number of applications.

Unlike a PostScript or HTML file, a PDF file is always self-contained, that is it contains all of the fonts, images, and other components.[1] A single file can contain a document of any length without the user having to worry about needing other files.

During PDF's development, Adobe attempted to address the known weaknesses in PostScript. Difficulties in processing PostScript have been handled by using a clever file structure, and the tendency for files to grow

---

1. Except for the base fonts which are not included since they are part of each Acrobat installation.

very large has been tamed with efficient organization of data and various built-in compression schemes.

Anyone creating a document using PDF can always be sure that it will appear correctly to the reader. Adobe has invested a lot in technology to ensure this, even if the target computer's configuration is unknown or not really adequate. For example, missing fonts are reconstructed using Multiple Master technology, and colors are matched to the monitor in use. Colors are matched not only on screen, but are also guaranteed for printing. PDF is the ideal format for sharing documents which need to be printed in high quality between users. This is one area where PDF's relationship to PostScript is a big plus.

On the other hand, the fact that the layout is fixed does mean that PDF documents can not be adapted flexibly for different media. PDF documents are optimized either for printing or for viewing on screen – dynamic adaptation for different media (as with HTML) is not possible. The only way to get round this problem is to prepare several versions of the document, which means much more effort for the document's originator.

PDF's biggest advantage is also its biggest drawback: it is purely layout-oriented and is not concerned with the text and overall structure of a document. The basic unit of a PDF document is the page. It can contain text, graphic and hypertext elements. The text is not saved as structural objects like paragraphs or headings, but, as in PostScript, in layout-related elements: as characters, words, or lines. This makes it much more difficult to modify or edit the text later on, as the structural information can not easily be recreated.

1.3 Comparison of HTML and PDF

It can be seen from the preceding short descriptions of both formats that HTML and PDF have strongly complementary properties. The totally differing predecessors of HTML and PDF – SGML and PostScript – with their strict emphasis on structure or layout give both HTML and PDF their own strengths and weaknesses. Since in the real world it can not be disputed that both meaningful, structured content and pleasing appearance are important, it is not surprising that both formats are drawing closer together. The HTML community is always adding new tags, which are supposed to add new layout controls. On the other hand, PDF already contains the same hypertext and form functions as HTML, but is still not capable of exporting a table from a document without creating a horrid mess. Adobe has been promising the integration of SGML into PDF for years. However, to do this, SGML-capable authoring programs, which support and stick to the definition of document structure, have to become established.

Table 1.1 contains a list of characteristics which allow an easy comparison of HTML and PDF taking into account various criteria which are important in the real world. I am well aware of the risks involved in such a simplistic comparison. There is much room for discussion in every single entry, depending on the intended use and the respective conditions of deployment.

In making this comparison (as in the whole book) it's not my intention to push PDF as a substitute for HTML – that would be a pointless exercise. However, the comparisons and examples ought to make it obvious that the two formats, with their complementary characteristics, supplement each other very well. Why should one try to adapt a format with extra functions for which it is not suitable? It makes more sense to examine the goals being set, the existing framework and the possibilities offered by existing formats. With respect to file size, it is often stated that PDF files are much larger than HTML documents. PDF's champions point out examples which contradict this. However, this can be like comparing apples and oranges – by choosing the test files carefully, either format's superiority can be "proved". It is true that PDF files are larger, but they usually have a complicated layout. PDF files, unlike HTML files, also compress text, but the size advantage can easily be lost because of font embedding.

Table 1.1. Comparison of HTML and PDF

Characteristic	HTML	PDF
Responsibility for format	W3 Consortium and manufacturers	Adobe
Standardization	many variants	unified standard
Viewers for different operating systems	free and commercial browsers	Adobe Acrobat Reader (distributed freely)
Software for creating documents	free and commercial tools	commercial tools (mostly); some free tools
Conversion of existing documents	time-consuming	easy using PostScript
Editing/altering documents	simple, using text or HTML editors	Acrobat (limited) or add-on programs
Information about a document	meta tags	document info fields
Creation of new documents (without using conversion routines)	with HTML authoring programs	hardly possible
Extension possibilities	plugins	plugins
Document structure	very good	poor
Searchability	good	OK
Search engines	excellent	excellent
Hypertext functions	excellent	excellent
Output quality	poor	very high
Who determines the appearance of the document?	user	author

Table 1.1. Comparison of HTML and PDF (continued)

Characteristic	HTML	PDF
Layout adapts itself to the viewing conditions	yes	no
Document is contained in one file	no (graphics are separate)	yes (with the exception of movie files)
Suitability for on-screen viewing	very high	high, if formatted correctly
Suitability for printing	low	high, if formatted correctly
Layout and typography	poor	very good
File format	simple tags	complicated
Dynamic generation on the server	easy	difficult
File size	small	medium to large
Form functions	good	very good

2 PDF in the Browser

2.1 Web Browsers and Acrobat

Every Web Browser can handle several file formats. Most browsers designed for Graphical User Interfaces (GUIs) can display HTML, text, GIF, and JPEG files in the program window. File formats which the browser does not "understand" itself can be coped with if the user configures an external program. The browser starts these programs as required and feeds them the data from the server. The browser and the server negotiate the type of data using the MIME protocol. MIME stands for "Multipurpose Internet Mail Extensions" and is a classification scheme for a multitude of file formats. When the server sends a particular MIME classification along with a requested file, the browser can do one of several things:

- ▶ Use its own program code to process the data and display the file in its program window.
- ▶ Start an external program configured for that MIME type which processes the data and displays the result.
- ▶ If a browser plugin is registered for that MIME type, the plugin is used to process the data.
- ▶ If the browser does not recognize the MIME type at all, the user can save the file to disk for later use.

Apart from the first one, in principle these are the options for PDF files. While earlier versions of Acrobat Reader could only be configured as a helper application, Adobe Acrobat 3.0 can be integrated much more closely with several Web browsers. From the user's point of view, the integration is virtually seamless. The browser starts Acrobat Reader as an external program, but displays the PDF file in the browser window. Before describing how this works with the most important browsers, I will examine how to configure Acrobat as a helper application. However, you should note that using this method with one of the current browsers is not recommended, but is included here for the sake of completeness. In-line display of PDFs, which is covered further on, is more important.

Acrobat as an external viewer for the browser.   Every Web browser can be configured to differentiate between MIME types and the helper applications to use. In a Windows or Mac browser the MIME configuration options can usually be found under the heading of "Helper Applications" in the settings or options menu. Under Unix, MIME types are defined in a *.mime.types* configuration file. The relevant applications have to be entered in the *.mailcap* file. The MIME type for PDF files is:

```
application/pdf
```

The exact name of the relevant application (Acrobat Reader or Exchange) is platform dependent. For example, under Windows the entry for Reader is:

C:\acrobat3\reader\acroread.exe

(The installation directory might have to be changed to match the particular machine.)

PDF files in the browser window. The more user-friendly technique displays PDF files in the browser's own window and integrates HTML and PDF. Depending on the browser in use, a plugin module (Netscape Navigator and compatible browsers) or an ActiveX Control (Microsoft Internet Explorer) has to be installed. This extension module interfaces between the browser and Acrobat. The browser is responsible for communicating with the server, while the plugin handles the PDF files which have been received. The plugin does not actually process the files itself, but passes them to Acrobat Reader, which in turn displays them in the browser window (see Figure 2.1). This means that whenever a PDF file is displayed in the browser, both programs have to be running and therefore there must be enough RAM to allow the Web browser and Acrobat to run at the same time.

When PDF files are displayed in the browser window, Acrobat is responsible for the window's content, but the menu entries remain those of the browser. This means that the user can not access Acrobat's menu functions. To compensate for this, the Acrobat toolbar (with navigation functions) appears above the document.

It is easier to install the browser extension if the browser is installed before Acrobat. Under Windows or on the Mac, Acrobat's installation routine detects which browser is installed and carries out the necessary steps during setup. However, even if Acrobat was installed before the browser, it is not much trouble to enable Acrobat support (see below).

Acrobat support for Netscape Navigator. Navigator has a plugin interface, used by Adobe, which allows extensive extra functionality to be added. The Navigator plugin for processing PDF files consists of a single file which simply has to be copied to Navigator's plugins directory. When the browser is restarted, PDF support is then available. After successfully installing Acrobat Reader or Exchange, proceed as follows (note that in most situations the Acrobat installer will take care of the plugin installation if the browser already is installed):

► Under Windows 95 or NT, copy the file *nppdf32.dll* (or *nppdf16.dll* for Windows 3.x) from the *browser* subdirectory of the Acrobat directory to the Netscape *plugins* subdirectory.
► On the Mac, copy the file *PDFViewer* from the *Web Browser Plug-in* subfolder of the Acrobat folder to Netscape's *Plug-ins* subfolder.

Fig. 2.1. Netscape Navigator displaying a PDF file in the browser window

▸ Under Unix, the Acrobat *Browsers* subdirectory contains the dynamic library for the plugin. For example, under Linux it is called *nppdf.so*. Copy this file into the Netscape *plugins* subdirectory (something like */usr/local/lib/netscape/plugins*). You can use the *netscape* shell script to start the browser, but this is not a requirement. After starting the browser, the plugin registers itself in the *plugin-list* in the user's HOME directory's *.netscape* directory, associated with the MIME type for PDF.

Follow the procedure above for browsers which are fully compatible with the Netscape plugin interface.

To check whether the plugin is correctly installed and working, enter the pseudo-URL *about:plugins*. Navigator will display a list of installed plugins and their associated MIME types.

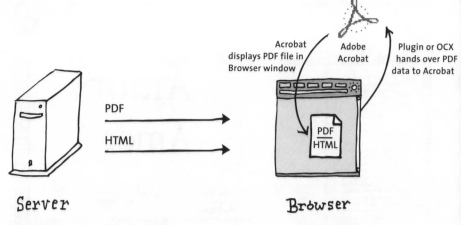

Fig. 2.2. The plugin or ActiveX Control interfaces between Acrobat and the browser

Acrobat support for Microsoft Internet Explorer.   Internet Explorer for Windows not only supports the Navigator plugin interface, but also allows the integration of ActiveX controls. The ActiveX interface has far reaching effects that I will go into below. For now, a few words about installing Acrobat support.

Acrobat Reader or Exchange (version 3.0 or above) contain not only a Netscape plugin, but also a corresponding ActiveX control. If Internet Explorer is already installed, the PDF module is automatically copied to the right browser directory during Acrobat setup. Note that Internet Explorer 4.0 and above requires a newer version of the PDF OCX control than the one contained on the Acrobat 3.01 CD-ROM. If you want to use IE 4, proceed as follows:

▶ Download the Acrobat OCX control from the following URL:

```
http://www.adobe.com/prodindex/acrobat/ocxreader.html
```

and install it on your machine. The OCX is included on the accompanying CD-ROM to save you download time. The new version of the OCX control is necessary for Explorer 4 and fixes a couple of bugs in the older versions. For example, search highlighting and form posting to a secure Web site now works.

▶ In case you have to re-install Internet Explorer: copy the file called *pdf41.ocx* (or other version number) from the *ActiveX* subdirectory of the Acrobat Exchange directory to the Internet Explorer plugin subdirectory, for example

```
\Program Files\Plus!\Microsoft Internet\Plugins
```

After restarting Internet Explorer, PDF functionality should be available. You can easily check this by opening a PDF file in the browser by using Drag & Drop.

Note that – although ActiveX support for the Mac is in the works – the Macintosh version of Internet Explorer 4 uses the Netscape-compatible plugin (instead of an ActiveX control) for PDF support.

ActiveX. ActiveX technology is based on the Windows techniques of OLE (Object Linking and Embedding) and COM (Component Object Model) and for that reason is well integrated with the Windows operating system. So far, it is only available for Windows, although ActiveX ports for other operating systems have been announced. ActiveX is not a programming language, but an interface specification for program modules which can be written in your favorite language – such as C, C++, Visual Basic, or Java.

Unlike Java applets, ActiveX controls (OCX modules) have full access to the Windows system. On one hand this means that, potentially, a huge number of tasks can be accomplished with ActiveX. On the other hand, this removes all protection to attacks from the Internet from the user's system. An OCX module can perform all kinds of malicious acts on the client machine from deleting files to snooping on confidential data. ActiveX does support digital signatures (security certificates) which are meant to ensure that a module does not get modified on the way from the originator to the user. As software manufacturers – and malicious hackers – can sign their own certificates, this does not really offer any effective protection.

One of the most useful properties of ActiveX further increases the security risk: if an HTML page contains a reference to an ActiveX module which is not installed on the client computer, the browser can download it from the Internet without further user intervention (the relevant URL is already on the HTML page). This gives an attacker the opportunity to attract unwitting Web surfers to a harmless looking Web site and load malicious ActiveX modules from that site. The only effective way of protecting yourself is to completely disable the downloading of OCX controls or running ActiveX modules in Internet Explorer's basic settings. Of course, this also shuts out useful applications. As Windows keeps OCX modules in their own cache area, deleting a module is no guarantee that it has been deactivated.

As ActiveX can currently only be used on Windows, its platform dependence is a great restriction for developers. Even the promised ports to other platforms will be of no use if, for example, no software manufacturer develops ActiveX modules for the Mac.

Each ActiveX module has its own unique identifier, the Class ID. When it is installed or started, an OCX registers itself, using this ID, in the Windows registry. This also plays a role when creating HTML pages with integrated PDF documents (see Section 8.2).

Internet Explorer quirks which affect Acrobat.   There are a couple of issues peculiar to Microsoft Internet Explorer which may affect your PDF experience on the Web. First, there are some configuration settings which prevent PDF viewing in the Browser. If you turn on the content advisor (via "View", "Internet Options", "Content" tab, "Content Advisor") Internet Explorer doesn't know about the rating of PDF files and consequently doesn't display them. Similarly, if you configure high security mode (via "View", "Internet Options", "Security" tab, "Security level high"), launching ActiveX controls – including the Acrobat control – is considered insecure and you cannot view PDF files in the browser (with the exception of local files dropped on the browser window).

Strangely enough, "File", "Open..." always displays the PDF in an external window instead of in the main browser window – even if downloaded PDFs are correctly displayed in the browser window. I am not aware of any workaround for this behaviour.

Conversely, you may occasionally want to disable in-line viewing of PDF files in the browser window and launch Acrobat as an external helper application instead. Since the Acrobat OCX control installs itself rather deep in the system, it may be hard to get rid of it once the Acrobat installer touched the registry. Here's the correct procedure for deinstalling the Acrobat OCX:

► Choose "Start", "Run..." and type the following command, changing the path name to the directory where your OCX control lives:

```
regsvr32 -u C:\Acrobat3\Exchange\ActiveX\pdf42.ocx
```

► Repeat the previous step for all *pdf*.ocx* files which may exist on your machine.
► Delete all *pdf*.ocx* and *pdf.tlb* files from your machine. Do not simply rename or move the files since they may still be accessible if you do so.

2.2 Optimized PDF and Page-at-a-Time Download

An important innovation in Acrobat 3.0 is page-at-a-time download, possible when using optimized PDF files. Page-at-a-time download makes it possible for the Web surfer to read the first page of a document while the rest of the document is downloaded in the background. This way, page-at-a-time download allows to use PDF files satisfactorily if bandwidth is limited. Further discussions of page-at-a-time download can be found in two other places: in Section 4.3 we will deal with creating optimized PDFs, and in Section 9.2 we will discuss the requirements on the Web server.

The structure of normal PDF files is not really suitable for use on the Web, as the browser has to load the whole PDF file so that it can read impor-

Fig. 2.3.
Rendering of a PDF page in the browser window: first the text appears, then images and embedded fonts, and finally the thumbnails

tant data at the end of the file. This means that the user has to wait for the whole file to be downloaded before viewing just one page. With HTML pages, a Web browser may display the start of the document straight away and loads the rest while the user is already reading. For GIF and JPEG files, there are methods of first showing a picture in coarse and then progressively finer detail (known as "interlaced GIF" or "progressive JPEG").

Optimized PDF files make similar advantages available for PDF files. Page-at-a-time downloading, in combination with a suitable Web server, makes it possible to access individual pages from a PDF file. While the user looks at the first page, the browser is downloading the rest in the background. Clever choice of the order in which objects are downloaded, along with progressive rendering (building up the page step by step) dramatically speed up PDF display. Rendering a PDF page in a Web browser takes place in several stages (see Figure 2.3):

- ► Firstly, hypertext elements of all sorts are activated, but their content is not shown. This means, for example, that links are already clickable.
- ► Next, the content of the page (text and line art) is built up: at this stage bitmap pictures are left out. Text which requires embedded fonts is initially displayed with a substitute font, so as not to have to wait until the font data arrives.
- ► After this, the hypertext elements are shown correctly.
- ► As soon as the data for the missing bitmap pictures is available, they appear on screen.
- ► To show the text as designed, the text which is already visible is then redrawn using the embedded fonts which are now available.
- ► Finally (if they are available and turned on) the thumbnails appear.

Psychologically, this procedure makes the loading process appear smoother: if the user can already read the first page he or she is less likely to notice that the pictures and fonts are still missing than if sitting in front of a blank screen doing nothing except watch a progress bar. Initially displaying the text in a substitute font (font blitting) has a similar effect: even if the proper font is still missing, the page is already legible.

One of the options in Acrobat Reader or Exchange's general preferences is important in connection with page-at-a-time downloading (choose "File", "Preferences", "General...", see Figure 2.4). The option "Allow Background Download of Entire File" determines whether the download stops when the first page is visible or whether the rest of the file continues to download while the user looks at the first page. Enabling this option only has an effect when browsing the Web and makes sense if the user wants the whole file on his or her computer.

This option also has an effect on the way that the browser caches files. If background downloading is enabled, the browser stores the PDF files in its cache and uses the copy in the cache, rather than downloading a new copy when the same file is accessed. In addition, when the browser's "Back" but-

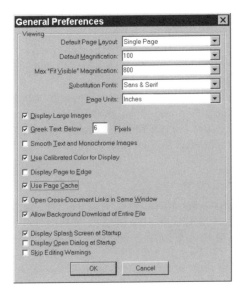

General Preferences

Viewing

Default Page Layout: Single Page

Default Magnification: 100

Max "Fit Visible" Magnification: 800

Substitution Fonts: Sans & Serif

Page Units: Inches

☑ Display Large Images

☑ Greek Text Below   6   Pixels

☐ Smooth Text and Monochrome Images

☑ Use Calibrated Color for Display

☐ Display Page to Edge

☑ Use Page Cache

☑ Open Cross-Document Links in Same Window

☑ Allow Background Download of Entire File

☑ Display Splash Screen at Startup

☐ Display Open Dialog at Startup

☐ Skip Editing Warnings

[OK]   [Cancel]

Fig. 2.4.
Acrobat General Preferences

ton is clicked on, the previously displayed page of the PDF file from the cache is used. If this option is not enabled, clicking on "Back" leads to the first page.

2.3 Using PDFs in the Browser

Acrobat Functions in the browser.   As previously mentioned, when a PDF file is loaded into the browser, controls from both Acrobat and the browser are available: Navigator or Internet Explorer supply the menu bar and (if configured to do so) additional toolbars; Acrobat's own toolbar appears above the top edge of the document. Acrobat 3.01 has, compared to Acrobat 3.0, additional buttons for the important functions "Select Text", "Copy", "Search", and "Repeat Search". A further feature introduced with Acrobat 3.01 is navigation in PDF documents using the keyboard. The arrow keys, Page Up and Page Down keys, etc., now work exactly the same in the browser as they do in Acrobat (refer to your Acrobat documentation). As the author of a document can specify whether or not the toolbar is displayed when a document is opened, PDFs loaded from a server can appear without Acrobat buttons. This setting is fixed, and can not be changed by the user.

Downloading PDFs.   If you want to save a PDF file from the Web on your own computer, merely viewing it with the browser is of course insufficient. Instead, a method to save the file to the local hard disk is needed. If the file has already been downloaded and is visible in the browser, you can use the browser's "File", "Save As..." menu function to save the file to disk. If you do not want to load the file into the browser at all, but instead save it straight to the hard disk, click on the link pointing to the file with the right mouse button (or the only button on a Mac), and choose "Save Link As..." (Navigator) or "Save Target As..." (Internet Explorer).

When downloading PDF files using a Mac, note that Mac files only save the file content and not the extra file information from the Mac file system (such as file type, creator and finder icon). For PDF files this can be corrected after the download using the *PDFTyper* utility which can be found on the Acrobat CD-ROM or on the Web at:

http://beta1.adobe.com/ada/acrosdk/utilities.html

After downloading a PDF file, drag its icon onto the PDFTyper icon. The program inserts the supplementary data identifying the file as a PDF file, so double-clicking on the file's icon will start Acrobat Reader or Exchange.

Printing PDFs from the browser.   To print PDF files straight from the browser, click on the Print button in the Acrobat toolbar (see Figure 2.1). This calls Acrobat's print function (which is optimized for PDF files), not the browser's print function. In Netscape Navigator and Internet Explorer 4, choosing "File", "Print..." starts Acrobat's print function too. In Internet Explorer 3 and earlier PDFs can not be printed via the browser's print function.

The author of a PDF document can also embed a print button in the document: a single mouse click on this button launches Acrobat's print dialog.

Forms.   From Acrobat 3.0 onward, you can define forms with input fields, action buttons, and so on in PDF files. These forms are used the same way as HTML forms, and do not require the user to learn new tricks: text is typed into text fields, check boxes are to be clicked, action buttons react to a mouse click and so on. Buttons which send the contents of a form to the server or reset the field contents to their default value have to be designed and implemented by the form's creator.

If you often use such forms you can save yourself a lot of effort in filling out PDF forms by preparing a file containing your personal data and adhering to the new PFN conventions. If required, you can import the prepared data into PDF forms again and again. Further details on the PFN standard and on creating a PFN profile can be found in Section 7.5.

Security aspects.   The possibilities of malicious attacks from the Internet on the Web user's computer are being discussed thoroughly in conjunction with the current techniques for making the Web more dynamic. Several terms always come up in this discussion, especially Java, JavaScript, and ActiveX. As PDF also allows external programs to be started from Acrobat documents, there is a risk that opening an unknown PDF file downloaded from the Internet could start a malicious program. However, the risk is no-

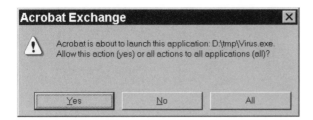

Fig. 2.5.
Security advice in Acrobat 3.01 when launching external programs

where near as high as with ActiveX, which gives a hacker complete access to the user's computer via the Windows API, but this does not mean that the problem can be entirely ignored.

Adobe has already reacted to the potential security risk and in Acrobat 3.01 has implemented a dialog which warns the user about the danger of starting external programs from a PDF file (see Figure 2.4). As in a browser, the user can choose whether to allow the action or not. Forbidding the start of all external programs does offer protection from attacks, but at the same time means that you can not take advantage of the extended functionality offered by using external programs.

2.4 Conversion from HTML to PDF

Often you want to save the results of a Web session on your own computer. However, HTML documents are usually made up of many individual files, which poses a big problem when trying to save the whole document on disk. This problem relates not only to complete documents consisting of several small HTML files, but also to the integration of GIF or JPEG graphics. To save the complete document, it is necessary to download each graphic file individually from the server. There are utilities which will "pull" a complete file tree from a server, but retrieving all the files using a browser's standard functions is very tedious. If an HTML document is printed, you don't get a complete version on disk, but instead increase the mountain of printed paper.

Conversion from HTML to PDF offers a solution to this problem, as PDF files contain all of the document's components in a single compact and convenient file. Two methods of achieving the conversion are described below: for the first, the commercial version of Acrobat is required; the second requires a Perl interpreter and Acrobat Distiller or Ghostscript.

PDF Writer. In your Web browser, select the PDF Writer (described more fully in Section 4.1) as the printer driver, and print the currently displayed HTML file. This produces, quickly and easily, a complete PDF version of the HTML document. Unfortunately, this method does not convert existing links: if they point to important URLs which you want to save as well, this

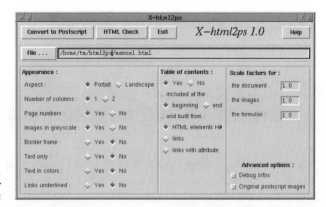

Fig. 2.6.
The graphical user
interface to html2ps

method is ruled out. In addition, the usual limitations apply when printing frames: the complete frameset is never printed (or converted to PDF), but only a single frame.

html2ps. The Swedish developer Jan Kärrmann has written a Perl script for converting HTML pages to PostScript. The PostScript output contains special pdfmark instructions for placing hypertext links into PDF files. This means that the HTML links are preserved when using this conversion method. To convert the PostScript output to PDF, Acrobat Distiller or Ghostscript is needed.

Apart from Perl, html2ps uses several utilities for different parts of the task: processing embedded graphics, loading referenced documents from the Web, and so on. The script uses several freely available programs – such as Ghostscript, TeX, ImageMagick – to achieve these tasks. As these are mostly Unix programs, html2ps is most suitable for Unix systems (although the Perl script itself is not platform dependent).

The script converts links in HTML pages to PDF links or Web links, so that the hypertext structure remains intact. If desired, links can be marked with a colored box. In addition html2ps generates a table of contents and bookmarks from existing headings. Formatting can be controlled with special configuration files similar to HTML's Cascading Style Sheets (CSS). You can find html2ps on the accompanying CD-ROM or at this URL:

http://www.tdb.uu.se/~jan/html2ps.html

2.5 Conversion from PDF to HTML

This chapter is called "PDF in the Browser", but a few remarks on using PDF files without Acrobat software seem appropriate. In particular the conversion of PDF documents to HTML is a topic which crops up again and again. Due to the basic differences between the formats – covered in Section 1.3 –

this is not a simple format conversion (like changing a GIF to a TIFF). A conversion program must attempt to extract as much structural information as possible from the PDF file's layout information and convert it to HTML. In addition, the PDF navigation controls – references, bookmarks, and so on – should be converted into HTML links.

In order to make PDF documents accessible to blind users (see below) Adobe has come up with two conversion methods, which are briefly discussed below.

The Access server.   Adobe offers a conversion service via the Web. The URLs of PDF documents are entered into an HTML form. Sending the form to the server activates a CGI script which loads the specified PDF file from the Web, converts it to HTML, and sends the result back to the browser. The form can be found at the following URL:

```
http://www.adobe.com/prodindex/acrobat/advform.html
```

This conversion service is also available via a special proxy server or by e-mail. The conversion preserves links to places in the document or to external documents. The resulting HTML file also contains extra links intended to make navigation easier:

- The "Document Outline" section contains links to all of the document's bookmarks.
- Each page contains links to the next or the previous page.
- The "Page Navigation Panel" at the end of the HTML document makes it possible to navigate the document page by page.

Figure 2.5 shows, as an example, a PDF file and the result of the conversion to HTML. Further conversion options can be specified on the form, for example the page range.

The conversion does enable access to the content of PDF files, in a purely text oriented environment (like Lynx, the text-only browser), but a hundred percent accurate conversion can not be expected. Apart from general formatting problems (with tables, multi-column text, hyphenation), there are problems with special characters. As the conversion process always uses the Windows character set, special characters from PDF documents which originated on a Mac are rendered incorrectly. Umlauts in bookmarks appear correctly as they are generated using the PDFDocEncoding character set, which is almost identical to the Windows character set (see Section 6.2).

The Access plugin.   To convert PDF documents to HTML on your own computer, Adobe makes available a plugin for the Windows versions of Acrobat Reader and Exchange. This plugin has similar functionality to the Access Server. In conjunction with a special screenreader program which reproduces parts of the screen content in a Braille cell, the plugin allows blind users to use PDF files. Additionally, the Access plugin adds export to HTML and ASCII text to Acrobat's functionality. By choosing "File", "Export",

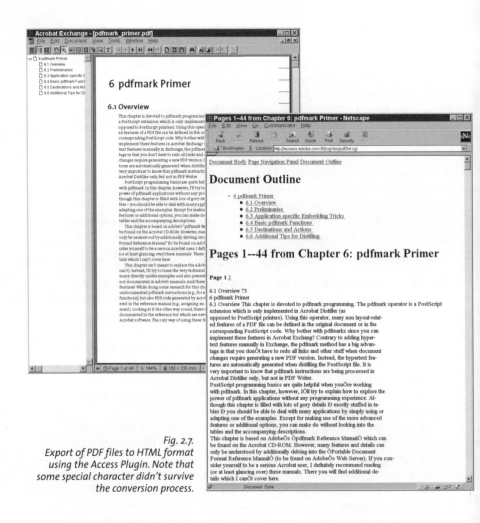

Fig. 2.7.
Export of PDF files to HTML format using the Access Plugin. Note that some special character didn't survive the conversion process.

"HTML" the text content of a PDF file can be saved in HTML 2.0 format. The plugin at least tries to place the text in the correct order for reading, which is very important when dealing with multi-column text. Using the plugin, umlauts are converted correctly but no additional links are generated for navigation within the document. You can find more information about the Access program and download the plugin, free of charge, at the following URL:

http://www.adobe.com/prodindex/acrobat/access.html

Acrobat Toolkit. With the Acrobat Software Development Kit, Adobe offers developers plenty of support for PDF programming. The Acrobat Toolkit, which can be obtained as part of this SDK, contains object libraries for working with PDF files. With the help of these libraries it is possible to write your own programs for converting PDF to HTML, plain text, or other formats. The Toolkit is available for Windows 95, Windows NT, HP-UX, SunOS, Solaris, AIX, and Irix.

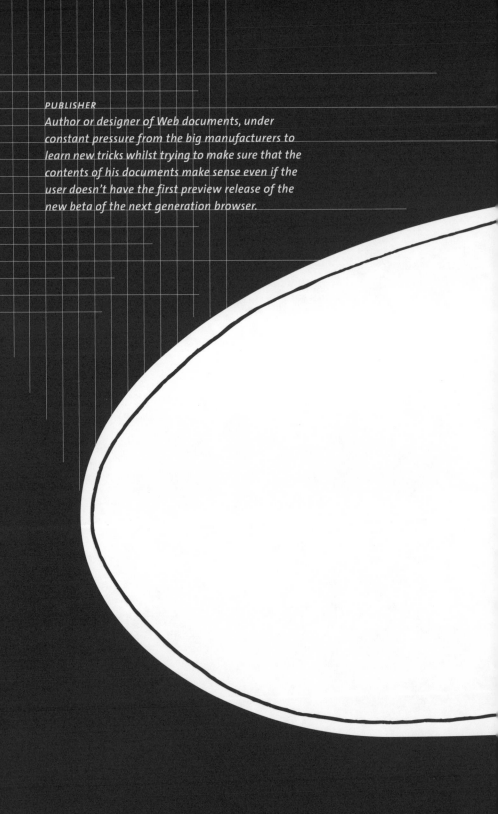

The Publisher's Point of View

3 Planning PDF Documents

3.1 PDF or HTML?

This book does not advocate the replacement of HTML with PDF, but a reasonable combination of both formats. A Web designer ought to consider which format will best fulfill the requirements for each individual job. Each problem has to be solved within the framework of prevailing logistical, financial, and technical conditions. Mostly, it is necessary to consider not only the final goal, but also the origins of the documents: does the data to be made available on the Web originate from a database, as a by-product of a conventional publishing process or even archived paper documents? Which format will meet the expectations of the target group better and allow the data to be presented more easily? The main role of the document should also be clear: are the files just a method for transferring data which the user will probably print out anyway, or are they purely for online use? It can make sense to offer two versions in parallel, which of course increases the resources needed.

Acrobat Reader is available free of charge, but downloading and installing it can be a daunting task for the user. If the target group is not prepared to download and install Acrobat Reader, then there is no point generating PDF files. On the other hand, in a closed or homogeneous user group, such as on an intranet or in a vertical market, it can often be assumed that the necessary software is already available.

If it is decided to offer PDF files on your Web site, then important sections like the home page should nonetheless be in HTML format with pointers to the PDF files. This avoids problems for users on whose machines Acrobat is not installed.

When to use PDF. For documents with complex formatting, which can not be realized satisfactorily or even at all with HTML, PDF is the format of choice. Careful graphic design and skilled use of typography make for an attractive document, but HTML can not accomplish this. Acrobat's strengths are particularly evident when the use of fonts is important. Apart from heavily formatted documents, long documents are also suited to being stored in PDF files. In HTML, large amounts of text are often hard to read and can not be printed out satisfactorily. HTML is only suitable for archiving long documents to a limited extent.

Some functions can not be achieved at all with HTML, such as access control using encryption or the conversion of paper documents for use on the Web.

When to use HTML.   HTML shows its strengths in documents which are not so heavily formatted, but where it is important to be able to navigate the document. Because of this, even a site with most of its pages in PDF should offer its contents pages in HTML format. On many sites, information with a short life span is better presented as HTML pages, using PDF for documents with a longer expected lifetime.

3.2 PDF Hypertext Features

Since this is not a design handbook I do not want to go into the question of formatting printed and online documentation in detail. Instead, I'd like to give a brief overview of the functions which PDF offers for preparing and enriching electronic documentation. First of all, you should be clear about the document's probable use:

- ▸ Printed documents: PDF is purely a means of transport. Usually, the user will print the files before using them.
- ▸ Online documents: The PDF files are primarily used on-screen and only rarely printed.
- ▸ Hybrid: the users have differing requirements and use the PDF files as a mixture of print and online documents.

The conversion of the electronic "added value" for PDF files described below partly depends on the above classification.

Page format and numbering.   Page size and orientation are the most affected by the "online or print?" decision. It is common knowledge that a letter portrait page is totally unsuited for use on screen. On the other hand, pages customized for online use do not print out well.

Acrobat numbers all pages consecutively, starting with page 1. In the case of multi-part documents or documents using mixed numbering schemes (such as roman numerals in the introduction and arabic ones in the main part) this means that the document page numbers will no longer agree with the page numbers displayed in Acrobat Reader.

In the case of longer PDF documents, it is more user friendly if the first page is kept relatively compact so that it loads quickly. While the user studies the introduction or the navigation elements on the first page, further pages can download in the background.

Bookmarks.   Bookmarks, which Acrobat displays in their own column to the left of the document, are an important aid to the structuring of PDF files. They offer not only navigational jumps, but at the same time give an overview of the document or multiple documents in a collection and are an indispensable help to the reader. To make the hierarchical order of sections or headings clear, you should use nested bookmarks according to the document structure.

A bookmark does not have to be associated with a jump or other action. Create a new bookmark in Exchange, select it and open the option list for possible actions by choosing "Edit", "Properties". Select "None" as the action type. You can, for example, label a no-function bookmark like this with hyphens and use it as a separator between groups of bookmarks, or label it with a heading which is not associated with a jump. Other possible uses of bookmarks include lists of figures, indexes, list of related topics, and many more.

When creating bookmarks manually, you can often save yourself some typing: to transfer the text from a heading into a bookmark, select the text with the selection tool. When you create a new bookmark, it will automatically be labeled with the selected text.

Note that bookmarks always use the PDFDocEncoding character set (see Section 6.2). Because of this, it is not possible to use certain Mac-specific characters in bookmarks (for example, ligatures and math symbols). The creator of a PDF document has no control over the font family and size used in bookmarks. The character set for bookmarks limits the use of bookmarks to documents written in Latin script. Documents using other languages,

Fig. 3.1.
HTML Frames, multiple ads, and bookmarks don't leave much space for the actual content!

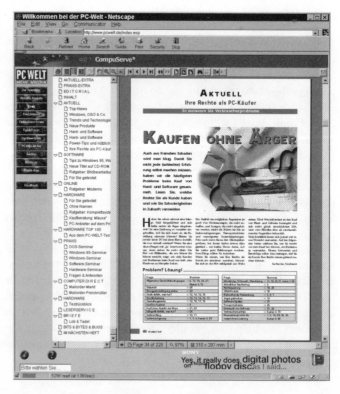

such as those written in Greek, Cyrillic, or Arabic, cannot have meaningful bookmarks in their native language.

Notes. Notes – Acrobat's yellow "sticky notes" – are perfectly suited for flagging alterations or amendments to the content of PDF documents if the change does not justify redoing the whole document. For example, notes may contain tips on how to optimize the printout of the document, a URL for updates, and similar information. Notes should not be used for large amounts of information as they make it harder to read the document and can not easily be printed (Exchange is capable of generating a notes summary).

Document information fields. The info fields – accessed in Acrobat by choosing "File", "Document Info", "General..." – provide the user with general information about a document (as opposed to its actual content). While displaying the info box for an individual document does not offer much added value, in conjunction with the search functions the info fields offer powerful search capabilities in larger documents collections (see below).

Naturally, this only works if the fields contain sensible entries. This can either be done manually in Acrobat Exchange or with the help of suitable pdfmark instructions (see Chapter 6). If the default fields "Title", "Subject", "Author", and "Keywords" are not sufficient, extra fields can be defined (see Section 4.4).

Full text index. If the author of a collection of PDF documents takes the trouble to generate a text index using Acrobat Catalog, users can save a lot of time every time they carry out a search. A text index makes it possible to quickly search large groups of PDF files. Apart from full text searches of the files' text contents, a text index also allows structured queries, using the document info fields (as long as the author has filled them out). Further hints on the use of index files on the Web server can be found in Chapter 11.

Article threads. Acrobat's article function is named after its main area of use, namely complex multi-column layouts, used above all for longer articles in newspapers and magazines. To read the text in the correct order, the user has to continually zoom and position to the respective document section on screen. To avoid having to do this, the author of a PDF file can indicate the text flow for an article using anchored rectangles. The user simply has to click in the text at the end of a column or press the return key – Acrobat will zoom in on the continuation of the text in the next column on the same or another page. Pressing shift-click or shift-enter moves the user through the article in reverse order. This is useful for returning to an earlier section of text for review. As article threads make life a lot easier for the user, this feature is recommended for layouts which are complex or which are not optimized for the screen.

Links and navigation.   Links and hypertext navigation are at the core of the added value which electronic documents have when compared to their paper counterparts. Acrobat makes it possible to jump to other places in the same document, to places in other PDF documents, to other types of documents, or to Internet URLs. In the case of jumps within or to other PDF documents, it is possible to specify the zoom factor as well as the target page. Using Acrobat 3.0, a wide range of additional actions can also be started by clicking on an active area. These include links to articles, various form functions, playing sound or movie files, or executing Acrobat menu commands.

When designing graphical buttons for links or actions, care should be taken to make them intuitive. However, a quick look at Acrobat's own online documentation will show that this basic rule is not always observed. Or do you know instinctively what a symbol consisting of two concentric circles might mean?

To avoid navigation controls getting in the way when the document is printed (in which case they serve no function) they can be defined as form fields, associated with the "Go to View" action. Form fields offer more dis-

Fig. 3.2.
HTML Frames
combined with PDF

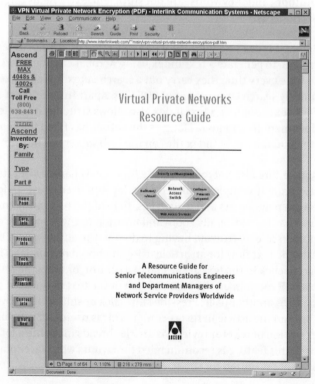

play options than links, including a setting which prevents them from being printed.

Thumbnails. Thumbnails give a visual overview of a PDF file. In highly structured documents they are a valuable navigation aid, as clicking on a thumbnail jumps to the corresponding page. In text-dominated documents, however, they do not offer any great advantage as the text in the thumbnails is not legible and navigation using page numbers is possible without thumbnails.

PDF developers should note that including thumbnails increases file size by about 3 KB per page. If the pages are to be used on the Web, consider whether they really add any value – there is no reason for using them with short documents.

Settings for opening a document. Using the menu sequence "File", "Document Information", "Open..." the author of a PDF file can specify how the document will be opened: which zoom factor, with or without bookmarks, with or without thumbnails, with or without menus and tool bars being

Fig. 3.3.
Single page documents do not need thumbnails to make navigation easier

displayed. Good use should be made of these settings. This starts with the zoom factor. The "Fit Width" setting (the pages are enlarged to fill the width of the whole screen) is often useful here. Thumbnails should only be turned on if the document actually includes them, as otherwise the unused thumbnail column just wastes screen space. Deactivating menus and tool bars should be thought about carefully: will the user be able to use the document without them? If Acrobat's own controls are not present, the document must contain all of the required navigation buttons on each page, such as links to the next or previous pages.

Multiple small files or a single large one? Often, it has to be decided whether documentation in digital format would be better as multiple small files or as a single large file. As many peripheral factors play a role, this question can not be definitively answered. Both variants have their pros and cons.

A collection of smaller documents offers the following advantages:

- ▸ Partial documents are easier to download. Users who are only interested in a particular detail do not have to download the whole document. As it is not possible to save single pages of a document, page-at-a-time download doesn't help in the case of long documents.
- ▸ It is easier for the author to make changes to the documents, or to swap individual files.
- ▸ It is quicker to edit and save small files using Acrobat Exchange.

On the other hand, a single large file offers these advantages:

- ▸ More straightforward to use and manage.
- ▸ Copying and archiving is easier with a single file.
- ▸ If a user requires a full set of documentation, it is easier to download a single file than many small ones.
- ▸ There is a limit to the number of files which Acrobat can open simultaneously. If there is just one big file, this limit isn't relevant.
- ▸ As embedded fonts only have to be stored once, having one large file will reduce the overall file size.

Fig. 3.4.
Settings for opening
a document

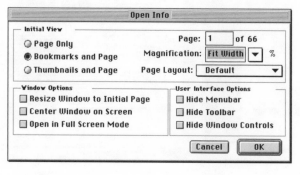

- Page numbering can be unified, if all the pages in a document are numbered consecutively. The page numbers used on the document pages are then identical with the page numbers displayed in Acrobat; with lots of small documents Acrobat will always start counting at page 1.
- When using encryption, the user only has to enter the password once for a large file, but if a lot of small files are used, the password will have to be entered every time a new file is opened.

Consider the pros and cons and the intended use of your PDF documents carefully before deciding the small versus large document issue.

4 Creating PDF Files

4.1 Several Paths to PDF

There are several ways of creating PDFs. They differ in the software required, functionality, and simplicity. In the following section I would like to introduce the most important variants.

Acrobat PDF Writer.   PDF Writer offers the simplest way of creating PDFs. It is installed at system level as a printer driver under Windows or on the Mac and makes all programs with a print function PDF capable. Unlike Distiller (see below), PDF Writer is not based on PostScript, but on the graphics interface of the respective operating system – QuickDraw on the Mac or GDI under Windows. As these imaging models are not as powerful as PostScript, PDF Writer has certain weaknesses when compared to Distiller.

PDF Writer has a whole load of functional weaknesses. The most serious of these is that it can not process EPS files satisfactorily. As the PDF driver does not interpret PostScript files, it only embeds the screen preview – a bitmap version of the graphic – in the PDF file which it produces. Because this EPS preview is rasterized at low resolution, it will not usually be of acceptable quality.

Another important difference is the preparation of hypertext functions before conversion to PDF. While Distiller makes use of the additional pdf-

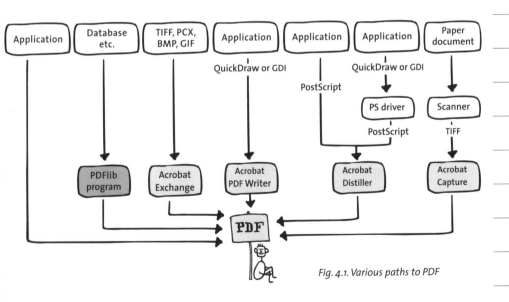

Fig. 4.1. Various paths to PDF

mark PostScript operator to do this (see Chapter 6), it is not possible to incorporate functions beyond pure layout control when using PDF Writer. Table 4.1 shows the limitations of PDF Writer when compared to Distiller. Because of the limitations listed, PDF Writer should only be used to convert documents to PDF when the graphic quality is not critical.

Table 4.1. Limitations of PDF Writer compared to Distiller

	Distiller	PDF Writer
EPS graphics	yes	no
Use of pdfmarks	yes	no
Font formats	Type 0, Type 1, Type 3, TrueType, Type 42	Type 1, TrueType
Limit for font subsets	user defined	always 35%
Downsampling resolution	user defined	fixed values
Prepress functions	yes	no

PDF Writer has further limitations on font handling. Because of the font conversion process involved, PDF files created using TrueType fonts might not be searchable or indexable.

Acrobat Distiller.   Distiller is the method of choice for conversion to PDF where requirements are higher. This program contains a full-blown PostScript Level 2 interpreter. This means that Distiller accepts the same page description files as a printer or an imagesetter. Unlike these output devices, Distiller does not rasterize the data (i.e., does not generate a pixel image) but converts the PostScript page description to a PDF file and stores it on the hard disk.

While PDF Writer makes a large number of programs "PDF capable", Distiller brings all programs which can create PostScript output into the PDF sphere. This also makes it possible to create PDF files on those platforms (Unix, for example) where there are no system level printer drivers.

Apart from "normal" PostScript instructions, Distiller also makes use of the pdfmark operator. This extension makes it possible to define PDF features in the PostScript code which would otherwise have to be added later using Exchange. These features include links, bookmarks, article threads, and many more. Some programs can generate these pdfmark instructions automatically (see Chapter 5). Alternatively, the document author can insert them, using various tricks, into the PostScript output (see Chapter 6).

In addition, Distiller offers several options for processing output files at the prepress stage, for example to control imagesetters or digital printing presses. The compression and font embedding capabilities are extremely important, however, with regard to Web or CD-ROM publishing. These capabilities are discussed further in Section 4.2.

Importing raster images in Acrobat Exchange. Acrobat Exchange 3.0 and above contains an import plugin which reads various raster image file formats and converts them to a PDF page. This import module supports the following file formats: BMP, Amiga IFF (Mac only), PCX, GIF, Photo-CD (Mac only), PICT (Mac only), TIFF, and Fax/DCX (Windows only). Each imported image appears on its own page, but it is not possible to scale or rotate the imported image.

Acrobat Exchange's documentation presents the program, thanks to this function, as a universal picture viewer, but in reality there are certain restrictions: firstly, the size of imported pictures is restricted to a maximum size of 14 inches (that is, 1008 points or 25.56 centimeters). The import function does allow more than one file to be selected, as long as they are in the same directory. Multiple file import is limited to 50 files at a time and does not work on the Mac. It would be better if there were a batch conversion facility to convert large numbers of pictures to PDF with a single command (or using Drag & Drop).

Converting scanned pages using Acrobat Capture. PDF Writer and Distiller only convert documents which are already in electronic form to PDF. Acrobat Capture, on the other hand, is for converting printed documents. This is done by scanning the printed pages and converting them to PDF. Capture includes an OCR (optical character recognition) module. Capture is available in two flavors: the "mini" edition is a plugin (contained in the standard Acrobat package) which gives Acrobat Exchange Capture functionality for single pages. The full-blown Capture package, sold separately, is suitable for converting large numbers of pages automatically.

Using PDF in conjunction with OCR offers several advantages: apart from the compact file format and the widely available viewer, this includes above all the combination of text and bitmap graphics. Most OCR software replaces characters which it doesn't recognize with a special symbol. Capture uses a bitmap image of the "doubtful" character instead, so that the document remains optically intact. Characters which were recognized are stored as text in the document, reducing the file size enormously when compared to a bitmap version, and has the advantage that the files can be indexed for full text retrieval. Also, portions of text can be copied using the selection tool.

Capture 1.0 had severe functional limitations, but the current version, Capture 2.0, is much enhanced. For example, color scans are now accepted as input. The text recognition module can be set up for languages other than English. Capture controls the scanner on its own and can convert large numbers of documents unattended if the scanner has an automatic feeder. The converted documents can be checked and manipulated to a limited extent in the Capture Reviewer (see Figure 4.3). Capture and Reviewer both use PDF Writer to actually generate the PDF files. Apart from direct scanner in-

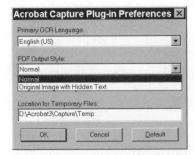

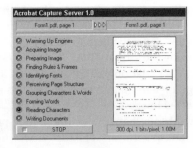

Fig. 4.2.
Converting scanned pages using the Capture plugin

put it is also possible to convert existing bitmap graphics in TIFF, BMP, or PCX format with resolutions from 200 to 600 dpi (black and white) or from 200 to 400 dpi (grayscale or color). In general, 300 dpi resolution is sufficient for Capture; at text sizes smaller than 8 points, this value should be increased to 400 dpi.

Several variants can be selected from when creating PDF files:

▶ "Normal": the PDF file contains recognized text as a normal text component, and can therefore be indexed and searched. In this format, a typical page takes up about 10 KB and is more suited for use on the Web than the other two variants.

▶ "Picture": the PDF file contains only a bitmap version of the page. This variant is generated, for example, by Exchange when importing raster image files.

▶ "Original Image with Hidden Text": This variant combines the text and picture variants. A bitmap version of the page ensures that scan and PDF file look the same. The recognized text is contained on a hidden layer behind the bitmap. This combination means that the text can be searched and indexed, while retaining the original layout. However, the image data takes up more space, and even with compression, 80 to 100 KB is usually needed for an average page.

Directly creating PDF using application software. All of the methods for generating PDF files described previously rely on Acrobat. However, there are also ways of generating PDF files without Acrobat software. More and more graphics and image processing applications include export modules for PDF. These export modules often do not support full PDF functionality so there are limitations on the files produced like this. For example, Adobe Photoshop can save images in PDF format, but always uses JPEG compression in the generated PDFs, which can lead to unwanted loss in quality and is therefore not always appropriate. Unfortunately, it is not possible to

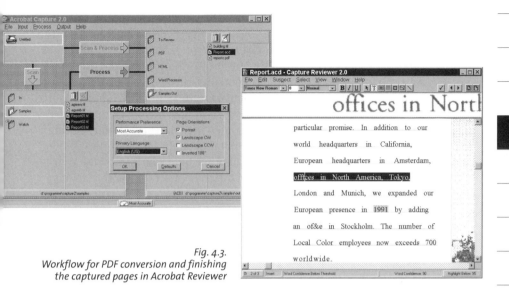

Fig. 4.3.
Workflow for PDF conversion and finishing
the captured pages in Acrobat Reviewer

change Photoshop's behavior in respect of PDF export. Further remarks on PDF support in graphics programs can be found in Section 5.7.

Generating PDF files using PDFlib programs.   In conclusion I would like to draw attention to my own PDFlib software package which can be found on the accompanying CD-ROM. PDFlib is a programming library for developing programs to generate PDF. PDFlib only acts as a back end for creating the PDF data. The actual data preparation and arrangement has to be carried out by other modules which have to be developed separately. PDFlib is particularly suited to creating PDF dynamically on a Web server, as described in Chapter 12.

The PDFlib package contains, apart from the actual program library, several demo programs which showcase PDFlib's functionality. These include converters for text and graphics files which can convert any number of ASCII, GIF, TIFF, and JPEG files to PDF, and can be used in batch mode. More information on these converters can be found in the PDFlib manual, also available from the CD-ROM.

.2 Distiller Settings

In this section I want to go in more detail into the settings and options available in Acrobat Distiller, the most important tool for creating PDF files.

Compatibility.   When Distiller is first started, decisions on compatibility settings must be made (the settings can always be changed later). The user has to decide between two types of PDF files: compatible with Acrobat 2.1, or compatible with Acrobat 3.0. If you are not sure whether all the users who will receive your files have Acrobat Reader 3.0 or higher, then you should choose Acrobat 2.1 compatibility. This means that you can not use some Acrobat 3.0 functions. The main functionality affected by the compatibility settings is Acrobat 3.0's more efficient compression, which is not supported by older viewers, and font embedding. As long as neither compression nor font embedding are used, PDFs generated with the compatibility setting 3.0 should also work in older viewers – but if in doubt, test your files before starting a CD-ROM production run or publishing your files on the Web. Table 4.2 shows the most important differences between both versions.

Table 4.2. Differences between Acrobat 2.1 and 3.0

	Acrobat 2.1	**Acrobat 3.0**
Web optimization[1]	*no*	*yes*
ZIP compression	*no*	*yes*
Font compression	*no*	*yes (CFF format or Type1C)*
Image downsampling	*downsampling only*	*downsampling and subsampling*
PostScript Level 2 patterns	*replaced by gray levels*	*replaced by gray levels on screen, print out OK*
Halftoning and transfer parameters preserved	*no*	*yes*
Prepress features, e.g. OPI	*no*	*yes*
Thumbnail creation in Distiller	*yes*	*no*

1. *Optimization is carried out in Exchange, not Distiller (see Section 4.3).*

Font embedding. Acrobat's refined method for handling font problems has a great bearing on the platform independence of PDF files. PDF 1.2 (which is the file format version created by Acrobat 3.0) supports all commonly used font formats: Type 1, Type 3, Multiple Master, TrueType, Type 0, *(composite fonts)* and CID (Far Eastern scripts). The new Type1C format (and also CFF, *compressed font format)* makes it possible for Type 1 fonts to be stored in a much more compact form. It is used by Distiller 3.0 for all Type 1 fonts, but is not compatible with Acrobat 2.1. Fonts can be embedded in PDF files so that they are available for screen display or printing even if they are not installed on the recipient's computer. As an alternative to font embedding, Distiller is also capable of generating a font descriptor, which describes several basic characteristics of a font: with or sans serifs, ascender and descender lengths, character set and, most importantly, character widths. If the font is not installed on the target system, Acrobat uses the font descriptor to generate, with the help of two special Multiple Master fonts (AdobeSansMM and AdobeSerifMM), a substitute font whose metrics match the missing font. Obviously, the substitute font cannot perfectly simulate any missing font, but will at least preserve line and page breaks and therefore ensure readability.

In the case of the most important font formats – Type 1 ("ATM fonts") and TrueType – there is in addition the possibility of embedding only those characters required by the document into the PDF file, not the whole font. As most fonts contain over 200 characters, such font subsets usually require much less space in the PDF file.

Details about the number and names of embedded fonts and subset structure can be found in an information box accessed with the menu sequence "File", "Document Info", "Fonts...". In the case of converted TrueType fonts this box usually contains unintelligible synthesized names.

Legal aspects of font embedding.   When embedding fonts in PDF files, both technical aspects such as file size (see below) and legal aspects have to be considered. Normally, you do not buy a font from a vendor outright, but only obtain a license to use it (exclusives, such as corporate fonts, might be different). Just as with software, you must observe the conditions and restrictions on use agreed upon and usually laid out in the license. As font design, realization, and marketing are financed by selling licenses, the vendors or manufacturers can naturally set their own conditions of use. The most common restriction is on the number of computers or output devices which a font can be used on. It should be immediately obvious that fonts, like software, should not be freely copied and passed on if we want the vitality and creativity of typography to be preserved – only if typographers are paid for their efforts will they be motivated to come up with new designs.

In conjunction with font embedding in PDFs, it is important to note that it is technically possible to extract embedded fonts from PDF files, and use them without paying a license fee. The fact that the process is not easy and requires both technical know-how and effort does not change the fact that type designers are understandably very critical of font embedding. A PDF document with embedded fonts, published on the Web, potentially makes the fonts available worldwide for free (even if – luckily for typographers – this has not yet happened). To preempt this danger, several smaller manufacturers and vendors have begun to define clearly in their licenses conditions and restrictions for the use of their fonts on CD-ROM or on the Web. Currently, several models are deployed:

- ► Font embedding is expressly forbidden by the license. If need be, a separate fee and conditions can be negotiated for each use.
- ► Two different licenses are offered for each font: one for conventional hard copy use and another for online use including embedding. The em-

bedding license fee is higher in order to compensate for potential loss of sales.

▶ Some manufacturers allow embedding in PDF, if Distiller's subset function is turned on and the minimum percentage is set to 99%. In this case, Distiller always creates subsets and never makes the full font available. From the manufacturers' point of view this minimizes the danger of piracy as the fonts are never complete.

▶ Some manufacturers have agreed with Adobe that all the fonts from their collections can be embedded in PDF files. For example, it is OK to embed the "Adobe Originals" series in PDF files. A list of the manufacturers participating in this scheme can be found in the Distiller documentation.

The legitimacy of font embedding is not simply an issue of fairness to typographers: there is also the question of whether you want to take a legal risk with your publication. It is often hard to prove the origins of pirated software, but it's usually very easy to prove the origins of a PDF file from the Web – after all, a publisher generally wants to reach as many people as possible.

Minimizing file size.   File size is an important factor for use on the Web. The temporary overloading of Internet backbones and possibly slow modem connections increase download times for Web surfers. Thanks to the integrated compression routines, Acrobat generally generates very compact files. This is illustrated by comparing PDF to PostScript: PDF files are usually smaller, by a factor of 3 to 5, than their PostScript counterparts. A further indicator that PDF's built-in compression is very good is the fact that PDF files cannot be compressed much by utilities like StuffIt, PKzip, gzip, compress and similar programs. Note that unlike PostScript, PDF compresses images as well as text. As well as compressing the files using compression routines, Acrobat has a few methods for reducing the amount of data before compression. Before looking into these, let's take a closer look at the compression routines supported in PDF.

Compression routines.   The LZW group of compression routines is named after Abraham Lempel, Jacob Ziv, and Terry A. Welch, and contains many related algorithms, used in many hardware and software packages. LZW compression is suitable for many types of input data and on average gives good compression ratios. As the LZ78 variant, used in PDF, is subject to a patent, more and more developers are abandoning LZW in favor of other algorithms. LZW is a lossless compression scheme, that is, after decompression you get exactly the same data as you had before compression. However, Acrobat Distiller also supports LZW 4-bit and LZW 8-bit variants. These reduce the color depth before compression, which results in a potential loss of image quality.

ZIP compression was developed by the Internet community as a reaction to the patent problems with LZW. It enjoys increasing popularity. Programmers can obtain freely available ZIP code and use it in their applications free of charge. Adobe supports this compression scheme in PDF 1.2. ZIP compression is not only usable free of charge but also generally performs more efficient compression than LZW. Because of this, ZIP is a good choice for PDF compression. The only drawback to using ZIP is that it is not supported in viewers for PDF below 2.1, which means that PDF files compressed with ZIP are not backwards compatible and can only be viewed with Reader or Exchange 3.0 or later. Like LZW, Distiller is also capable of 4-bit or 8-bit ZIP compression, which do not preserve all of the original file information. This means that uncompressed files are not identical with the original file before compression.

JPEG or DCT compression is an international standard which is widely used. JPEG is very complicated, but gives a very good compression ratio. The most important JPEG flavor, baseline JPEG, is a lossy technique and so the algorithm is only usable for images and never for text. JPEG compression was developed with the aim of only removing from the picture to be compressed that information whose absence has little or no impact on the quality of the display. When using JPEG, the user can choose between quality and compression level. The more the data is compressed, the more the compressed image differs from the original. The compression ratio is not so

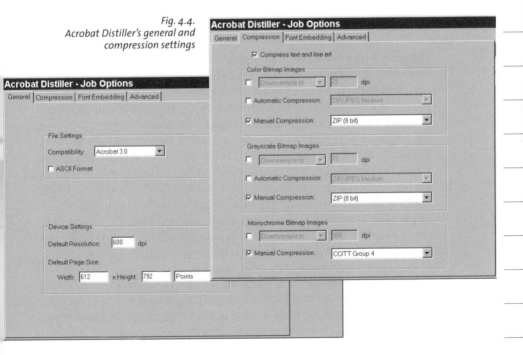

Fig. 4.4.
Acrobat Distiller's general and
compression settings

good if the quality loss is low. The best setting depends on the type of image and its intended use. JPEG is really only suitable for images with continuous colors, and should never be used for images with sharp edges or embedded text, such as screenshots. Unfortunately, books and newspapers often use screenshots compressed using JPEG – unsightly ghosting around the edges and around text lets the authors down.

CCITT Group 3 and 4 are the methods which are also used in fax protocols to transmit black and white data. These processes are optimized for bitmap images with small amounts of black on a white background. This is the case for most black and white office documents. CCITT is not really satisfactory for other uses.

RunLength compression is a very simple method which was also originally developed for black and white data. It gives the best results with original images that have long "runs", i.e., many pixels of the same color.

File size and fonts.   Embedding fonts naturally impacts the file size. A complete embedded font adds 40 to 60 KB to the PDF file. Font subsets, discussed earlier, help here. As only those characters which are actually needed in the document are embedded, the use of font subsets reduces the size of the embedded font by up to half. However, by default the limit for subset generation is 35 percent. This means that the complete font will be embedded if more than 35 percent of its characters are used. To take full advantage of font embedding the minimum should be set to 99 percent, even if this is counterintuitive (higher threshold value makes the fonts smaller). The 99 percent setting ensures that fonts are always embedded as subsets if the full character set is not used.

Reducing image resolution.   An important way of reducing the amount of data involved in raster images is to reduce the resolution of embedded images. To achieve this, two schemes are available which are called downsampling and subsampling. Both processes look at a group of several pixels to calculate a value for one pixel in the image to be generated. For example, if the original pixel group contains 3 x 3 = 9 pixels, the process reduces the resolution to one third of its previous value and the amount of data to one ninth. The new image contains less information and therefore fine detail is are lost in the conversion. When downsampling, Distiller calculates the color of the new pixel as the average of all the pixels in the original pixel group. When subsampling, a single pixel is used as a representative of the group to deliver the new value; the others are simply ignored. As no average needs to be calculated, subsampling is much quicker than downsampling (although downsampling gives better results).

Both variants can give disastrous results when used on unsuitable data. Just think of a checkerboard pattern of alternating black and white pixels. Downsampling gives an average value of all the pixels, that is a uniform gray. Subsampling choose either all black or all white, also a uniform colored area. With "normal" images, reducing the resolution reduces only the amount of detail but preserves the overall structure of the image.

Sensible downsampling values depend on the intended use for the PDF file. Documents which are mainly for on-screen use do not profit much from resolutions over 100 dpi (the exact value also depends on the zoom level). In this case, it makes sense to reduce the resolution, as only data will be lost which can not be used properly on screen anyway. If the final PDF use requires high quality, then the resolution should not be reduced.

Binary format.   Differentiation between ASCII and binary format also plays a role in determining PDF file size. While the first version of the PDF specification prescribed the ASCII format to avoid transfer problems – for example in email – from PDF version 1.1, binary data has been allowed. Binary files are smaller than ASCII files, but need to be handled "more carefully". This is no longer an important issue, and so the majority of PDF files contain binary data, which results in a much smaller file size.

Last but not least, Acrobat 3.0's optimization function, described in Section 4.3, also affects file size.

Watched folders.   Acrobat Distiller's "watched folders" are an extremely useful feature for network use. When in use, Distiller runs on a server and periodically checks directories to which users send PostScript files for conversion to PDF. Distiller carries out PDF conversion for all files which are sent to the watched directories and sends the PDFs to an output directory. It's interesting to note that different options can be specified for each watched directory. This means that, for example, one directory can be used for files to be viewed on-screen (with downsampling) and one for files to be converted for printing (with higher quality requirements).

Running Distiller as a Windows NT service.   Distiller's watched folders are quite a useful feature, but you can even further automate the distilling process on a server. Although you could launch Distiller from the AutoStart group of a particular user, running the program as a service in Windows NT is advantageous. In this case Distiller is started during boot-up time; it's not necessary to log in as a particular user in order to launch the program. Additionally, you can specify the desired account under which Distiller is to operate. To implement Distiller as an NT service, you need the Windows NT Resource Kit. Proceed as follows:

► Copy the program *srvany.exe* from the Resource Kit CD-ROM to the server's hard disk, e.g., to the *Program Files* folder.

► Create a new service called *DistillerService* using the following command in a command shell:

```
instsrv DistillerService "D:\Program Files\srvany.exe"
```

- Choose "Start", "Settings", "Control Panel", "Services" and click on "Distill-erService", "Startup". In the upcoming menu, click on "Log On As: Sys-temAccount" (or choose another account). If you want to see the Distill-er window, click on "Allow Service to Interact with Desktop". If you leave this box unchecked, Distiller will silently process its watched folders in the background without displaying any window or progress bar.
- Now you have to define the Distiller service. Launch the registry editor *regedt32* and locate the following registry entry:

```
HKEY_LOCAL_MACHINE\SYSTEM\CurrentControlSet\Services\
DistillerService
```

Add a new key with the name "Parameters" of type REG_SZ and value "Application" which holds the path to Distiller's executable file:

```
Application:REG_SZ:D:\Program Files\Acrobat3.01\Distillr\
Acrodist.exe
```

- You can check the Distiller service by manually starting it from the Ser-vice applet of the Control Panel. Next time you boot your server the Dis-tiller service will start up automatically.

If you want to remove the service, issue the following command from a command shell:

```
instsrv DistillerService remove
```

4.3 Optimized PDF Files

Exchange 3.0 offers an optimization option when saving PDF files. Optimiz-ing a PDF file has several consequences:
- The file is linearized which increases apparent download speed from the Web. Linearization is described in detail below.
- Redundant document resources are combined. This affects, for example, multiple subsets of the same font or multiple instances of the same im-age. For example, in the case of a screen presentation with the same background image on each page, the data for the background is stored only once. This enormously reduces the file size: I was able to reduce a 30 MB PostScript output file for a 60-page presentation with the same background on each page to a 9 MB PDF file. Applying optimization fur-ther reduced this to only 1 MB!
- Uncompressed document components are compressed. As this process uses ZIP compression, this can make optimized documents unreadable by older versions of Acrobat.

Exchange's optimization function needs to make several passes through the document; this is shown by the progress bar which goes up and down to show the progress for each individual stage.

Linearized PDF files. To increase apparent display speed on the Web and enable page-at-a-time download, Adobe has introduced linearization of PDF files. To understand this issue it is necessary to delve a little deeper into the PDF file structure.

Unlike PostScript files, which are always organized page by page, a PDF file contains a collection of objects which can be arranged in any order in the file. The objects – fonts, pictures, text, etc. – are needed to display one or more pages. So that the viewer does not have to read the complete file when a PDF document is opened, every PDF file has a cross-reference table at the end which shows where in the file the individual objects are located. When reading PDF files from the local hard disk, Acrobat first of all reads the end of the file. Using this information, the viewer calls the specific objects required for a particular page. To make it easier for Distiller to generate the PDF, the table is placed at the end of the file, as the object positions are then known.

To accelerate Web access – described in Section 2.2 – there are special rules for the numbering and ordering of objects in an optimized PDF file. In addition, parts of the table (and the so-called hint tables) are copied to the beginning of the file. The browser uses these tables to determine where the data for the first page is located. It then requests the relevant objects from the server. A more detailed description of the byteserver protocol used in this process and the requirements which it places on the Web server can be found in Section 9.2.

Optimizing PDF files. Distiller can not generate optimized or linearized PDF files. Optimization always has to be carried out later using Exchange. As the optimization of large numbers of files using "File", "Save As..." is very tedious, Exchange allows multiple files to be optimized without further user intervention. Using "File", "Batch Optimize..." all PDF files in a directory and its subdirectories can be optimized in one go.

Fig. 4.5.
Optimizing PDF files. Left: Saving a single file.
Right: Optimizing all files in a directory

4.4 Full Text Retrieval

Acrobat's simple search tool (the binocular symbol) is useful for finding a phrase in a single file, but fails when confronted with large collections of documents. Even in large individual documents, the linear search can take far too long. A solution to this problem is provided by indexing the document with Acrobat Catalog and carrying out the search using the Search plugin. Adobe licenses the underlying text search engine from Verity. An index file holds a structured collection of all phrases which occur in the source documents. The index allows quick searches to be performed in large collections of documents, and the results to be displayed quickly. The index can be regarded as a database which ensures quick access to the information stored in the PDF files. As when using the well-known Web search engines, the user enters a query consisting of key words which can be linked using Boolean operators. In fact, Acrobat Search internally uses the same software as many Web search engines (see Chapter 11).

Queries can be related to both the actual content and certain meta-information (i.e., information about a document). While most users are familiar with searching for content from the Web, the use of meta-information unfortunately remains a closed book for most of them. Meta-information allows a structured search, especially with large quantities of documents, while a content-oriented search is likely to be unstructured and turn up irrelevant matches. In Acrobat the following meta-information can be used for searches:

- The standard document information fields: "Title", "Subject", "Author", "Keywords".
- User-defined document information fields. More information on custom fields can be found below.
- Date and time: when was the file created or last changed?

If the input fields for document and date information (see Figure 4.6) are missing from the search mask, they can be activated using "File", "Preferences", "Search..." Searches for meta-information can also be carried out with empty text fields; that is, only documents with fields that match the search criteria – regardless of the actual content – will be returned. Note that queries for meta-information can also be performed on the Web server (see Chapter 11).

A requirement for meta-information to be used successfully is, of course, that the fields are filled out consistently when the document is created, and that the users are familiar with the scheme used. Usually a preexisting reference scheme – such as product or procedure numbers, internal file references, and job numbers – has to be inserted into the predefined document information fields. If this is not possible or difficult (for example, because the existing reference scheme requires more fields), it is a good idea to define additional information fields. Document information fields

Fig. 4.6.
Dialog box of the Search plugin

are filled out when creating PDFs from certain programs using internal information which is present in the original documents. The fields can also be filled out manually in Acrobat Exchange, but this is very tedious if there is a large number of files. Using suitable pdfmark instructions (see Section 6.4), the fields can be prepared in the PostScript code.

Possible index trouble.   In some cases you may experience problems with PDF indexes which apparently don't work: the search tool doesn't find any text at all, or highlights completely different text. There are several classes of files for which PDF indexing doesn't work:

- ▶ The page may have been scanned. Catalog is unable to retrieve any text from scanned pages. You may run Capture in order to convert the scanned page image to text. You can verify whether a page contains a scanned image either by zooming in or by trying to use the selection tool ("abc") to select some text. Text selection doesn't work with scanned page images.
- ▶ The text may use a non-standard encoding vector (character set). Since the search dialog box uses the system character set, the search text must match this encoding. Several applications are known to use completely different encodings, i.e., not even the lower half (ASCII range) complies with the Mac or Windows character set. The most notorious among such applications is InterLeaf which uses a completely non-standard encoding for some text fonts. You can check the text encoding by checking the "Encoding" entry in the font info box for "Custom", or by selecting some text and copying it into a text processing application. If the copied text looks like total gobbledygook, the character sets don't match.

- PDF files with converted TrueType fonts – called Type 42 fonts – may have the characters in the "wrong" places, as in the encoding problem above. You can identify converted TrueType fonts by checking the font info dialog box. Such fonts usually have artificial names instead of their "real" names.
- Encrypted files (see Section 4.5 for more info on PDF encryption) don't work well with Acrobat Catalog. This causes a chicken-and-egg problem: If you apply the encryption before indexing the documents, Catalog cannot open the files because of the encryption. However, if you encrypt your files after generating the index, the documents' contents are changed by the encryption process. The search engine realizes that the files have changed and accordingly doesn't highlight any matches. You can break this vicious encryption/indexing circle by checking the "Optimize for CD-ROM" option in Acrobat Catalog before generating the index. This option (besides other functions) disables the file-has-changed check and therefore makes encrypted files accessible for the search engine (of course you still have to supply the password to open the file).

Attaching an index file. So that the user does not have to specify the index file to use when working with a collection of PDF documents, you can permanently attach an index file to use with "File", "Document Info", "Index...". The AutoIndex plugin then makes sure that the appropriate index file is activated when the document is opened. This process can also be automated using pdfmark instructions (see Section 6.4).

When using automatic index attaching, it should be noted that once an index has been loaded, it is not automatically unloaded, which means that the user might find surprising matches in the wrong index.

Custom info fields. By following the instructions you can add as many fields as desired in addition to the standard "Title", "Subject", "Author", and "Keywords" fields, and use these fields in search queries. As an example, let's define custom fields called "Department", "Cost Center" and "Transaction Date". Proceed as follows:
- The fields are defined and filled out using pdfmark instructions in the PostScript code. Any number of fields can be defined and have any content allocated to them. Obviously, all the documents should contain these fields with the same spelling so that the search function can find them. An example of a suitable pdfmark instruction can be found in Section 6.4. By using the pdfmark instructions, the custom information fields are inserted during distillation.
- Before indexing the PDF files, Acrobat Catalog has to be told about your new fields. On the Mac, this is done by choosing "Edit", "Preferences...", "Custom Fields" (see Figure 4.7). Type the new field names into this dialog and choose a type for each field, choosing between "String" (up to 255 characters), "Integer" (Number between 0 and 65535), and "Date".

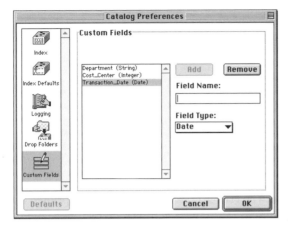

Fig. 4.7.
Defining custom info
fields in Catalog

▶ In Windows edit the file *acrocat.ini* in the Windows directory and add a
new line in the [Fields] section for each new field. Use the descriptions
"str", "int", and "date" for the three possible field types. In our example
the lines look like this:

```
Field0=Department,str
Field1=Cost_Center,int
Field2=Transaction_Date,date
```

▶ Next, restart Acrobat Catalog (only necessary under Windows) and cre-
ate the index file for the PDF files which contain the new info fields.
▶ To search for the new fields' contents, enter a search phrase in the form
"Field name = Term" into the search mask, for example:

```
Department = Marketing
```

Advanced query functions can also be used, for example the ~ operator
which means "contains":

```
Department ~ Mark
```

Using the Acrobat SDK, the interface can also be extended so that the custom fields can be filled out or queried using a dialog box.

4.5 Encrypting PDF Files

Since Acrobat 2.x appeared, it has been possible to protect PDF files by en-
crypting them. This encryption is a part of the file format and is handled by
the viewer (it is of course possible to use a separate encryption program on
any file type). In Exchange you can decide when you save a file whether it
can only be opened when a password is entered, or whether to forbid certain actions:

Fig. 4.8.
Settings for
protecting a PDF

- ▸ "Printing": the file can be viewed on screen but can not be printed.
- ▸ "Changing the Document": Exchange's editing tools can not be used and fields in forms can not be filled out.
- ▸ "Selecting Text and Graphics": This deactivates the selection tool.
- ▸ "Adding or Changing notes and form fields": Fields and notes can not be edited with the form tool, but they can still be filled out.

Entering a password is not always necessary to be able to use such a document. If the file's creator did not specify a password for opening the file when saving it, the file will be encrypted but can be used without a password – only the restrictions specified in the dialog box still apply.

So that a user can not simply reverse these settings, they are protected by a second password. Exchange only allows security settings to be changed if the second password is entered.

If the security restrictions are active, you should note that the Viewer and not the PDF file format is responsible for maintaining the restrictions. It is conceivable that somebody will develop a PDF viewer which simply ignores the security settings.

The password for opening the document behaves differently. The file can only be unlocked by entering the correct password, but contrary to the editing restrictions, the security lies in the PDF file, not in the viewer.

PDF's encryption is based on the RC4 algorithm developed by the well-known cryptographer Ron Rivest. In addition, the hash algorithm MD5 is used. Both procedures are used in many other software products. MD5 is defined as an Internet standard in an RFC ("request for comment"). Due to the restrictive US export conditions for cryptographic products, RC4 can only be exported with a key length of up to 40 bits. Because of this, Acrobat (and many other products such as Netscape Navigator) uses 40-bit keys derived from the key chosen by the user.

With regard to the security of PDF's encryption, it is worth looking at the decoding contest run by the RSA crypto company: an RC5 encryption with a 40-bit key was cracked within 3.5 hours, and a 48-bit key in 313 hours! RC4 and RC5 can not be directly compared since RC4 is a stream algorithm and RC5 is a block algorithm, but the figures can not be ignored. In another experiment, Netscape Navigator's 40-bit encryption was cracked by a number of networked workstations. PDF encryption is by no means totally secure!

Finally, two remarks on the practical use of PDF encryption: as Distiller does not create encrypted PDF files, the encryption has to be carried out later using Exchange. Unfortunately, there is no batch encryption function. The Compose plugin partially solves this by adding a lot of batch processing functions.

It should also be noted that protected files can not be opened by Acrobat Reader or Exchange 1.x.

.6 Acrobat Plugins

The Acrobat plugin interface for Reader and Exchange is a means of extending the software's functionality. Many companies have taken the opportunity to develop Acrobat add-ons for a host of applications. This section lists the most important Acrobat plugins.

It is important to note that although Acrobat Reader and Exchange support the plugin interface, most commercial plugins work only in Exchange. The reason for this is a licensing and encryption scheme which Adobe implemented in the interface. In order to somehow control which Reader plugins are offered, developers must present their modules to Adobe and obtain a special license. This way, Adobe wants to make sure that nobody comes up with a Reader plugin that essentially duplicates Exchange's functionality, thereby encroaching Adobe's sales.

Using PDF documents more effectively.   Aerial (Windows) offers a wealth of practical navigation tools. With these tools you can navigate through a PDF document using actual page numbers instead of Acrobat's fixed physical page numbers; search document indices, tag frequently referenced pages with dog-ears; print only a selected portion of a single page or split a single page across two or more pages; paper clip pages for quick reference; copy tables to the clipboard, and convert PDF to RTF.

Re:mark (Windows and Macintosh) contains markup, review, and security tools. It offers extensive tools for marking up PDF pages. For example, you can type text right on the document page, rubberstamp or highlight important passages, strike out text, mark out text and reviewer comments with circle, line, and square symbols, and attach files. The annotation management functions let you sort and filter annotations. With the security features you can set read, write, delete, and print options for annotations.

xToolsOne (Mac and Windows) is a set of plugins for automatically creating links and bookmarks. Additionally, the xTools plugins make it easy to administer hypertext features.

Automating document generation.   Compose (Windows) consists of ten plugins. You can add multiple links and bookmarks to an entire document in a single click, copy hypertext links, build tables of contents, add custom headers and pagination, and set security and file-open options quickly for a selected set of PDF files. Batch Meister performs a set of operations in batch mode on a set of files in one go. InfoFill can fill in the document info fields in a PDF file with information provided in an ASCII text file.

QuickLinx (Windows) automates hypertext link generation. Use Quick-Linx to instantly draw hypertext links around tables of contents, index entries, figures or illustrations, and internal page references. QuickLinx will automatically transfer the links you create to the Acrobat bookmark list.

DigiDozen (Mac and Windows) is a collection of plugins for optimizing the Acrobat workflow. The features include: create hypertext links and bookmarks for every entry in a PDF table of contents, set multiple destinations (e.g., different language versions) for a single link, and embed a non-PDF source document in a PDF file.

FaceIt! (Windows) enables users to dynamically change images in existing PDF files.

Text extraction.   Redwing (Windows) extracts text and tables from even the most complex, compound PDF documents. Tables can be edited before export with a customized table editor. Cells can be edited, merged, split, and deleted. Columns and rows can be merged and deleted. All text exported by Redwing is fully editable.

Content licensing.   Signet (Windows) is an integrated security solution. Signet uses Acrobat's built-in document encryption to secure documents, but end-users never see this. Signet handles all the password details, so users don't have to remember or enter any passwords when they read a secure document. Signet consists of three components: Signet Author is a plugin that allows the publisher to encrypt documents and set document expiration parameters; Signet Authenticator is a plugin for end-users that decrypts only those documents the end-user is authorized to read; Signet Registry is an application for end-users that updates and manages the Signet password registry file.

Prepress plugins.   Crackerjack (Mac; Windows version announced) provides tools that give graphic arts professionals control over their output for PDF documents. Crackerjack generates output compatible with PostScript Level 2 or PostScript 3 RIPs. The plugin lets you position, scale, screen, and separate PDF content. It makes use of Level 2's in-RIP separation capability for color separations (process and spot color), and also supports composite output. Using Crackerjack's screening controls you can choose screen frequency and spot functions.

The PitStop plugin (Mac and Windows) opens any Acrobat PDF document for editing, and saves changes to the file. It preserves all object attributes and lets you move, scale, and rotate any object, and edit text lines.

CheckUp (Mac and Windows) generates a preflight report with details on colors, fonts, and images used in a PDF file, and offers a list of specific problems and areas of concern.

pdfToolbox (Mac and Windows) lets you easily configure Distiller settings and control the final PDF file for prepress. pdfBatchMeister is a batch processing tool which controls Acrobat Distiller 3.0 with predefined and thoroughly tested Distiller options. pdfInspektor is a preflighting tool which flags potential problems regarding color usage, image resolutions, and rotations. pdfOutput creates completely self-contained cross-platform EPS files from PDF files.

Acrobat plugin vendors.   Table 4.3 lists company names and Web sites for vendors and developers of the Acrobat plugins mentioned above.

Table 4.3. Acrobat Exchange plugin vendors

Company	Product or service	Web site
Adobe Plug-in shop	Plugin vendor	www.pluginsource.com
Ambia Corporation	Aerial, Compose, Re:mark, Signet	www.ambia.com
Callas Software GmbH	pdfToolbox	www.callas.de
Datawatch Corp.	Redwing	www.datawatch.com
DigiDox	Collage, DigiDozen	www.digidox.com
Emerge	Plugin vendor	www.emerge.pdfzone.com
Enfocus Software Inc.	CheckUp, PitStop	www.enfocus.com
Lantana Research Corp.	CrackerJack	www.lantanarips.com
Net Formation Inc.	FaceIt!	www.netformation.com
xman software	xToolsOne	www.xman.com

4.7 Testing PDF Files

After successfully generating PDF files, some resources should be set aside for testing. This test should check navigational functionality and platform independence.

If possible, test links, bookmarks, etc., on different platforms to check that they are working correctly and do not depend on the functionalities of any particular operating system. When used on the Web, all internal and external links must be thoroughly tested for reliability. The consistency of links can also be tested with Web administration programs like Adobe SiteMill. A common cause of defective links is a changed directory structure which leaves Acrobat searching for a file which is no longer there, or case differences in file names.

The test for platform independence should ensure that the documents display and print correctly in all environments. It is best to carry out the test on a computer where the fonts required by the document are not installed. If the PDF file includes embedded fonts, then they will be used for display. If they are missing, then either Acrobat's font substitution comes into play or (in a few cases) an error message appears, which the user should naturally be spared.

Testing on various monitors ensures that online documents can be used on lower resolution systems. For documents which are intended to be printed, the effect that compression and downsampling have on output quality should be tested. If the test is thorough and printed appearance is important, then printing should be tested on both PostScript and non-Post-Script printers.

5 PDF Support in Applications

5.1 PDF-savvy Applications

In this chapter we will examine creating PDF files with various text, DTP and graphics programs. Of course, almost every program is "PDF capable" if you create PostScript output and run it through Acrobat Distiller. However, converting the data to PDF requires a lot of effort to insert the hypertext features using Exchange. If there are a large number of documents, or if the files need to be updated often, it is a good idea to specify as much PDF-relevant information as possible in the original document file. Ideally, these features (for example URLs for links to Web sites) are converted automatically to the corresponding PDF features. Adobe has defined the "pdfmark" PostScript operator which allows hypertext elements to be described in the PostScript code. Using pdfmark instructions, the PostScript data can be prepared so that Distiller will generate PDF files including links, bookmarks, and other hypertext elements – without the need for any post-processing in Exchange. A PDF-savvy program has two characteristics:

► It offers access in the user interface to functions for generating those hypertext features which are supported. These include internal links or URLs included in the document. Many DTP programs support such functions by default.

► When it outputs PostScript code, suitable pdfmark instructions to define these properties are included automatically. Programs which do this are still uncommon; several applications can be enabled with plugins or other extensions.

Apart from generating pdfmark instructions via the program interface, it is possible to embed your own pdfmark instructions in the PostScript output by making use of EPS files or program-specific tricks. The whole of the next chapter is devoted to this very powerful method. In this chapter, I want to discuss the PDF features which can be defined in the original document without pdfmark programming. Programs such as Adobe FrameMaker, Adobe PageMaker, and Corel Ventura already support these functions by default. Others – such as Microsoft Word – require extensions.

As the program used to create a file generally has much more data about a document than strictly layout-oriented information, various types of structure and meta-information can be incorporated into the PDF document.

The opposite direction is also very exciting: placing PDF pages in a DTP document. "Placed PDF" is a very recent development implemented in products slated for the near future. At the time of printing, Adobe had already implemented placed PDF support in a PageMaker 6.52 extension.

Similarly, Quark announced that they will provide PDF import and export filters for QuarkXPress, probably in version 4.1.

Article threads.   Defining article threads using Acrobat Exchange's tools is very tedious for long documents. The necessary information is usually already present in the source document as the article rectangles generally follow the text columns exactly. PDF article threads corresponding to the text columns in the document can be generated automatically.

Links.   Without a doubt, links are the hypertext means par excellence. Many DTP programs allow internal links, links to other files, or links to Internet resources. Ideally, these links should be preserved when the document is converted to PDF. This is also the case for automatically generated links, like those used by some programs for tables of contents or indexes, where clicking on an entry takes you to the corresponding place in the document.

Document information.   In many programs it is possible to store general information about the document – author, subject, keywords, etc. – along with the document. Such meta-information should be integrated into a PDF file's document information fields.

Bookmarks.   Bookmarks are an important aid to orientation for a PDF document's readers. In many cases, first, second, and possibly third level headings are suitable for use as bookmarks. The bookmark hierarchy follows the heading hierarchy. If the headings are very long, or if the document is unusually structured, it can make sense to alter the heading text before it is used as a bookmark, or possibly to define a completely different bookmark structure.

Document open info.   Settings related to opening of the PDF file – such as zoom factor, or one or two column layout – are hardly ever found in current DTP programs, but can sometimes be defined in the document as part of PDF preparation.

Other PDF features.   PDF features which are not supported by a program can be inserted later using Acrobat Exchange, or using pdfmark tricks. There are special tricks for incorporating pdfmark code directly into the document.

As pdfmark instructions are only processed by Acrobat Distiller, and not by PDF Writer, you always have to follow the PostScript-and-Distiller route to use them. Programs like PageMaker (see below) integrate Distiller to such an extent that the creation of the intermediate PostScript files is almost invisible to the user.

5.2 Adobe FrameMaker

FrameMaker has for many years occupied an important position in the field of technical documentation and book production. Even before Frame was bought by Adobe, the program had capabilities which simplify the conversion of Frame documents to PDF. As FrameMaker itself contains a powerful hypertext system (used, for example, in FrameMaker's on-line help) many of its features can be carried over when FrameMaker documents are converted to PDF. Since version 5.0, FrameMaker has supported automatic translation of these functions to PDF (the following description relates to FrameMaker 5.0 and 5.1, see below for details on additional features in FrameMaker 5.5):

- ▸ Article threads are generated from text frames.
- ▸ Bookmarks are created from headings.
- ▸ Manually inserted and automatically created links are converted to PDF links.
- ▸ Most of FrameMaker's hypertext commands are converted to their PDF counterparts.

To activate the preparation of these PDF functions, you must check the "Generate Acrobat Data" check box in FrameMaker's print dialog. This ensures that FrameMaker inserts pdfmark instructions corresponding to the above functions in the PostScript code. Acrobat Distiller uses these to generate the desired PDF features.

When Acrobat support is activated in the print menu, it should be noted that some output options are not compatible with PDF preparation. If Acrobat support is turned on, then all pages must be output in the normal order. That is, both odd and even pages must be printed, and the options "Skip Blank Pages" and "Last Sheet First" are not allowed. This restriction is due to the links, which no longer work if pages are missing or are in a different order.

Under Windows 95 it is important to make sure that the PostScript tab of the PostScript driver properties is set to "Optimize for portability – ADSC" (Start Menu, "Settings", "Printer", select the printer, "File", "Properties") as otherwise Distiller may report error messages.

Article threads. FrameMaker uses (if the Acrobat option in the print dialog is activated) the geometry of the text frames as rectangles for PDF article threads. This gives the PDF publisher, without further intervention, article threads which exactly follow the text reading order. Each text flow generates its own article thread, and the name of the text flow is used as the name of the thread. By default, Frame simply labels the flows with capital letters, but this is easy to change in the text frame properties dialog.

Although the automatic generation of article flows is very practical, problems can arise in some situations:

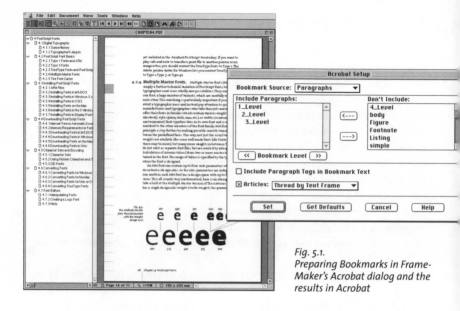

Fig. 5.1.
Preparing Bookmarks in Frame-Maker's Acrobat dialog and the results in Acrobat

▸ If a frame has several text columns, one article rectangle is generated for the whole frame, not for each column. This means that a mouse click in Acrobat does not follow the column order – the functionality of the article thread is therefore lost.

▸ Articles in the document always run from front to back even if the frames are linked in reverse order.

In these situations it is desirable to turn FrameMaker's article function off completely. However, if you still want to retain the automatic generation of bookmarks and links (see below), the article function has to be deactivated with a small pdfmark trick which is described in Section 6.2.

Bookmarks.   FrameMaker can convert headings directly into bookmarks. To do this, the user specifies, in the print dialog's Acrobat settings, which paragraph formats should be used to generate bookmarks (see Figure 5.1). In general, the first two or three heading levels are suitable. In addition nesting – that is, the indentation between the lower and higher level book–marks – can be specified. This nesting (in Figure 5.2 the paragraph formats "1_Level", "2_Level", "3_Level") appears in the PDF document in the hier-archically arranged bookmarks.

FrameMaker does try to make an educated guess based on the font size, but in general, it is necessary to adjust the allocation of paragraph formats to bookmarks manually. As these settings are saved in the FrameMaker doc-ument, this only has to be done once. Finally, a tip which saves many mouse clicks: if you click on one of the arrows while holding down the shift key, all of the paragraph formats are transferred to the other window.

Links and other hypertext commands.   FrameMaker has comprehensive tools for creating links in documents. These links, and most of Frame's other hypertext elements, are also converted to PDF if Acrobat support is turned on in the print dialog. This means that in the ideal scenario a working hypertext document structure can be transferred straight from Frame to Acrobat.

Frame's hypertext capabilities are described fully in the product documentation. Table 5.1 shows all of Frame's hypertext commands and the corresponding PDF elements which are generated automatically.

The few elements which are not translated directly can either be simply replaced by others (for example "matrix" can be replaced with multiple individual links) or can be simulated by Acrobat functions. These functions can be inserted using Exchange, but for large numbers of documents it is much more efficient to prepare them in the Frame file using pdfmark instructions. For this reason the table contains the PDF functions corresponding to those Frame functions not converted automatically as well as hints on generating them using pdfmark instructions. The instructions required to do this are described fully in Chapter 6.

A particular important use of links are internal references which Frame-Maker uses for the table of contents, index or cross references in the text (in the book file, select "File", "Set Up File...", and click on "Create Hypertext Links"). These links are also transferred to PDF, which saves a lot of work.

Named destinations.   FrameMaker uses a PDF feature called "named destinations". This feature identifies document locations by name and is discussed in more detail in Section 8.6. FrameMaker generates named destinations for automatic and user defined links. This occasionally causes Distiller to display a warning that multiple named destinations with the same name are defined. However, you can safely ignore this message as it does not impact the results of the PDF conversion.

Frame derives the symbolic names from the actual text or hypertext command (see Figure 5.2). Links to a heading have spaces replaced by periods, and use the result as a symbolic name. "Newlink" hypertext commands also generate a named destination from the user defined name. For links to a specified page, Frame generates a named destination of the type "P.5" (for page 5).

Frame's "newlink" hypertext command therefore offers an easy method of defining your own named destinations (which is not possible in Acrobat Exchange).

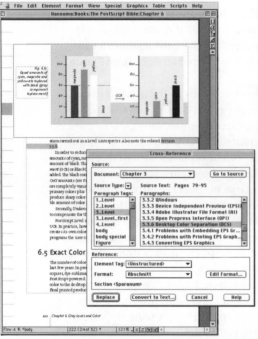

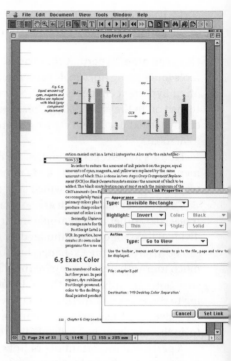

Fig. 5.2.
How a cross-reference in FrameMaker relates to a
named destination in the Frame-generated PDF

File names. When converting FrameMaker files to PDF, certain peculiarities regarding file names have to be observed. FrameMaker always assumes that if there is a file name suffix (for example *.fm* or *.fm5*), it is to be removed for the PDF file and replaced with *.pdf*. This affects not only output files but also links. Because of this, the names of the PDFs generated have to adhere this scheme!

If you want to generate platform-independent file names – as for a CD-ROM in ISO 9660 format – the source files must be set up so that after conversion they have the names which Frame expects. The file names can not be changed later, because doing so would mean that the links would no longer work.

The easiest situation to deal with is if there is no suffix, as then automatic conversion does not take place and *.pdf* is simply appended. The suffix *.fm5* is replaced by *.pdf* while other file name extensions are retained. The suffix *.pdf* is then added as well (for example, *intro.doc.pdf*).

Table 5.1. *FrameMaker 5.1's hypertext commands and their PDF equivalents*

Hypertext Command	Automatic Conversion	Remarks, Substitute Functions
alert	note	The note is always closed.
alerttitle	note	The alert title appears in the note window.
exit	–	Use the menu command "File", "Quit" instead.
gotolink	link	File name suffix is changed (see text).
gotolink firstpage	link	–
gotolink lastpage	link	If it refers to another document, always jumps to the first page of that document.
gotolinkfitwin	link	Like gotolink, window is not resized
gotopage	link	Target is defined as a named destination.
matrix	–	Use individual links instead.
message	–	Only works for Frame API Clients.
message system	–	Use program call with /Launch key instead.
message winexec	–	Use program call with /Launch key instead.
message URL	Web link	URL links are availably only in FrameMaker 5.5.
newlink	named destination	Named destinations can not be created in Acrobat Exchange.
nextpage	link	–
openlink	link	Like gotolink, no new window
openlinkfitwin	link	Like openlink, window is not resized
opennew	–	New documents can not be created in Acrobat.
openpage	link	Like gotopage, no new window
popup	–	–
previouslink	–	Use menu command "View", "Back" instead.
previouslinkfitwin	–	Like previouslink, window is not resized
previouspage	link	–
quit	–	Use menu command "File", "Close" instead.
quitall	–	Use menu command "Window", "Close All" instead.

When printing a book file, FrameMaker allows the user to choose between creating a single PostScript file for the whole book or one file per chapter. To achieve the latter, simply enter a "*" as the name of the PostScript file in the print dialog. This will produce files with the same names as the original chapters, but with the original file name extension replaced by *.ps*.

If different operating systems are in use, the different handling of upper and lower case file names on Mac, Windows, and Unix have to be considered. Further information on this topic can be found in Section 8.6.

Common source documents for all media. Usually, both online and print versions of a document should be made from the same source file in order to avoid duplicate content and conversions. As the two media place different requirements on the documents, the respective versions have to be differently formatted. The main problems are different page formats and the optical indication of links.

Although FrameMaker does have a useful "conditional text" function, the problem of "conditional formats" can only be partially solved using workarounds.

You cannot switch between page formats by clicking on a button, but importing another document's formats helps. To do this, create two extra documents in FrameMaker which contain the desired page formats for the printed and PDF versions. Using "File", "Import", "Formats..." you can apply the desired page size to your document.

To prepare links when the text is being typed in, it is best to define a character style called something like "Link", which you apply to text which will be a link in the online version. For the printed version, where links are not usually highlighted, the settings for this style are the same as for normal text. As above, define the character format "Link" in an extra file, but this time (for example) define the text color as blue to highlight it. Before distilling the file, import the character style from the extra file to color all the links blue. Of course, this procedure only works if you have formatted all of the links with the corresponding style.

For navigational elements such as arrows and the like, the "conditional text" function, with which you can make document components disappear, is very useful. This function can easily be used to prevent navigation buttons from appearing in print.

Extensions in FrameMaker 5.5.   It is not surprising that Adobe has improved PDF support in FrameMaker after taking over its manufacturer. Some of the problems addressed above have been dealt with in FrameMaker 5.5. In addition, this version contains a complete set of Acrobat software. The following improvements with respect to PDF conversion are implemented in FrameMaker 5.5:

- ▸ Under "File", "Save as..." PDF is offered as an output format. As before, FrameMaker does not generate the PDF code itself, but uses Distiller to process previously generated PostScript files.
- ▸ Article threads can be turned on or off separately in the enhanced Acrobat settings dialog.
- ▸ You can specify, in the same dialog, whether article flows for multicolumn text should follow the text frame or the individual columns.
- ▸ URLs can be inserted directly into the text using the hypertext marker "message URL http://...". These are changed to Acrobat's Weblinks when the document is converted to PDF.

- In FrameMaker+SGML, bookmarks can be created not only from headings but also from SGML's structural elements. As with headings, the number and hierarchy can be specified.

Missing features. Even with the extra functions in FrameMaker 5.5 several features remain on the wish list. As there is no corresponding function in FrameMaker, for example, you can not enter general document information. However, this function, and many others, can be forced using pdfmark instructions. Using PostScript frames and dummy EPS files, there are powerful (if somehow clumsy) methods of inserting these instructions into Frame documents. Details about pdfmark instructions in FrameMaker's PostScript frames can be found in Section 6.3.

5.3 Adobe PageMaker

From version 6 PageMaker, Adobe's other DTP program, has had extensive PDF support. The PDF export function (see Figure 5.3) generates PostScript files enriched with pdfmark instructions, and allows Acrobat Distiller to convert them to PDF. Generating PostScript, opening and closing Distiller, and optionally testing the PDF files in Exchange are so well integrated with PageMaker that the process is transparent to the user. PageMaker offers significantly more options for controlling PDF conversion than FrameMaker.

It is almost unnecessary to note that links in the document are translated to the corresponding links and Weblinks. This applies equally to manually defined links within the document and to URL links inserted into the document using the hypertext palette. PageMaker also converts the automatically generated links for the table of contents and the index. The user can control how links are generated very precisely from the "PDF Options" dialog (see Figure 5.4): it can be specified separately for each of the four types of links (table of contents, index, internal and external links) whether or not they should be taken into account during PDF conversion.

In general, bookmarks are created from those headings which are also in the table of contents. If these are too long, or unsuitable for use as bookmarks for other reasons, you can also define other text for bookmarks. For

Fig. 5.3.
PageMaker's PDF
export options

Fig. 5.4.
General PDF options and bookmark
options in PageMaker

bookmark destinations, PageMaker even allows the zoom factor to be specified.

Coupling bookmarks to the table of contents makes it easier to create bookmarks. But how do you create bookmarks if the PageMaker document does not have a table of contents? In this case, you can get round the problem by creating a dummy table of contents which is only used as a data source for bookmarks:

- ► Mark all paragraphs for the bookmarks for inclusion in the table of contents.
- ► Generate the table of contents and place it on a new page at the end of the document. Make a note of this page number.
- ► In the PageMaker PDF options dialog, specify a page range which does not contain the page with the table of contents, as this page should not be included in the PDF file.

If possible, the dummy table of contents should not contain headings as otherwise all bookmarks derived from the table of contents will be demoted by one level (with the heading as the highest bookmark).

The PDF document info fields for title, subject, author, and keywords are taken from the document information. As well as the viewing options for opening the PDF file, a note can be attached to the first page of the PDF file – all this is done in the PageMaker document without any additional work in Exchange!

Placing PDF files in PageMaker documents. In early 1998, Adobe published a plugin for PageMaker 6.52 which allows placing single pages from PDF files in a document, just as you can place an EPS graphic on a page created in PageMaker. The plugin, which is freely available from Adobe's Web server, creates a screen preview from the PDF which is used for the screen layout. The user can control the resolution and color depth of the preview. Although the PDF contents are not editable and hypertext features in the PDF are not preserved, this PageMaker plugin is certainly an important step

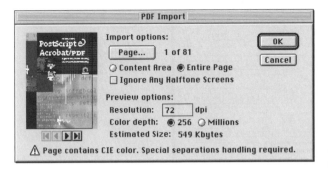

Fig. 5.5.
*Placing a PDF file in Page-
Maker works similarly to
placing an EPS graphic*

towards a PDF-based workflow in the graphics and prepress trade. We may
expect other vendors to offer similar features for their programs as well.

.4 QuarkXPress

QuarkXPress does not offer any direct support for PDF generation. This de-
plorable situation has not changed with version 4.0. There is, however, one
piece of good news: The plugin "PDF Design XTension" from the Dutch
company Techno Design facilitates the most important aspects of converting Quark documents to PDF:

- ▸ Bookmarks
- ▸ Links
- ▸ Article threads
- ▸ Document info fields

The XTension does not itself generate PDF, but prepares PostScript files for
conversion by inserting pdfmark instructions, and therefore requires Acrobat Distiller. The Project Manager allows several files to be collected as a single project, such as the individual chapters of a book. With the help of the
project file, bookmarks and links which span all documents can be defined
across files.

Bookmarks can be generated automatically by defining complete or partial paragraphs using particular styles as bookmark source. This makes it
very easy to use headings as bookmarks. Alternatively, you can specify the
typographic properties which text must have to be used as a bookmark,
such as bold text with a size of at least 18 points.

Links can also be defined manually or automatically. When generating
links automatically it is often a good idea to relate this to a property like
text color. If – with a view to how they will appear in a Web browser – links
are highlighted in color, you can specify that text in this color will become a
link in a dialog field in the PDF Design XTension. Links support the same
range of hypertext actions as bookmarks, namely jumps to another page in

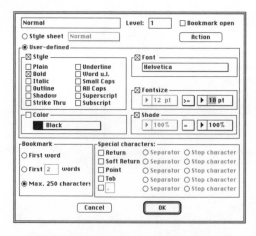

Fig. 5.6.
Bookmark and Link options with the PDF
Design XTension for QuarkXPress

the same document, opening another document, or a link to a Web server. It is also possible to define references which go to the next or previous page.

The article threads which the PDF Design XTension generates generally correspond to the order in which the QuarkXPress document's text frames are linked. This order can be changed manually if need be.

The document information field contents for the individual documents in a project can be specified in the Quark file too. When the document is converted to PDF, they are used in the Acrobat version of the document.

5.5 Microsoft Word

Macros for the PDF Writer. If Microsoft Word is already present on the computer when Acrobat is installed, the setup routine installs Word and Excel macros which simplify the use of the PDF Writer for Word documents. Using the new menu entry "File", "Create Adobe PDF..." in Word you can force the conversion of a document to PDF. However, this is the simplest type of PDF conversion, namely using the PDF Writer printer driver. The macros do not offer any additional functionality for the actual conversion, but simply make the PDF Writer the current printer, send the document to the printer, and then make the original printer the default printer again. The macros save the user a few mouse clicks if simple documents have to be converted frequently, but are not suitable for high-quality documents or incorporating hypertext functions.

Adobe PDFMaker. PDFMaker is a free Word add-on which makes many PDF features available from within the Word document. PDFMaker is implemented as a Visual Basic Application for Word 97. As Word 97 uses a new macro language, PDFMaker does not work with older versions of Word. On the plus side, PDFMaker has no problems with non-English Word versions. PDFMaker is available from the following URL:

`http://www.adobe.com/prodindex/acrobat/resources.html`

PDFMaker includes support for conversion to PDF with both Acrobat Distiller and PDF Writer. The latter is quicker, but does not offer any supplementary functions. The list of functions supported when converting using Distiller is indeed impressive:

- ► Headings are converted to bookmarks.
- ► Internet links are converted to PDF Weblinks.
- ► Cross references are converted to PDF links.
- ► Page numbers in the table of contents and other places are linked to the relevant page.
- ► Links to other documents are converted to PDF links.
- ► Footnote and endnote symbols are linked to the corresponding footnote or endnote.
- ► Comments are converted to notes.
- ► Text boxes are converted to article threads.
- ► The document properties are used in the PDF file's info fields.

PDFMaker interprets the Word file's contents and uses them to generate the corresponding pdfmark instructions which are then passed to Distiller via

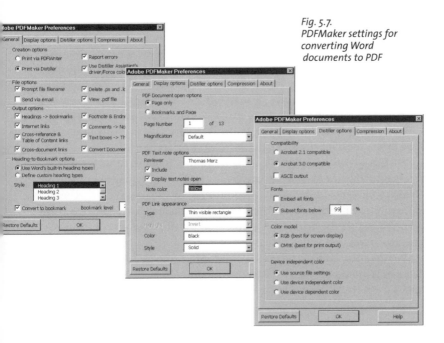

Fig. 5.7.
PDFMaker settings for converting Word documents to PDF

the PostScript printer driver. Many aspects of the PDF conversion can be controlled from comprehensive dialogs (see Figure 5.7). Even Distiller's preferences can be specified from within the Word document.

5.6 TEX

The TEX typesetting system has a long history of producing high-quality output and is widely used in academic publishing. Many users and programmers have expanded TEX's functionality by writing macro packages and auxiliary programs. Several DVI drivers are available for producing PostScript output from TEX documents for printing or distilling. However, there are two issues related to TEX-generated PDF which should be addressed. The first relates to font configuration, the second to hypertext enhancements.

Bitmap and outline fonts in TEX .   In many TEX installations, if you produce a PostScript file from your TEX source and distill it to PDF, the resulting Acrobat file displays slowly and does not render well on screen, and the characters look very ugly when the page is zoomed into. Besides, the PDF files grow quite large.

These problems are related to the font handling in several DVI drivers which are optimized for printer output. Many TEX output drivers generate PostScript bitmap fonts by default, which are optimized for the printer's resolution, e.g., 300 dpi. When distilling such a PostScript file, the bitmap fonts are included in the PDF and are used for screen display in Acrobat. However, Type 3 (bitmap) fonts in PDF don't match the screen quality of Type 1 (outline) fonts. Type 3 fonts increase PDF file size and make the character shapes look irregular. It is therefore recommended to install Type 1 outline fonts in the DVI driver in order to get the best possible output.

Several drivers, such as Tom Rokicki's dvips and the TeXtures driver from Blue Sky Research can handle bitmap fonts as well as outline fonts, and the user can choose which kind is preferred. Other drivers, such as the commercial ones from Y&Y, are not able to use Type 3 fonts at all, which means the font problem in TEX doesn't exist with these drivers.

PostScript outline versions of the Computer Modern fonts for TEX are freely available for Mac, Windows, and Unix. The high-quality fonts from Blue Sky Research and Y&Y are administered by the American Mathematical Society (which also holds the copyright), and are included in the CTAN archives. Before these fonts were available, the outline fonts in the BaKoMa package have been widely used.

For details related to installing and configuring outline fonts, check out Kendall Whitehouse's paper "Creating quality Adobe PDF files from TEX with DVIPS". It has been available as a Technical Note from Adobe's Web server. However, since they rearrange the files on their server frequently, ask the search machine to locate the document.

You can find out whether Type 1 or Type 3 fonts are used in your documents by clicking "File", "Document Info", "Fonts...". The font info box displays the name and type of each font used in the document.

The hyperref package.   Sebastian Rahtz's hyperref package for LATEX 2e lets you define PDF hypertext features in the TEX source. Simply include the line

```
\usepackage [driver_name]{hyperref}
```

in the document preamble. This results in LATEX's symbolic references being transformed to PDF links. Hyperref also makes PDF bookmarks for the sections of the document, and generates hyperlinks from index and bibliography entries to the corresponding source location. Additionally, you can specify the appearance of links (border color, etc.) as well as general document information and viewing options.

Hyperref generates pdfmark instructions and can be configured to a number of backend processors, for example those following the HyperTeX conventions.

PDFTeX.   PDFTeX is an enhanced version of TEX that can output either DVI or PDF. The PDF output is created directly, avoiding the intermediate formats DVI and PostScript. Although still in a beta version at the time of writing, PDFTeX is available as part of several TEX packages, including MikTeX and the widely used Web2c package for Unix and Windows 32-bit. By the time you read this, PDFTeX will probably already be contained in the CTAN archives.

The ConTeXt package.   Although I can't judge it from my own experience, the ConTeXt macro package is worth mentioning since it is considered the most advanced TEX way to make PDF. Sebastian Rahtz, who is deeply into all TEX-related matters, says "ConTeXt PDF documents make your hair stand on end". The package is available from

```
http://www.ntg.nl/context
```

5.7 Graphics Programs

As PDF becomes more widespread, the most important graphics software manufacturers are also implementing PDF support within their programs. Using PDF-capable graphics programs, you can produce PDF files without Distiller or PDF Writer, and edit existing documents. However, there are limits on the PDF functions which can be used: most hypertext functionality is lost; platform independence and font embedding are also poorly served. As PDF files usually contain text in many small portions, it is usually difficult or impossible to edit large passages of text. Graphics programs can be used to correct typos in PDF files whose source documents are unavailable – but this can also be done in Version 3.0 and later of Exchange.

As the graphics programs generate the PDF code themselves (without Distiller), it is not possible to use pdfmark instructions. To be able to use EPS files with pdfmark instructions, the normal method of generating a PostScript file and running it through Distiller must be used rather than the program's "Export as PDF" or "Save as PDF" function.

Adobe Illustrator.   Since version 5.5, Illustrator has been able to read and write PDF files. As Illustrator can only work on one page at a time, in the case of multipage documents the page number of the page to be worked on must be specified when the page is opened. For multipage documents without thumbnails, this can become a blindfold chase through the document (see Figure 5.8). After opening and editing a page, it must be resaved in PDF format and, if need be, the original page in the document must be replaced with the modified one using Acrobat Exchange.

The usual Illustrator text and graphics tools can be used to modify the page contents. Hypertext elements can be neither edited nor defined; links and form fields which are already defined are lost when the file is resaved, and have to be redefined in Exchange. By way of replacement, individually corrected pages can be replaced in the document using Exchange's replace function. This function does preserve the links.

Text can only be edited reliably if the relevant font is installed on the system. If the fonts are embedded, and particularly in the case of subsets and character sets from other platforms, you can expect problems.

With embedded EPS files, Illustrator only uses the preview part of the graphic in the PDF output (in a similar way to output on a non-PostScript printer). Besides, this bitmap data is compressed using JPEG compression. This algorithm removes some image information, thereby reducing image quality. For these reasons, Distiller should always be used to convert Illustrator files with embedded EPS files to PDF.

Fig. 5.8.
When importing PDF files in Illustrator you have to select a single page from the file, but without thumbnails you can only make an educated guess as to the correct page number

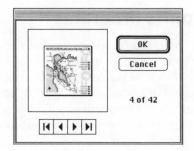

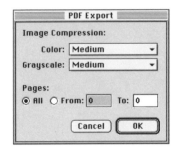

PDF Export

Image Compression:

Color: Medium

Grayscale: Medium

Pages:
● All ○ From: 0   To: 0

Cancel   OK

Fig. 5.9.
FreeHand offers several options
when exporting to PDF

Macromedia FreeHand. FreeHand has also offered PDF support since Version 5.5. Freehand, unlike Illustrator, can only use Acrobat 2 files, not PDF 1.2's or Acrobat 3's optimized files. Optimized files have to be saved in unoptimized format using Acrobat Exchange before they can be edited in Free-Hand.

As FreeHand can also process multi-page documents, you do not have to specify a page when opening a PDF file. Instead, the program reads the whole file and any page can be edited. This is very useful, but in the case of large or complex files often causes a memory shortage.

CorelDRAW. As of version 7, CorelDRAW has its own PDF import and export filter. Using this filter, you can edit existing PDFs or generate PDF files from Corel documents. The PDF filter processes text, graphics, and raster images. However, Corel's filter suffers from major restrictions. It only supports PDF 1.1, which means Corel refuses to interpret Acrobat 3.0's optimized files. Even worse, in one of my tests an old PDF 1.0 file was imported as a text file consisting of PDF instructions and code, instead of being interpreted! Hypertext features for PDF are completely missing in CorelDRAW 7.

6 pdfmark Primer

6.1 Overview

This chapter is devoted to pdfmark programming. The pdfmark operator is a PostScript extension which is only implemented in Acrobat Distiller (as opposed to PostScript printers). Using this operator, many non-layout-related features of a PDF file can be defined in the original document or in the corresponding PostScript code. Why bother with pdfmarks since you can implement these features in Acrobat Exchange? Contrary to adding hypertext features manually in Exchange, the pdfmark method has a big advantage in that you don't have to redo all links and other special effects when document changes require generating a new PDF version. Instead, the hypertext features are automatically generated when distilling the PostScript file. It is very important to know that pdfmark instructions are processed in Acrobat Distiller only, but not in PDF Writer.

PostScript programming basics are quite helpful when you're working with pdfmark. In this chapter, however, I'll try to explain how to explore the power of pdfmark applications without any programming experience. Although this chapter is filled with lots of gory details – mostly stuffed into tables – you should be able to deal with many applications by simply using or adapting one of the examples. Unless you wish to make use of the more advanced features or additional options, you can get by without looking into the tables or the accompanying descriptions.

This chapter is based on Adobe's *pdfmark Reference Manual* which can be found on the Acrobat CD-ROM. However, many features and details can only be understood by additionally delving into the *Portable Document Format Reference Manual* (to be found on Adobe's Web server). If you consider yourself to be a serious Acrobat user, I definitely recommend reading (or at least glancing over) these manuals. There you will find additional details which I do not cover here.

This chapter isn't meant to replace the Adobe manuals (in fact, it surely can't). Instead, I'll try to tame the very technical contents by introducing many directly usable examples and also present additional information not documented in Adobe's manuals. And there are lots of undocumented features! While doing research for this chapter, I not only discovered undocumented pdfmark instructions (e.g., for executing Acrobat menu functions), but also PDF code generated by Acrobat software but not covered in the reference manual (e.g., assigning an index file to a PDF document). Looking at it the other way round, there are PDF features which are documented in the reference but which are nevertheless inaccessible with Acrobat software. The only way of using these features is by generating the respective pdfmark operators (e.g., named destinations; these are link targets labeled with a symbolic name, see Section 8.6). But you should take care when using such features – undocumented features usually don't warrant any support by the manufacturer of the software.

So you ask yourself why an author or editor should bother with technical details such as pdfmark programming? You're definitely on the right track. In my not so humble opinion, pdfmark only serves as a temporary kludge as long as application software is unable to generate the necessary pdfmarks automatically. In Chapter 5 you can find an overview of the current status of pdfmark support in several important application programs.

Function overview.   Using pdfmarks, you can define a wealth of Acrobat features in the PostScript code. This chapter presents many functions along with working examples and extensive explanations. To avoid your getting lost in a plethora of samples, Table 6.1 gives an overview of all pdfmark features covered in this chapter.

.2 Preliminaries

Embedding pdfmarks in the PostScript code.   Before delving into pdfmark descriptions I'd like to present several means of including pdfmark statements in a document's PostScript code. The techniques covered in this chapter do not relate to certain application software. Chapter 5 has already covered automatic pdfmark generation in application programs; Section 6.3 talks about application-specific methods for embedding pdfmarks in the PostScript stream.

As you can see in Figure 6.1, several components are involved in creating the PostScript code. The exact number and kind of these components not only varies with the operating system in use, but also with the kind of application software.[1] The location at which to embed pdfmarks in the Post-Script generating chain depends on the scope of the feature to be realized by pdfmarks. Consider the following examples:

- ▸ A URL link is expected to show up on a certain page only.
- ▸ Automatically attaching an index file may affect a certain file or several files in a group.
- ▸ It may be desirable for all files created with a certain program to contain document info fields with appropriate contents.
- ▸ The name of the creator (the person, not the program) may be inserted in the document info fields of all generated files, independently of the program used to create the file.

The following pages present important ways of embedding pdfmarks along with some examples. The remaining sections of this chapter will explain in more detail how these examples work. For now we will only consider how to embed pdfmark statements. The embedding techniques presented here require varying degrees of experience on the user's part.

Protecting your printout.   I already mentioned the fact that the pdfmark operator is only implemented in Acrobat Distiller and not in any type of PostScript printer. For this reason, using pdfmarks implies getting Post-Script errors when you try to distill and print the very same PostScript files (which is normally the case). This problem can be solved with a couple of PostScript statements which don't have any effect in Distiller but cancel the

---

1. You can find much more information on these topics in my book "PostScript & Acrobat/PDF – Applications, Troubleshooting, and Cross-Platform Publishing" (Springer-Verlag 1997).

pdfmark operator when printing the document. To achieve this effect I recommend placing the following line of PostScript code in front of any pdfmark operator, or – better still – in modified PostScript prolog:

```
/pdfmark where {pop} {userdict /pdfmark /cleartomark load put} ifelse
```

To achieve the protection it suffices to include these statements once at the beginning of the PostScript code – this cancels all forthcoming pdfmarks when printing the document.

Another source of error is related to older printers equipped with a PostScript Level 1 interpreter: pdfmark sequences often make use of the << and >> operators which are only defined in Level 2. On Level 1 devices these two operators give rise to a syntax error – even if you followed the above advice and included the protection line! However, it's not very difficult to deal with this problem by adding a few more PostScript lines before using any pdfmark statement:

```
/pdfmark where {pop} {userdict /pdfmark /cleartomark load put} ifelse
/languagelevel where {pop languagelevel}{1} ifelse
2 lt {
    userdict (<<) cvn ([) cvn load put
    userdict (>>) cvn (]) cvn load put
} if
```

Including pdfmarks in the native document.   Often it is more convenient to define pdfmark statements directly in your native DTP or word processor document. This requires application software which is capable of embedding user-defined PostScript code, or which at least offers some feature which may be (mis-) used for this purpose. Obviously, it's not sufficient to write the pdfmark statements in the document's text since the text is getting printed instead of being interpreted as PostScript code.

Two samples of nice embedding features are FrameMaker's PostScript frames and Microsoft Word's print fields. You may find similar functions in other programs, although these functions originally may have served a completely different purpose. According to the embedding technique, additional information for use in pdfmarks may be available, e.g., the enclosing text frame's coordinates which may be used for defining a link rectangle. You can find a more detailed explanation of embedding pdfmarks for several programs in Section 6.3.

Startup directory of Acrobat Distiller.   Before it processes a document's actual page descriptions, Acrobat Distiller interprets all files found in its startup directory. This gives an easy way to activate or deactivate certain features by simply moving the respective PostScript file in or out of the startup directory. Note that startup files are only processed once at Distiller's launch time. For this reason, they generally remain active during Distiller's life time, independently of the number of files processed. Unfortu-

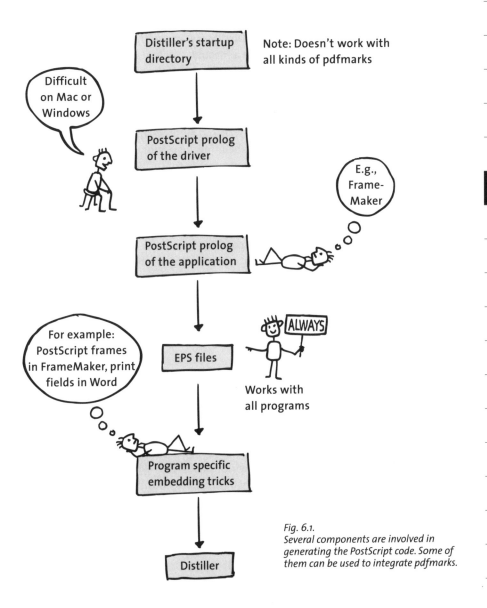

Fig. 6.1.
Several components are involved in generating the PostScript code. Some of them can be used to integrate pdfmarks.

nately, this also means that the document-related pdfmark stuff doesn't work. An example that works in the startup directory is the canceling of specific pdfmark variations as described on page 83.

To avoid confusion, I recommend displaying a descriptive message according to the following pattern:

```
(Article threads deactivated!\n) print flush
```

This way you can easily see which startup files are active when launching Distiller.

A note of warning: all files in Distiller's startup directory are loaded in an undocumented order. If you edit a file and your text editor leaves a backup file in this directory, both files will be loaded. If the old file is loaded after the new one, the old values will be used!

EPS files. Graphics files in the Encapsulated PostScript (EPS) format are supported within all major text, DTP, and graphics applications. By definition, they provide a means of embedding PostScript code in the document. EPS files therefore offer great opportunities for including pdfmark operators. Aside from being supported in all current programs, this method has the additional advantage of very easy handling via a program's "import" or "place". The disadvantage is an EPS file's rather limited scope: EPS files don't act globally, but are restricted in operation to one particular page. In some cases, however, it's possible to bypass this restriction. Another complication is that of the formal requirements for EPS files which have to be obeyed for pdfmarks too. Since EPS files don't know anything about their location on the page they can't use absolute coordinates within the page.

Sounds complicated? In many cases embedding pdfmarks in EPS is as easy as using the following template and simply adjusting the contained pdfmark operators:

```
%!PS-Adobe-3.0 EPSF-3.0
%%BoundingBox: 0 0 72 72
%%EndProlog
/pdfmark where {pop} {userdict /pdfmark /cleartomark load put} ifelse
[ {ThisPage} << /Trans << /S /Dissolve >> >> /PUT pdfmark
%%EOF
```

This dummy EPS file defines a size of 72 × 72 points (equalling 1 inch = 2.54 cm) within the "%%BoundingBox" comment. This is the EPS graphic's size in the document. The graphic can be arbitrarily positioned on the page. Since the EPS doesn't produce any printout, it doesn't matter where it is placed on the page. Generally, you can place it somewhere near the edge of the page in order not to disturb the layout.

Note that the EPS sample above already includes the additional line of PostScript code for eliminating PostScript errors when printing the document.

You can further reduce the size of the graphic in order to make it appear less prominent. The following line:

```
%%BoundingBox: 0 0 1 1
```

defines a size of 1 × 1 points, making the graphic nearly disappear from the screen. However, this small size makes it close to impossible to click the graphic with the mouse if you want to move or delete it.

pdfmark operators relating to a rectangular area – for example links, notes, or form fields – should use the BoundingBox's coordinates as values in the /Rect array. This simplifies changing the link's size by simply changing the size of the embedded EPS.

There is, however, a small glitch related to pdfmarks in EPS "graphics": you won't be able to see any screen preview of the EPS. But what should a hypertext function's preview look like anyway?

PostScript prolog of operating system or application. The PostScript prolog is a set of PostScript procedures loaded ahead of the actual page descriptions by the operating system, printer driver, or application program. The prolog is required for successfully printing the document and may also be modified to include pdfmark operators.

Firstly, you have to check whether the driver's or program's prolog is accessible at all or hidden deeply in the driver, only surfacing in the final PostScript output. Note some samples:

► In addition to the printer driver's prolog, FrameMaker for Windows uses another small prolog which can be found in the program's init directory. In Unix – which doesn't have any system-wide printer drivers – FrameMaker uses the prolog in the file *ps_prolog*.

► As an optimization, some PostScript drivers allow generating the prolog separately, and later create the print data without any prolog. The prolog must of course be available when printing the document. For PDF conversion, it may be possible to adjust the prolog.

When patching prolog files, note that pdfmark operators relate to all documents being distilled with the manipulated prolog. This is not always what you want.

Windows NT separator pages. Windows NT offers a hook for including custom instructions in the printer output stream. This feature is called separator pages because its most prominent use is to print exactly that: informative sheets between individual print jobs. In order to use separator pages for pdfmarks, we have to adhere to the syntax of the separator pages interpreter – the contents of a separator file are not simply copied to the output stream but may also contain certain variables. This means you have to insert a couple of special characters into your pdfmark code before installing it as a separator page.

As explained above, we include the printout protecting code (only to be sure) and the familiar "%!PS-Adobe-3.0" line (because our code will be sent ahead of all other PostScript instructions). For example, to define general document information in a separator page, create a file named *docinfo.sep* which contains the following lines:

```
@
@L%!PS-Adobe-3.0
@L/pdfmark where {pop} {userdict /pdfmark /cleartomark load put} ifelse
@L[ /Title (User Manual)
@L  /Author (Michael Heinzel)
@L  /Subject (Adjusting the electronics of MH-screen)
@L  /Keywords (screen display MH-screen)
@L  /Creator (DocMaker 1.0)
@L  /ModDate (D:19980110205731)
@L/DOCINFO pdfmark
```

The "@" character in the first line defines the special character used in this file. "@L" instructs the driver to include the entire line in the PostScript output without changing it. To make use of this separator page, select "Start", "Settings", "Printers", right-click your PostScript printer driver, choose "Properties", and click the "General" tab. In this menu, click "Separator Page…" and browse to locate the file defined above. (NT's default separator pages live in \winnt\system32*.sep.) The selected separator page is included in your PostScript output as long as you don't deselect it in the printer driver settings.

Note that PostScript drivers for Hewlett-Packard printers include some PJL code at the start of the output stream which does not contain PostScript. In order to avoid problems with Distiller, I recommend selecting a non-HP printer.

PPD files. Most current PostScript drivers are configured via PPD (PostScript printer description) files. The drivers read the PPD file in order to find out a device's features, and the PostScript code to activate these features. Therefore, such drivers may be instructed to include pdfmarks via the PPD file. Since a PPD may also configure the driver's user interface, PPDs may be used for constructing a convenient method for including pdfmarks. However, manipulating PPD files is an error-prone process which may result in damaged PostScript output or the driver not working any more. For this reason I only mention this method for specialists without exploring further details.

Post-processing the PostScript code after generation. In some cases it's reasonable to completely generate the PostScript files and do some processing afterwards. Automated text processing tools like Unix's sed and awk or the Perl programming language are quite useful for this task. Note that most text processing tools can't deal with binary data. For this reason, the PostScript data have to be generated in ASCII format to allow post-processing.

The method isn't suited for all pdfmark applications and may require a good deal of work for implementing it. As an example, let's define an article thread for which the columns (beads) have identical widths on each page.

This task may be achieved by inserting the following line at the beginning of each page's PostScript code:

```
[ /Title (A) /Rect [ 100 100 500 700 ] /ARTICLE pdfmark
```

Since the pages in PostScript files are separated by "%%Page:" comments (at least in DSC conforming PostScript files), it's easy to accomplish this. The following sed script implements the task on Unix systems (it requires the "%%EndPageSetup" comment to be present):

```
/%%EndPageSetup/a\
[ /Title (Main text) /Rect [100 100 500 800 ] /ARTICLE pdfmark
```

Canceling certain pdfmark operators. In some cases it may be useful to cancel certain pdfmarks which are automatically generated by an application, but which are not wanted. For example, FrameMaker (up to version 5.1.x) generates pdfmarks for bookmarks, links, and article threads. It's impossible to selectively activate or deactivate these features – you get either all or none. If you want to get rid of automatically generated article threads without sacrificing links and bookmarks, you can use the following code to cancel a single kind of pdfmarks (in this case the article feature):

```
/pdfmark where { pop
    /_origpdfmark /pdfmark load def
    /pdfmark {
        dup /ARTICLE eq {
            cleartomark
        }{
            _origpdfmark
        } ifelse
    } bind def
} if
```

Data types for pdfmarks. Since pdfmarks are part of the PostScript code they share data types and syntax with the page description language. In order to spare you reading PostScript programming books, I'll try to briefly explain the most important data types used in pdfmark instructions. You can separate instructions with arbitrary numbers of spaces, tabs, or line-end characters. Note that case is significant in PostScript and pdfmark programming.

Concerning *integers* and *floating point numbers* there's nothing more to note except that they work as expected. *Boolean values* can take on the values "true" or "false". An *array* is an arbitrary long collection of (possibly different) data types delimited by square brackets:

```
[ /XYZ null null null ]
```

A *name* (don't confuse names with the strings presented below) is an identifier for a function or a parameter, always starting with a slash "/". Names can be up to 127 characters long (including the leading slash). Names

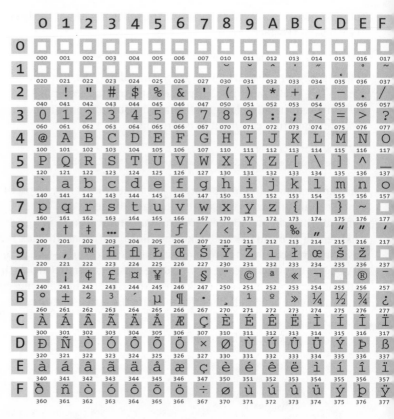

Fig. 6.2.
The PDFDocEncoding
character set for PDF
bookmarks and
notes also has to be
used in pdfmark
strings. The octal
codes are shown be-
low each character.

mustn't contain one of the characters %, (,), <, >, [,], {, }, /, or #. Neither must they contain any special characters.

Strings are text in parentheses. Parentheses themselves, line-end characters, or backslashes inside strings must be "escaped" with a leading backslash:

```
(This is a string with two \(2\) parens.)
```

Strings have to obey a certain character set. Unlike the actual page contents, PDF internally uses a fixed character set called PDFDocEncoding (see Figure 6.2) which is different from the Mac or Windows character sets. PDF bookmarks and notes use this character set. Therefore, strings used in pdfmark instructions must also use PDFDocEncoding. Since this character set shares many (though not all) character positions with the Windows character set, you can use many Windows special characters within pdfmarks since their Windows code equals their PDFDocEncoding code.

On the Mac, however, octal notation has to be used for special characters, i.e., the octal value of the character after a leading backslash. Here are several examples:

```
™=\222, ‰=\213, •=\200, «=\253, »=\273, ©=\251, ®=\256
```

You can determine the codes of other characters by looking at the table in Figure 6.2. There, you can also find out whether a certain character is supported in PDFDocEncoding at all. For example, the French word "Télégramme" as a PDF string looks like this:

```
(T\3511\351gramme)
```

Colors in pdfmarks are defined as RGB triples in an array. Translating to plain talk, this means three numbers in the range 0 to 1 for the red, green, and blue components. The following array defines 100 percent blue:

```
[ 0 0 1 ]
```

Dictionaries are data structures containing an arbitrary number of key/value pairs (note that /URI is used as a value in the first pair, and as a key in the third pair):

```
<< /Subtype /URI /IsMap true /URI (http://www.ifconnection.de/~tm) >>
```

Dictionaries are delimited by two angle brackets ("less than" and "greater than" characters – not to be confused with French quotes "«" and "»") on either side. Dictionaries may be nested, requiring the appropriate number of angle brackets. The order of pairs in a dictionary isn't significant. However, the ordering key/value must be strictly obeyed for each pair.

Finally, *comments* may contain remarks on the sometimes otherwise incomprehensible pdfmark instructions. Comments are introduced with a percent character and continue until the end of the line:

```
% The following code defines a bookmark:
[    /Page 1
     /View [/XYZ 44 730 1.0]
     /Title (Start)
/OUT pdfmark
```

In order to keep track of your pdfmark tricks I recommend using comments for all pdfmark instructions. Since all examples in this chapter are explained in the text, however, I will do without comments.

Coordinate system.   Many pdfmark instructions involve geometrical coordinates, especially when you define rectangles for a link's active area. pdfmarks use the PostScript coordinate system which has the origin in the lower left corner, the first coordinate increasing to the right, and the second coordinate to the top. The unit of measurement is the well-known DTP point, defined as follows:

```
1 point = 1/72 inch = 25.4/72 mm = 0.3528 mm
```

For example, a U.S. letter page measures 612 x 792 points.

6.3 Application-Specific Embedding Tricks

The method described above for embedding pdfmark instructions in EPS files works in all programs which support EPS embedding. In addition, there are some program-specific options for embedding pdfmarks in the native application document which I'd like to present in this chapter.

Adobe FrameMaker. You may already have wondered about the somehow strange "PostScript Code" option in a text frame's properties dialog. In FrameMaker's infancy, this was meant to include graphical tricks to be manually programmed in PostScript (e.g., rotated text – considered highly innovative at that time). Today – since every man and his dog is able to do sexy text and graphics effects (FrameMaker supports rotated text by default) – PostScript frames are rarely used.

Including pdfmarks for preparing PDF conversion puts the PostScript frames back to work in our days. PostScript frames are a simple and convenient way of defining PDF effects in the native Frame document. The advantage is that you can see and edit the pdfmark code in your documents (contrary to the EPS technique). Additionally, FrameMaker makes available the frame's coordinates which may be used for defining a rectangular area for a link or another type of active area, e.g., a form field.

The following sections of this chapter contain tons of pdfmark samples. Pick the appropriate code for your particular PDF feature of interest and type it into a newly created text frame. To make life easier and prevent typos, you may want to open the PDF file of this chapter from the accompanying CD-ROM and cut-and-paste the samples. Take care not to hyphenate or otherwise alienate the pdfmark code. I found it convenient to define a paragraph style called "pdfmark" which uses a small font size and deactivates hyphenation. Now select your text frame with the arrow pointer and click "Graphics", "Object Properties...". This brings up the dialog box shown in Figure 6.3 where you activate the "PostScript Code" check box. The option results in the text being passed through as PostScript instructions instead of being printed as text. Note that you have to de-select the "PostScript Code" option before you can again edit the frame's contents. It's also possible to position PostScript frames on a master page. This is particularly useful, for example, for defining page transitions for PDF presentations.

The PostScript frame's size depends on whether or not the respective PDF feature needs geometrical layout information. For example, document info fields don't relate to a specific location on any page but to the whole document. In this case, place a frame with code similar to the following snippet somewhere near one of the page edges (so that it doesn't disturb your on-screen layout when working on the document):

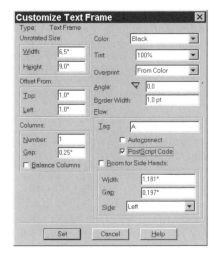

Fig. 6.3.
Defining a PostScript
frame in FrameMaker

```
pop pop pop pop
/pdfmark where {pop} {userdict /pdfmark /cleartomark load put} ifelse
[    /Title (Installation Instructions)
     /Author (Thomas Merz)
     /Subject (Preparing and Starting the Engine)
     /Keywords (Introduction Manual Troubleshooting)
/DOCINFO pdfmark
```

Since the four coordinates of the PostScript frame which are supplied by
FrameMaker are not needed here, we get rid of them via pop instructions at
the beginning of the code.

For links, form fields, and other PDF features the situation is quite different since we need a rectangular area for defining their size. pdfmarks
specify this area by means of the /Rect parameter. The following sample defines a URL link which has the size of the PostScript frame as its active area.
The PostScript gobbledygook after /Rect is necessary to adapt Frame coordinates to the notation required for pdfmarks:[1]

```
/pdfmark where {pop} {userdict /pdfmark /cleartomark load put} ifelse
[    /Rect [ 7 -4 roll 4 -2 roll pop pop 0 0 ]
     /Action << /Subtype /URI /URI (http://www.ifconnection.de/~tm) >>
     /Subtype /Link
/ANN pdfmark
```

If you want to use pdfmark instructions which make use of /Rect, place
/Rect as first parameter after the opening bracket (parameter ordering isn't
relevant for pdfmarks) and use the /Rect line shown above instead of the

---

1. Note to readers fluent in PostScript: FrameMaker resets the coordinate system's origin to the lower left
corner of the frame, and pushes the offset of this corner from the page origin on the stack, as well as width
and height of the frame.

one with four explicit numbers as used in the other examples in this chapter. If /Rect is missing from the pdfmark description, enter "pop" four times at the beginning of your pdfmark code to delete the FrameMaker coordinates from the PostScript stack.

Note that it's quite useful to include FrameMaker variables inside pdfmark instructions. This is very efficient for repeating commands, such as the author field in the document info. Cross-references used for placing a chapter heading inside an info field also work nicely.

Section 5.2 explains FrameMaker's integrated PDF support which spares you pdfmark programming in many cases.

Microsoft Word.   Word too has some means for incorporating your own pdfmark code in a document. Firstly, use "Tools", "Options...", "View" to activate screen display of field codes. This makes life easier in the following steps. Using "Insert", "Field...", "Field name: Print" you can insert pdfmark instructions (surrounded by double quotes) in a dialog box (see Figure 6.4). The following code in a print field defines PDF document information:

```
{print "[ /Title (Manual) /Author (Thomas Merz) /DOCINFO pdfmark "}
```

You will need the coordinates of the position on the page or the size of the paragraph containing the print field in order to use pdfmark instructions which make use of rectangles. The "\p" option tells Word to define some variables which can be useful for defining a link's active area. A complete list of these variables can be found in Word's online help. The most important variable is "wp$box" because it's perfectly suited for defining a rectangle. This variable supplies a PostScript definition of a rectangular shape around the current paragraph. You can use it in a pdfmark instruction as follows:

```
{print \p para "[ /Rect [ wp$box pathbbox ] /Page 3 /Subtype /Link /ANN
pdfmark "}
```

Fig. 6.4.
pdfmark code in a
Microsoft Word print field

The group instruction "para" results in Word's PostScript relating to the current paragraph. The code above transforms the paragraph containing the print field in a PDF link with a jump to page 3. Remember to include the additional line with the print protection code if you want to print and distill the resulting PostScript file (see Section 6.2).

Finally, here's an example for defining a URL link inside a Word print field:

```
{print \p para "[ /Rect [ wp$box pathbbox ] /Action << /Subtype /URI
/URI (http://www.ifconnection.de/~tm) >> /Subtype /Link /ANN pdfmark "}
```

This code transforms the current paragraph into a Weblink's active area.

Section 5.5 informs about more comfortable ways of generating hypertext-enhanced PDF from Word documents.

TEX. The powerful TEX typesetting system also has a mechanism for including user-defined printer instructions into the output stream. The \special instruction can be used to embed PostScript code. It is also suited for pdfmark programming. The following example defines PDF document information within a (device-driver-dependent) \special sequence:

```
\special{ps::
[   /Title (User Manual)
    /Author (Michael Heinzel)
    /Subject (Adjusting the electronics of MH-screen)
    /Keywords (screen display MH-screen)
/DOCINFO pdfmark
}%
```

The macro package hyperref can automatically insert pdfmarks for hypertext links and for certain document information. You can find more information on creating PDF from a TEX source in Section 5.6.

.4 Basic pdfmark Functions

Now that we've dealt with the necessary preliminaries, let's take a closer look at the specific instructions. This section and the next one contain a list of all pdfmark instructions, including descriptions of the PDF features they achieve. Since there is a wealth of link and action related options which are used in many pdfmark operators, these options are discussed separately in the next section.

The information presented in this and the next section relates to Distiller 3.0 and higher. Older versions support a subset of these pdfmarks.

There's a common scheme for all descriptions: Following a heading which briefly identifies the topic, a functional description is given along with usage samples. These samples illustrate important applications of the operator. The tables given last in the descriptions contain more detailed information concerning additional variations or options. Note that the samples only contain the "pure" pdfmark code. Don't forget to include additional instructions which may be necessary depending on the software in use, e.g., for protecting against printing errors, or including the pdfmarks in the program (like coordinate transformations in a FrameMaker PostScript frame).

Keys in the tables which must be present are labeled as such, others are optional. For most optional keys the default value is shown which is used when the key is missing.

Notes. The /ANN pdfmark instruction generations PDF annotations. These include notes, links, and special goodies such as sound and video, Acrobat menu items, and Weblinks (URLs). The /Subtype key defines the particular kind of annotation to create. If /Subtype is missing, a PDF note is generated.

The following code creates an open note with red window border:

```
[   /Rect [ 75 400 175 550 ]
    /Open true
    /Title (Important note)
    /Contents (This document is a preliminary version!)
    /Color [1 0 0]
/ANN pdfmark
```

Table 6.2 contains all keys for notes which may be used with /ANN if /Subtype is missing or has a value of /Text. Along with other /Subtype values, /ANN is used for many other functions too which are explained in the rest this chapter.

Table 6.2. Keys for notes with /ANN, if the /Subtype is /Text or is missing altogether

Key	Explanation
/Contents[1]	The note's text string
/Rect[1]	Array of four numbers specifying the note's rectangle
/SrcPg	Number of the page on which the note appears. If this key is missing, the note appears on the current page.
/Open	If "true", the note is open and the text visible. If "false", only an icon is displayed for the note. If the key is missing, the note will be closed.
/Color	Array of three RGB values defining the color of the note's icon or frame.
/Title	The note's title
/ModDate	Date and time the note was last modified.
/Subtype	For notes always has a value of /Text (this is the default too).

1. This key is required.

Links. Early Distiller versions used the /LNK key for defining links. In Distiller 3.0, this is accomplished with /ANN and a /Subtype value of /Link.

The following code creates a link inside the given rectangle with a blue border. The link jumps to the next page and retains the viewing parameters (zoom factor):

```
[    /Rect [ 70 550 210 575 ]
     /Border [ 0 0 1 ]
     /Color [0 0 1]
     /Page /Next
     /View [ /XYZ null null null ]
     /Subtype /Link
/ANN pdfmark
```

The following code creates a link inside the given rectangle with a red border. The link jumps to the document named *chapter02.doc*:

```
[    /Rect [ 70 600 210 625 ]
     /Color [1 0 0]
     /Action /Launch
     /File (chapter02.doc)
     /Subtype /Link
/ANN pdfmark
```

I'd like to restrict myself to describing the actual link definition here. Many ways of selecting a link destination or action to be triggered when the link is clicked on are described in Section 6.5 (along with many samples).

With the exception of destinations and actions, Table 6.3 lists all keys for /ANN, when /Subtype has a value of /Link.

Table 6.3. *Keys for links with /ANN and the /Subtype value /Link*

Key	Explanation
Destination or action for this link (see Section 6.5)[1]	
/Rect[1]	Array of four numbers defining the link's active area
/Subtype[1]	For links always /Link
/Border	Array defining the link rectangle's appearance (line width and line dash). The array [0 0 0] means no border at all.
/SrcPg	Number of the page on which the link is to appear. If the key is missing, the link appears on the current page.
/Color	Array of three RGB values defining the link rectangle's color.

1. This key is required.

Bookmarks.   Bookmarks (outline entries) contain text which is related to a particular location in the document or an action. This means that the information in Section 6.5 applies to bookmarks too.

The following code creates a bookmark for jumping to page 1:

```
[ /Page 1 /View [/XYZ 44 730 1.0] /Title (Start) /OUT pdfmark
```

The following code creates a bookmark with the title "Introduction" which jumps to the article thread labeled "A" if clicked on:

```
[ /Action /Article /Dest (A) /Title (Introduction) /OUT pdfmark
```

The following code creates a bookmark with a URL link:

```
[    /Title (Home page)
     /Action << /Subtype /URI /URI (http://www.ifconnection.de/~tm) >>
/OUT pdfmark
```

With the exception of destinations and actions, Table 6.4 lists all keys for /OUT. For nested bookmarks, you first have to define the higher-level bookmarks with the correct /Count value, and then the subordinate bookmarks.

Table 6.4. Keys for bookmarks with /OUT

Key	Explanation
Destination or action for this link (see Section 6.5)[1]	
/Title[1]	The bookmark's text (a maximum of 32 characters is recommended)
/Count	If there are subordinate bookmarks, /Count specifies their number, otherwise this key is missing. If /Count is negative, the bookmark is closed, otherwise open.

1. This key is required.

Article threads. A PDF article consist of several rectangular areas, called beads, which are placed on one or more pages. They are linked via their common title. Additionally an article thread can have some meta-information associated with it (keywords, for example) which you can view or edit in the "View", "Articles...", "Info..." menu of Acrobat Exchange.

The following code defines a rectangle for an article bead with the title "Introduction" and additional meta-information:

```
[    /Title (Introduction)
     /Author (Thomas Merz)
     /Subject (Brief Overview of Engine Maintenance)
     /Keywords (Maintenance Overview)
     /Rect [ 225 500 535 705 ]
/ARTICLE pdfmark
```

More rectangles for the same article may follow this first definition. They are linked to the other parts by a common /Title key. Subsequent rectangles don't have /Subject, /Author, and /Keywords keys. Table 6.5 lists all keys for /ARTICLE.

Named destinations. PDF link targets can not only be defined in a layout-oriented manner (i.e., by specifying a page number and geometric coordinates), but also symbolically. A location in a document may be assigned a symbolic name. This name may later be used as a link target. A target with a

Table 6.5. *Values for article beads with /ARTICLE*

Key	Explanation
/Title[1]	The title of the article
/Rect[1]	Array of four numbers specifying the current bead of the article
/Page	Number of the page on which the bead will be defined
/Subject	The article's subject
/Author	The article's author
/Keywords	The article's keywords

1. This key is required.

symbolic name is called a "named destination". This technique has the advantage that the target location may change without invalidating the link. For this reason programs which automatically generate pdfmarks use symbolic names for their link targets. These names are visible in Acrobat Exchange too; however, you cannot create named destinations in Exchange, nor change existing names or their locations. More information on named destinations can be found in Section 8.6.

The following code defines a link target with a symbolic name of "chapter01" which is located on the current page. Jumping to this target doesn't change the zoom factor:

```
[ /Dest /intro /View [ /XYZ null null null ] /DEST pdfmark
```

Table 6.6 contains all keys for /DEST.

Table 6.6. *Values for named destinations with /DEST*

Key	Explanation
/Dest[1]	The destination's symbolic name
/Page	The target page's number. If this key is missing, the named destination is defined on the current page.
/View	Viewing parameters for the link target

1. This key is required.

PostScript instructions.   It is well known that PostScript and PDF are very closely related to each other. However, there are some PostScript features and tricks which are not possible in PDF, and which are lost when converting from PostScript to PDF and back to PostScript.

In order to solve this problem you can use pdfmarks to store PostScript instructions in a PDF file. Acrobat ignores the PostScript when rendering the file on screen, but when printing to a PostScript device the included instructions are embedded in the print data.

Probably a more practical use of this feature than exploring somehow obscure PostScript features in PDF files is a "don't display, but print" effect:

If certain objects on the page are to appear in the printed version only but shouldn't be displayed on screen, PostScript pass-throughs might be used.

```
[ /DataSource (100 100 50 0 360 arc fill) /PS pdfmark
```

Table 6.7 contains all keys for /PS.

Table 6.7. Values for "pass-through" PostScript instructions with /PS

Key	Explanation
/DataSource[1]	String or file containing the PostScript code
/Level1	Alternative PostScript code for printing to a PostScript Level 1 device

1. This key is required.

Page cropping.   Using pdfmarks you can define the size of one or more pages in a PDF document. Distiller crops the page according to the pdfmark values, independent of the page size defined in the printer-relevant Post-Script instructions. These values can be found in Exchange's status line at the bottom of the window.

The following code crops all pages of the document to letter size. The line should be inserted at the beginning of the PostScript file (at the end of the prolog):

```
[ /CropBox [0 0 612 792] /PAGES pdfmark
```

Using /PAGE instead of /PAGES crops only the current page. Again, this code should be inserted at the beginning of the PostScript page description.

The following code defines a cropping rectangle for the current page:

```
[ /CropBox [54 403 558 720] /PAGE pdfmark
```

Table 6.8 lists the key for /PAGE and /PAGES.

Table 6.8. Key for cropping pages with /PAGE or /PAGES

Key	Explanation
/CropBox	Array of four numbers specifying location and size of the visible page area. The page size may vary from 1 to 45 inches (72 to 3240 points).

General document information.   Using "File", "Document Info", "General..." you can view or change a PDF's general document information fields. According to the documentation, these fields can be defined with pdfmark instructions of type /DOCINFO at an arbitrary location within the PostScript code. However, I found /DOCINFO only to work reliably if placed on the first document page.

The following code defines the document information fields of a PDF file:

```
[   /Title (User Manual)
    /Author (Michael Heinzel)
    /Subject (Adjusting the electronics of MH-screen)
    /Keywords (screen display MH-screen)
    /Creator (DocMaker 1.0)
    /ModDate (D:19980210205731)
/DOCINFO pdfmark
```

Table 6.9 lists the keys for /DOCINFO. Additionally, custom key names can be inserted. Although they can't be viewed in Acrobat, custom fields are quite useful in index queries (you can find more details about custom info field names in Section 4.4). In order to define a custom field called "Department", for example, add the following line to the pdfmark code above:

```
/Department (Marketing)
```

If such a custom info field exists in all documents, you can restrict an index query to all files created in a specific department.

Note that Distiller attempts to extract some information from the DSC comments at the beginning of the PostScript file if there are no /DOCINFO pdfmarks present. These comments are listed in parentheses in the table.

Table 6.9. *Keys for document info fields using /DOCVIEW*

Key	Explanation
/Author	Author of the document (%%For)
/Creation-Date	Document creation date and time
/Creator	Name of the program used to create the original document (%%Creator)
/Producer	Name of the program used to convert the original document to PDF
/Title	Document title (%%Title)
/Subject	Subject of the document contents
/Keywords	Keywords for the document
/ModDate	Date and time of last document change

Viewer properties.   A PDF file may specify the Acrobat viewer's behavior. This includes bookmark or thumbnail display as well as full-screen mode. In Acrobat Exchange, you can edit these settings via "File", "Document Info", "Open...".

The following code results in Acrobat opening the document at page 3 with thumbnail display enabled:

```
[ /PageMode /UseThumbs /Page 3 /DOCVIEW pdfmark
```

For a screen presentation it may be useful to open the document in full-screen mode:

```
[ /PageMode /FullScreen /DOCVIEW pdfmark
```

Table 6.10 lists all keys for /DOCVIEW.

Table 6.10. Keys for viewer properties using /DOCVIEW

Key	Explanation
Document open action (see Section 6.5)	
/PageMode	/UseNone (default): The document is displayed without bookmarks and thumbnails. /UseOutlines: The document is displayed with bookmarks. /UseThumbs: The document is displayed with thumbnails. /FullScreen: The document is displayed in full-screen mode.

Page transitions. In Acrobat you can choose among several page transitions in order to make the process of replacing a page with the next more attractive. Unfortunately, these effects cannot be set in Acrobat Exchange. Although you can choose a page transition in "File", "Preferences", "Full Screen", this setting relates to the whole document, not to individual pages in the file. Similarly to named destinations, individual page transitions are a PDF feature not supported in Acrobat's user interface. Even the pdfmark reference manual remains silent about this topic – you have to take a look at the PDF specification.

The following code specifies a mosaic-like transition from the old page to the new page. The old page contents "dissolve" to reveal the new page:

```
[ {ThisPage} << /Trans << /S /Dissolve >> >> /PUT pdfmark
```

The following code specifies a wiping effect which generates the new page by wiping over the old page from left to right:

```
[ {ThisPage} << /Trans << /S /Wipe /Di 180 >> >> /PUT pdfmark
```

{ThisPage} is a symbolic name for the current page. This entry always has to be included exactly as shown. The page transitions are always activated when opening the page, irrespective of the previous page. Therefore it doesn't matter whether the page is displayed through manual navigation, by page number, or a link.

Table 6.11 lists all keys for page transitions supported in Acrobat 3.0.

Table 6.11. Keys for page transitions with /PUT

Key	Explanation
/Split	Two lines sweep across the screen to reveal the new page similar to opening a curtain.
/Blinds	Similar to /Split, but with several lines resembling "venetian blinds"
/Box	A box enlarges from the center of the old page to reveal the new one.
/Wipe	A single line "wipes" across the old page to reveal the new one.
/Dissolve	The old page "dissolves" to reveal the new one.

Table 6.11. Keys for page transitions with /PUT (cont.)

Key	Explanation
/Glitter	Similar to /Dissolve, except the effect sweeps from one edge to another.
/R (Replace)	The old page is simply replaced with the new one without any special effect. This is the default.

For some of the transitions additional parameters may be specified. The following code results in a split effect with the lines moving horizontally (/H) from the inner parts of the page to the outer parts (/O). The duration of the effect is two seconds (/D):

```
[ {ThisPage} << /Trans << /S /Split /D 2 /Dm /H /M /O >> >> /PUT pdfmark
```

Table 6.12 lists all supported parameters for /Trans, along with the kind of transition on which the parameters may be applied.

Table 6.12. Additional parameters for page transitions with /Trans

Key	Explanation
/D	Duration of the transition effect in seconds (applies to all effects)
/Di (Direction)	Direction of the movement (multiples of 90° only). Values increase in a counterclockwise fashion, 0° points to the right (for /Wipe and /Glitter).
/Dm (Dimension)	Possible values are /H or /V for a horizontal or vertical effect, respectively (for /Split and /Blinds).
/M (Motion)	Specifies whether the effect is performed from the center out or the edges in. Possible values are /I for in and /O for out (for /Split and /Box).

Generally, a page transition will be defined for the current page. However, it's also possible to define transitions for another page. Table 6.13 lists all keys which can be used with /PUT. Note that only direct page specification may be used for page transitions. {Catalog} and {DocInfo} are reserved for other /PUT applications.

Table 6.13. Selecting pages with /PUT

Key	Explanation
{Catalog}	(reserved for other /PUT applications)
{DocInfo}	(reserved for other /PUT applications)
{PageN}	Page N (replace N with a page number)
{ThisPage}	Current page
{PrevPage}	Previous page
{NextPage}	Next page

Viewer preferences. A PDF document may specify several Viewer preferences which apply when opening the file in Acrobat Reader or Exchange.

You can edit these settings in Exchange with "File", "Document Info", "Open..."

The following code instructs the viewer to hide the toolbar when opening the document:

```
[ {Catalog} << /ViewerPreferences << /HideToolbar true >> >> /PUT pdfmark
```

You can also specify the page layout mode in the document. The following code makes Acrobat open the file in two-column layout (two pages are displayed side-by-side):

```
[ {Catalog} << /PageLayout /TwoColumnRight >> /PUT pdfmark
```

Note that the syntax is different to the preceding example. The /PageLayout description in the PDF specification doesn't match the implementation in Acrobat.

Table 6.14 lists all entries for the /ViewerPreferences dictionary. The default settings are given in parentheses. These apply when the respective entry is missing. Except for the last two entries, all keys are populated with Boolean values.

Table 6.14. *Additional parameters for /ViewerPreferences*

Key	Explanation
/HideToolbar	Hide toolbar (false).
/Hide-Menubar	Hide menu bar (false).
/Hide-WindowUI	Hide other user interface elements (false).
/FitWindow	Adjust window size to the size of the first page (false).
/Center-Window	Place window in the middle of the screen (false).
/PageLayout[1]	Specify page layout. Possible values are: /SinglePage: Display single pages /OneColumn: Display pages in columns /TwoColumnLeft: Display pages in two-column layout, starting with a left page /TwoColumnRight: Display pages in two-column layout, starting with a right page
/NonFull-Screen-PageMode	Specifies how to display the document when exiting full-screen mode. Except /FullScreen the same values are allowed as for the /PageMode key in a /DOCVIEW instruction (see Table 6.10).

1. /PageLayout isn't documented correctly in the specification and is used differently than the other parameters (see example).

Encapsulating graphics. Acrobat's optimization function compresses PDF data and rearranges the objects for page-at-a-time download from a Web server. There is another optimizarion that is not as well known even though it further decreases file size in certain situations. Exchange checks for images in the document which are repeatedly used on multiple pages, for example a logo on each page header. If such an image is found, its PDF data is included only once in the file. Other pages reference the image data already included for another page. If an image is used several times in a document, this feature dramatically reduces the overall file size.

Similar optimization can be achieved by means of pdfmarks, although more programming is needed which requires a good command of the PostScript language. For this reason, I'd like to restrict myself to explaining the basic principle without working out a full-blown example.

Let's suppose we have an EPS file with the image to be included in the document. /BP (BeginPicture) and /EP (EndPicture) instructions surround the image's PostScript code. The image is assigned an arbitrary symbolic name in /BP. Using the /SP (ShowPicture) pdfmark operator along with the symbolic name, the image can be referred to on arbitrary pages without repeating the actual PostScript instructions:

```
[ /BBox [100 100 400 600] /_objdef {company_logo} /BP pdfmark
...the company logo's PostScript instructions...
[ /EP pdfmark
```

Use the following code to reuse the image on another page in its original size and on the original position:

```
[ {company_logo} /SP pdfmark
```

If you want to change the image's location or size, you have to transform the PostScript coordinate system with appropriate PostScript language commands before issuing the /SP instruction.

Table 6.15 lists the keys for /BP. The /EP instruction doesn't need any additional parameters. /SP only needs the symbolic name defined in /BP.

Table 6.15. Keys for embedding EPS graphics with /SP

Key	Explanation
/BBox	Array of four numbers defining the graphic's bounding box
/_objdef	The graphic's symbolic name in curly braces

Attaching an index file. Using "File", "Document Info", "Index..." in Exchange you can attach an index file to a PDF file. This index is activated without any further user intervention when the document is opened.

The PDF specification doesn't mention the instructions necessary to define the index's name in the PDF file. However, it's easy to find out the instructions by manually attaching an index in Exchange, and analyzing the resulting PDF file. As it turns out, you can achieve the same effect with pdfmarks.

The following code attaches an index called *cms.pdx* to the PDF file. Carefully take into account the many angle brackets in order to avoid error messages from Distiller.

```
[   {Catalog} << /Search << /Indexes
        [ << /Name /PDX /Index (cms.pdx) >> ]
    >> >>
/PUT pdfmark
```

Page open actions. Using "Document", "Set Page Action..." in Exchange
you can define actions which automatically take place when opening the
page. This effect can also be achieved with pdfmarks. You can find an example in the next section which describes actions. Note the difference between "page action" and "page transition": page transitions define how the
previously displayed page is replaced with the new page.

Creating form fields. Exchange's form tool offers plenty of features for
defining PDF form fields. However, defining fields manually is a time-con-
suming and labor-intensive process. This effort can be reduced by using
pdfmarks. Although not all form features are supported, creating fields and
defining some of their features is indeed possible with pdfmarks. To facilitate changing the size and position of the fields, I recommend the EPS technique for including the form pdfmarks in the PostScript code. Detailed descriptions of the various field types can be found in Section 7.2.

Since form fields have many attributes, and not all field properties can
be defined with pdfmarks, I'd like to restrict myself to some examples for
defining field types. More detailed information can be found in the *PDF Reference Manual*. With the code shown below you can at least prepare and exactly position the form fields in the original file. Setting the field attributes
is best done in Acrobat Exchange.

Setting font and other field attributes requires so-called widget definitions. These are additional pdfmark instructions which must precede the
following examples (on the first page of the document). You can find an EPS
file called *afrmdict.eps* in the PFN directory on the Acrobat CD-ROM. This
EPS file contains the necessary widget definitions.

The following code defines a text field with a border width of one point.
The default value is "Thomas Merz", the field's size is specified in /Rect:

```
[   /T (text input field)     % title
    /Subtype /Widget
    /FT /Tx                    % field type text box
    /DV (Thomas Merz)          % default value
    /Rect [ 0 0 216 18]
    /F 4                       % field is printable
    /BS << /S /S /W 1 >>       % border style solid, width = 1
    /MK <<
    /BC [ 1 0 0 ]              % border color red
```

```
    /BG [ 1 1 1 ] >>        % background color white
/ANN pdfmark
```

The following code defines a list box with two list elements called
"element1" and "element2". When activated, the elements export the values
"e1" and "e2", respectively. "e1" is the default value:

```
[   /T (list box)
    /Subtype /Widget
    /FT /Ch                 % field type choice: list box
    /Rect [ 0 0 216 18]
    /F 4
    /DV (e1)                % default value
    /DA (/Helv 12 Tf 0 g)
    /Opt [ [ (e1)(element1)] [ (e2)(element2)] ]
/ANN pdfmark
```

Including a suitable /Ff flag value in the preceding example results in a
combo box. This means the list elements are editable by the form user:

```
[   /T (combo box)
    /Subtype /Widget
    /FT /Ch                 % field type choice: combo box
    /Rect [ 0 0 216 180]
    /F 4
    /Ff 393216              % special flag signals combo box
    /DV (e1)                % default value
    /DA (/Helv 12 Tf 0 g)
    /Opt [ [ (e1)(element1)] [ (e2)(element2)] ]
/ANN pdfmark
```

Next, let's create a check box:

```
[   /T (check box)
    /Subtype /Widget
    /FT /Btn                % field type button: check box
    /Rect [ 0 0 216 18]
    /F 4
    /BS << /S /S /W 1 >>
    /MK << /BC [ 1 0 0 ] /BG [ 1 1 1 ] >>
/ANN pdfmark
```

Finally, a push button:

```
[   /T (button)
    /Subtype /Widget
    /FT /Btn                % field type button: check box
    /Rect [ 0 0 216 18]
    /F 4
    /Ff 65540               % special flag signals push button
    /BS << /S /S /W 1 >>
    /MK << /BC [ 1 0 0 ] /BG [ 1 1 1 ] >>
    /DA (/Helv 12 Tf 0 g)
/ANN pdfmark
```

Since I can't cover creating form fields with all options and variations, Table 6.16 only gives an overview of possible field types. These main field types are further refined using several values in the /Ff flag (see examples above). More information can be found in the "PDF Reference Manual".

Table 6.16. Possible form field types (/FT key) with /ANN and /Widget subtypes

Key	Explanation
/Tx	Text field
/Ch	(choice) List box
/Btn	(button) Check box, radio button, or push button.

6.5 Destinations and Actions

Destinations and actions are used in three areas, all of which can be set up in an interactive manner in Acrobat Exchange or with pdfmarks:

▶ Links are created with the /ANN pdfmark and a /Subtype of /Link. In Exchange simply use the link tool to define a rectangle and select the type of action from a pull-down menu (see Figure 6.5).

▶ Bookmarks are created with the /OUT pdfmark. In Exchange choose "Document", "New Bookmark", select the bookmark, "Edit", "Properties...", and choose the desired type of action.

▶ Page actions – actions which are performed when the page is opened – are defined with the /AA and /PUT pdfmark instructions. The corresponding menu sequence in Exchange is "Document", "Set Page Action...", "Add...", choose type of action.

Figure 6.5 shows the dialog box for creating a link.[1] It contains all link destinations and actions covered in this section.

Before delving into the many and somehow confusing variations for link destinations and page actions, I'd like to give an example for each of the three applications outlined above. We'll use an intradocument link, a URL link, and playing a sound file as actions.

The following code creates a link which jumps to page 5 of the document:

```
[   /Rect [ 70 550 210 575 ]
    /Page 5
    /View [ /XYZ null null null]
    /Subtype /Link
/ANN pdfmark
```

The following code creates a bookmark. Clicking this bookmark results in jumping to the specified URL:

---

1. *In case you wonder what the "JavaScript" entry is supposed to do – read Section 7.6.*

```
[    /Count 0
     /Title (Click here for home page)
     /Action << /Subtype /URI /URI (http://www.ifconnection.de/~tm) >>
/OUT pdfmark
```

The following code results in the sound file *melody.snd* being played as
soon as the first page is opened (generally, when opening the document):

```
[    /Rect [0 0 0 0]
     /Subtype /Movie
     /Title (Greeting sound)
     /Movie << /F (melody.snd) >>
/ANN pdfmark
[    {Page1} << /AA << /O << /S /Movie
        /T (Greeting sound) /Operation /Play  >> >> >>
/PUT pdfmark
```

Note that the greeting sound is attached to an annotation, although a
sound doesn't need an active area on the page. We use a size of 0 for this
area to make sure it doesn't disturb anybody. The page action simply relates
to the name of the annotation.

Overview.   Following the three application examples, I'd like to give an
overview of all link destinations and page actions. More detailed descriptions of all flavors can be found after the overview.

Table 6.17. Keys for links and actions

Key	Explanation
/View	Array describing a document location which serves as a destination for a bookmark or link. See Table 6.19 for more details.
/Page	Describes a link destination along with /View. /Page specifies the number of the page (counting from 1). A value of 0 means no destination at all. For links and article threads, the values /Next and /Prev relate to the next or previous page. /Page is only required if the destination is not located on the current page.
/Action	Most general specification. See Table 6.18 for more details.
/Dest	Symbolic name of a named destination defined with /DEST. If used as a destination for an article, /Dest contains the title or number of the article (counting article numbers from 0).

A closer look at Figure 6.5 clarifies the relationship of pdfmarks and Exchange's user interface elements: The "View" link type relates to the /View
and /Page keys. All other types are implemented with the /Action key. Links
to named destinations cannot be defined in Exchange at all but only with
the /DEST pdfmark operator.

   Table 6.18 lists all keys for /Action. The samples and tables on the following pages explain how to use them, and which subkeys are involved.

Fig. 6.5.
All of the actions which can be defined in
Exchange using a link, a bookmark, or a page
action can also be defined using pdfmarks.

Table 6.18. Direct and indirect keys for /Action

Key	Explanation
/GoTo	Jump to a page in the current document. Requires the /Dest key or both the /Page and /View keys.
/GoToR	Jump to a page in another PDF document. Requires the /Dest key or both the /Page and /View keys, and the /File key.
/Launch	Launches a non-PDF document or an application program. Requires /File.
/Article	Link to an article in the current or another PDF document. Requires /Dest and additionally /File, if the article is contained in another PDF file.
/URI[1]	URL for linking to a document on the WWW
/Sound[1]	Play a sound file
/Movie[1]	Play a movie or sound file
/SetState[1,2]	Store viewing definitions for an annotation
/Hide[1]	Hide or show an annotation
/Named[1]	Execute one of Acrobat's menu functions
/SubmitForm[1]	Send form contents to a URL
/ResetForm[1]	Reset form contents to default values
/ImportData[1]	Import form fields from a file
/JavaScript	Insert JavaScript for the whole document or a form field

1. These actions cannot be activated directly by a key, but must be defined indirectly via a dictionary entry
   for the /Action key. This is already taken into account in the following descriptions.
2. Acrobat Exchange doesn't offer any user interface for this feature.

Linking to a page in the same document. The following code defines a
rectangular link area. Clicking on this area results in jumping to the next
page:

```
[    /Rect [ 70 550 210 575 ]
```

```
        /Page /Next
        /View [ /XYZ -5 797 1.5]
        /Subtype /Link
/ANN pdfmark
```

Table 6.19 lists all keys for the /View array, as well as the corresponding values.

Table 6.19. Keys for the /View array

Key	Explanation
/Fit	Fit page to window size.
/FitB	Fit visible page contents to page width.
/FitH	top Fit width of the page to window size. "top" specifies the desired distance from the page origin to the upper edge of the window. If "top" has a value of -32768, Acrobat calculates the distance from the page origin to the upper edge of the window automatically.
/FitBH	top Fit visible page contents to window size. "top" specifies the desired distance from the page origin to the upper edge of the window.
/FitR	x_1 y_1 x_2 y_2 Fit the rectangle specified by the four numbers to the window.
/FitV	left Fit page height to window size. "left" specifies the desired distance from the page origin to the left edge of the window.
/FitBV	left Fit height of visible page contents to window size. "left" specifies the desired distance from the page origin to the left edge of the window.
/XYZ	left top zoom "left" and "top" specify the desired distance from the page origin to the upper left corner of the window. "zoom" specifies the zoom factor (1 means 100%). A value of "null" for one of the three numbers instructs Acrobat to retain the old value.

Link to another PDF document. Links can jump not only to a page in the current document, but also to a page in another PDF file.

The following code defines a link rectangle. Clicking on the link's active area jumps to a document with a file name of *chapter06.pdf*:

```
[   /Rect [ 70 600 210 625 ]
    /Action /GoToR
    /File (chapter06.pdf)
    /Subtype /Link
/ANN pdfmark
```

Table 6.20 lists all keys for /GoToR. The platform dependent keys can be used to specify platform-specific variations of the file name. These are only used on the respective platform and override the generic /File key.

Table 6.20. Keys for /GoToR

Key	Explanation
/File[1]	Path name of the PDF file (relative names are allowed)
/DOSFile	MS-DOS path name (overrides /File if present)
/MacFile	Mac path name (overrides /File if present)
/UnixFile	Unix path name (overrides /File if present)
/URI	URL of the PDF file (note: "URI" for "Universal Resource Identifier, not "URL")
/ID	ID number of the PDF file (rarely used)
/New-Window	If this key has a value of "true", Acrobat opens a new window for the file.

1. This key is required.

Launching another document or application. The next step in generalizing link destinations is a document in a format other than PDF, or another application program. Acrobat launches an external program and passes the file name given in the pdfmark link or bookmark.

The first example illustrates the main problem with such a construct – it is no longer portable. This means the link doesn't work on all operating system platforms. The names of the programs as well as the details of launching a program depend heavily on the underlying operating system (the user's, not yours!).

The following code defines a link. When activated, it starts the Windows Paintbrush program (without a document file name):

```
[    /Rect [ 70 600 210 625 ]
     /Border [ 16 16 1 ]
     /Action /Launch
     /File (pbrush.exe)
     /Subtype /Link
/ANN pdfmark
```

Table 6.21 lists all keys for /Launch.

Table 6.21. Keys for/Launch

Key	Explanation
/File[1]	Path name of the file or executable program (relative names are allowed). Under Windows 95 and NT, when /File points to a directory, Explorer is launched to explore this directory.
/DOSFile	MS-DOS path name (overrides /File if present)
/MacFile	Mac path name (overrides /File if present)
/UnixFile	Unix path name (overrides /File if present)
/URI	URL of the PDF file (note: "URI" for "Universal Resource Identifier, not "URL")
/Dir	For Windows: initial directory of the application

Table 6.21. Keys for/Launch (cont.)

Key	Explanation
/Op	(open) or (print). Only supported in Windows
/WinFile	File name of the document or application
/Params²	Parameters for a Windows application
/Unix	Parameters for a Unix application
/New-Window	If this key has a value of "true", Acrobat opens a new window for the file.

1. This key is required.
2. This key doesn't work in Distiller 3.01.

Linking to a named destination. Symbolic names for document locations defined with a /DEST instruction (named destinations) can also be used as destinations. As already explained, Acrobat Exchange doesn't offer any user interface for defining such named destinations. Although existing named destinations in a document are displayed, you cannot edit or create them in Exchange.

The following code defines a link to the destination with the symbolic name "chapter5" in the file *target.pdf*:

```
[   /Rect [ 70 650 210 675 ]
    /Color [ 0 0 1 ]
    /Dest /chapter5
    /File (target.pdf)
    /Subtype /Link
/ANN pdfmark
```

Linking to a file on the WWW. A bookmark or link may also reference a document (more generally, a resource) on the Internet. In this case, the target is defined by its URL (Universal Resource Locator). If Acrobat doesn't already display in a Web browser's window, the browser is launched. Note that URLs in PDF are always labeled URI (Universal Resource Identifier).

The following code defines a link rectangle. When activated, it jumps to a home page:

```
[   /Rect [ 50 425 295 445 ]
    /Action << /Subtype /URI /URI (http://www.ifconnection.de/~tm) >>
    /Subtype /Link
/ANN pdfmark
```

Note that the /IsMap key allows you to define an image map for interactive graphics. Clicking in the link's area can trigger different actions according to the mouse pointer's location inside the link graphic. More information on PDF image maps can be found in Section 8.6. Table 6.22 lists all keys for /URI.

Table 6.22. Keys for /URI

Key	Explanation
/Subtype[1]	For Internet links always /URI
/URI[1]	The target's URL in 7-bit ASCII encoding
/IsMap[2]	"true" if the mouse coordinates are to be appended to the URL (image map feature). Default is "false".

1. This key is required.
2. It's not possible to define image maps in Acrobat Exchange.

Defining a document's base URL. Like HTML, PDF supports the concept of a base URL and relative URLs. This is useful when a large document collection is to be moved to another server. If base URLs and relative links are used, not all links have to be adjusted but only the base URLs. Any PDF document can be assigned a base URL. In Acrobat Exchange this is achieved via "File", "Document Info", "Base URL...". Attaching a base URL can also be implemented with pdfmarks in the original file. Absolute URLs – WWW locations with complete server addresses – remain unchanged by such a base URL definition.

The following code defines the given URL as base URL for all relative Internet links in the document:

```
[ {Catalog} << /URI << /Base (http://www.ifconnection.de/~tm) >> >>
/PUT pdfmark
```

Inserting JavaScript instructions. Using Acrobat 3.01 and the Forms extension it's possible to insert JavaScript instructions in a document. These are executed when the user clicks on a link, opens a PDF file, or fills form fields. More information on JavaScript in PDF can be found in Section 7.6.

JavaScript can also be embedded using pdfmarks. The following code defines JavaScript code which is activated by clicking on a link:

```
[   /Rect [ 400 400 500 450 ]
    /Action << /Subtype /JavaScript
        /JS (console.show\(\)\r console.println\("Cuckoo!"\);) >>
    /Subtype /Link
/ANN pdfmark
```

As can be seen in the example, the JavaScript instructions are contained in a string. This means that several special characters, mainly (,), and \, must be "escaped" with a backslash character \. Line-end characters in the Java-Script are labeled with \r.

JavaScript instructions can be defined for use in PDF forms so that they are executed when filling out the fields. The following example defines a text field with additional JavaScript instructions which are executed for calculating field values, verifying and formatting the field input, and checking the keyboard input for valid characters.

```
[    /Rect [ 400 400 600 450 ] /T (text input) /Subtype /Widget
    /FT /Tx /F 4 /Ff 65540 /BS << /S /S /W 1 >>
    /AA <<
    /C << /S /JavaScript /JS (AFSimple_Calculate\("SUM", "F1, F2, F3"\);) >>
    /V << /S /JavaScript /JS (AFRange_Validate\(true, 0, true, 1000\);) >>
    /F << /S /JavaScript /JS
        (event.value=util.printx\("999",\revent.value\);) >>
    /K << /S /JavaScript /JS (var valid = new String\("-0123456789"\);\rif
        \(valid.indexOf\(event.key\) == -1\)\r{\r\tsys.beep\(1\);\revent.rc
        = false;\r}) >>
    >>
    /MK << /BC [ 1 0 0 ] /BG [ 1 1 1 ] >>
/ANN pdfmark
```

Finally, it's possible to embed JavaScript instructions which are executed
when the document is opened. The script is assigned the symbolic name
"TMScript" and stored in the "Catalog" data structure of the PDF document:

```
[ /_objdef {TMScript} /type /dict /OBJ pdfmark
[   {TMScript} << /JavaScript << /Names [ (Cuckoo)  << /S /JavaScript
        /JS (console.show\(\)\rconsole.println\("Cuckoo!"\);) >> ]
    >> >>
/PUT pdfmark
[ {Catalog} << /Names {TMScript} >> /PUT pdfmark
```

To insert multiple scripts, adjust the example above according to the following scheme:

```
[   {TMScript} << /JavaScript << /Names [
        (script1)  << /S /JavaScript /JS (...) >>
        (script2)  << /S /JavaScript /JS (...) >>
    ] >> >>
/PUT pdfmark
```

The names of the JavaScripts are stored in the "names tree" of the PDF document which also holds destination names. If the document contains named
destinations, the names of the JavaScripts must be inserted in the existing
names tree. Since this is not possible with pdfmarks, the above technique
does not work for PDF file containing named destinations.

More details on JavaScript programming in PDF, especially on additional
objects and methods, can be found in Section 7.6 of this book, and in the Acrobat Forms documentation. Table 6.23 lists the keys for several kinds of
JavaScript instructions which can be bound to form fields.

Table 6.23. Keys for JavaScript instructions with /AA

Key	Explanation
/K	(keystroke) JavaScript for checking the validity of the keyboard input
/F	(format) JavaScript for formatting the input
/V	(validate) JavaScript for checking the field values when the field is exited
/C	(calculate) JavaScript for calculating field values when the field is exited

Linking to an article.   When jumping to an article, the first bead of the article is displayed. The article thread may be identified by title or number.

The following code defines a bookmarks labeled "Lead story" which jumps to the article thread of the same name:

```
[ /Dest (Lead story) /Title (Lead story) /Action /Article /OUT pdfmark
```

When jumping to an article, all /GoToR keys (Table 6.20) are allowed. /File is necessary only when the article is located in another PDF file. Additionally, the key in Table 6.24 is required.

Table 6.24. Additional key for /Article

Key	Explanation
/Dest[1]	Article target. A string containing the article's title. Alternatively, a number may be specified which is the number of the article in the document (the first article in the document is numbered 0).

1. This key is required.

Playing sound and video files.   Given suitable hardware and software (sound card, QuickTime) Acrobat is capable of playing sound and video files. External sound files and video clips both are stored with the /Movie key in the PDF. Strictly speaking, there's another key called /Sound for directly embedding the sound data in the PDF file. In practice, however, both types of data are treated as external data of type /Movie. Actually, embedding the movie or sound data in the PDF file isn't possible, only linking.

To be sure to include movies successfully, note that not all file formats are supported on all platforms. A list of supported sound and video formats can be found in the Acrobat documentation. Since videos can only be scaled proportionally, the movie rectangle must be created proportional to the movie's edges.

The following code plays the film from the external file *vacation.mov* in the specified rectangle:

```
[   /Rect [ 216 503 361 612 ]
    /Type /Annot
    /Subtype /Movie
    /Movie << /F (vacation.mov) >>
/ANN pdfmark
```

The following code plays the sound file "melody.snd" when the rectangle's active area is clicked:

```
[   /Rect [ 216 503 361 612 ]
    /Type /Annot
    /Subtype /Movie
    /T (My composition)
    /Movie << /F (melody.snd) >>
/ANN pdfmark
```

Table 6.25 lists the keys for /Movie.

Table 6.25. Keys for /Movie

Key	Explanation
/Subtype[1]	For videos and external sounds always /Movie
/A	false: Play the movie when clicked true: Play the movie with the default activation values (this is the default for /A) Alternatively, a dictionary may be used as value for the /A key. See Table 6.26 for details.
/Movie[1]	Dictionary describing the movie. It may contain the following keys: /F: Name of the movie file /Aspect: Array of two values describing the movie's size in pixels /Rotate: Number of degrees the movie has to be rotated clockwise (multiples of 90° only, 0° is top) /Poster: Boolean which indicates whether or not to display the poster from the movie file
/Operation	/Play: start playing the movie (default value) /Stop: stop playing the movie /Pause: pause playing the movie /Resume: resume playing a paused movie
/T (Title)	The movie's title

1. This key is required.

The information in the /A dictionary describes the dynamics of playing the movie. Table 6.26 lists all keys for the /A dictionary. All keys are optional (details on the keys not described in the table can be found in the PDF specification).

Table 6.26. Keys for the optional /A dictionary in a /Movie instruction

Key	Explanation
/Show-Controls	Boolean indicating whether or not a movie controller bar is shown when the movie is displayed
/Mode	/Once: Show the movie once and stop /Open: Show movie and leave controller open /Repeat: Repeat movie until stopped by user /Palindrome: play back and forth until stopped by user
/Syn-chronous	If true, the user must wait for the movie to be finished before further Acrobat interaction is allowed
/Start	Starting time of the movie segment
/Duration	Duration of the movie segment
/Rate	Initial relative speed of the movie
/Volume	Volume setting for the movie

Table 6.26. Keys for the optional /A dictionary in a /Movie instruction

Key	Explanation
/FWScale	For floating window movies, the magnification at which to play the movie
/FWPosition	For floating window movies, the screen position at which to play the movie

Hiding and showing fields.   Hiding and showing form fields is quite a useful feature for implementing context-sensitive help and similar interactive elements. The field to be hidden or shown is identified by its name.

When the link generated by the following code is activated, the contents of the field called "help" are displayed if the field was hidden before:

```
[   /Rect [ 50 425 295 445 ]
    /Action << /Subtype /Hide
        /T (help)
        /H true >>
    /Border [ 1 1 1 ]
    /Subtype /Link
/ANN pdfmark
```

Table 6.27 lists all keys for /Hide.

Table 6.27. Keys for /Hide

Key	Explanation
/Subtype[1]	For showing/hiding fields always /Hide
/T[1]	Name of a form field or array of several field names to be hidden or shown
/H (Hide)	"true" means hide, "false" means show the field. The default is "true".

1. This key is required.

Submitting a form to a URL.   The ability to submit a form's contents to a certain URL is the cornerstone of PDF form usage on the Web. The form's contents can be sent in either FDF (Forms Data Format) or HTML to the server.

The following code submits the form data in FDF format to the specified CGI script on the server:

```
[   /Rect [ 50 425 295 445 ]
    /Action << /Subtype /SubmitForm
        /F (http://www.ifconnection.de/~tm/cgi-bin/order.pl#FDF) >>
    /Flags 0
    /Subtype /Link
    /Border [ 1 1 1 ]
/ANN pdfmark
```

Table 6.28 lists all keys for /SubmitForm.

Table 6.28. Keys for /SubmitForm

Key	Explanation
/Subtype[1]	For submitting form data always /SubmitForm
/F (File)[1]	URL of the Web server script for processing the data
/Fields	(used internally)
/Flags	Integer for specifying FDF or HTML as submission format. Flags = 0 means FDF, Flags = 4 means HTML. Default is 0 (FDF).

1. This key is required.

Resetting a form to its default values.   A button for resetting a form to its default values makes it easy for the user to start over with a form. Resetting means all fields with predefined default values are set to this value, and fields without any default value remain empty.

The following code resets all fields of the document to their default values:

```
[   /Rect [ 50 425 295 445 ]
    /Action << /Subtype /ResetForm >>
    /Subtype /Link
    /Border [ 1 1 1 ]
/ANN pdfmark
```

Table 6.29 contains all fields for /ResetForm.

Table 6.29. Keys for /ResetForm

Key	Explanation
/Subtype[1]	For resetting form fields always /ResetForm
/Fields	(used internally)
/Flags	(used internally)

1. This key is required.

Importing form data from a file.   Importing form contents from a file facilitates filling multiple similar forms, especially when the forms adhere to the PFN standard (Personal Field Names; a description of the PFN standard can be found in Section 7.5). The creator of a form may further facilitate importing form data from a file by supplying an import push button.

The following code defines a rectangle for importing all form fields from a FDF file called *myprof.fdf*:

```
[   /Rect [ 50 425 295 445 ]
    /Action << /Subtype /ImportData
    /F (myprof.fdf) >>
    /Subtype /Link
    /Border [ 1 1 1 ]
/ANN pdfmark
```

Table 6.30 lists all keys for /ImportData.

Table 6.30. Keys for /ImportData

Key	Explanation
/Subtype[1]	For importing form data always /ImportData
/F (File)[1]	Name of the file from which to import the form data

1. This key is required.

Executing menu items. Although the PDF specification "officially" only supports the menu items "Next Page", "Previous Page", "First Page", and "Last Page", actions in a PDF file may execute all menu items of Acrobat Reader or Exchange. In order to determine the corresponding PDF code and

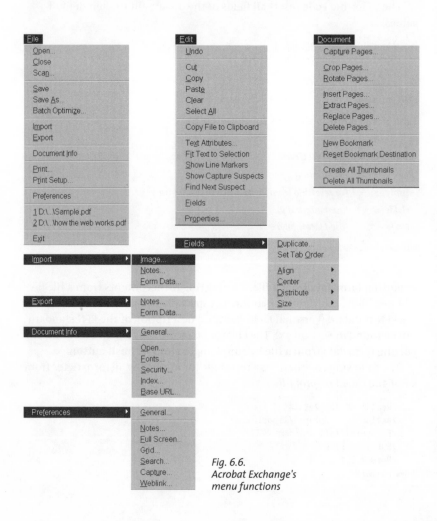

Fig. 6.6.
Acrobat Exchange's
menu functions

the pdfmarks for these undocumented menu items, I manually created actions for all menu items in Exchange. Unlike the specification, the resulting PDF file reveals all the required keys.

Note that not all menu items are available in Acrobat Reader. Items which are only available in Exchange are marked in the table. Another remark relates to subordinate menus: pdfmark cannot predefine the settings in higher-order menus. For example, although you can launch the print menu, you cannot define the print menu's settings (page range, etc.). The user must adjust these settings manually and confirm the menu before the print action is launched.

The following code creates a rectangle which, when clicked, closes the current PDF document:

```
[    /Rect [ 50 500 150 600]
     /Action << /Subtype /Named /N /Close >>
     /Subtype /Link
/ANN pdfmark
```

Table 6.31 lists all keys for activating Acrobat Exchange's menu items when used as /N value for the /Subtype /Named. Since the key names correspond to the menu items and are given in the same order as they appear on screen, the table doesn't need any additional explanation for the key names.

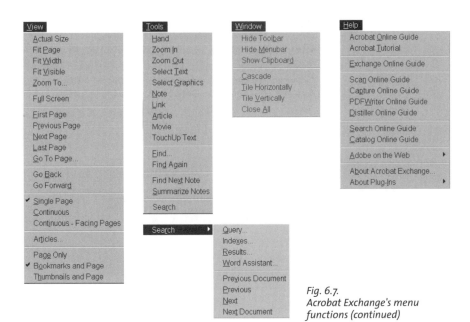

Fig. 6.7.
Acrobat Exchange's menu functions (continued)

Table 6.31. Keys for /N for executing menu functions with /Named

Acrobat menu	Keys for the menu function
File	/Open, /Close, /Scan[1], /Save[1], /SaveAs[1], /Optimizer:SaveAsOpt[1], /Print, /PageSetup, /Quit
File → Import	/ImportImage[1], /ImportNotes[1], /AcroForm:ImportFDF[1]
File → Export[1]	/ExportNotes[1], /AcroForm:ExportFDF[1]
File → Document Info	/GeneralInfo, /OpenInfo, /FontsInfo, /SecurityInfo, /Weblink:Base[1], /AutoIndex:DocInfo[1]
File → Preferences	/GeneralPrefs, /NotePrefs, /FullScreenPrefs, /Weblink:Prefs, /Acro-Search:Preferences (Windows) or /AcroSearch: Prefs (Mac)[2], /Cpt:Capture[1]
Edit	/Undo, /Cut, /Copy, /Paste, /Clear, /SelectAll, /Ole:CopyFile[1,3], /TouchUp: TextAttributes...[1], /TouchUp:FitTextToSelection[1], /Touch-Up:ShowLineMarkers[1], /TouchUp:ShowCaptureSuspects[1], /TouchUp:FindSuspect[1], /Properties
Edit → Fields[1]	/AcroForm:Duplicate[1], /AcroForm:TabOrder[1]
Document[1]	/Cpt:CapturePages[1], /AcroForm:Actions[1], /CropPages[1], /Rotate-Pages[1], /InsertPages[1], /ExtractPages[1], /ReplacePages[1], /Delete-Pages[1], /NewBookmark[1], /SetBookmarkDest[1], /CreateAllThumbs[1], /DeleteAllThumbs[1]
View	/ActualSize, /FitVisible, /FitWidth, /FitPage, /ZoomTo, /FullScreen, /FirstPage, /PrevPage, /NextPage, /LastPage, /GoToPage, /GoBack, /GoForward, /SinglePage, /OneColumn, /TwoColumns, /Article-Threads, /PageOnly, /ShowBookmarks, /ShowThumbs
Tools	/Hand, /ZoomIn, /ZoomOut, /SelectText, /SelectGraphics, /Note[1], /Link[1], /Thread[1], /AcroForm:Tool[1], /Acro_Movie:MoviePlayer[1], /TouchUp:TextTool[1], /Find, /FindAgain, /FindNextNote, /Create-NotesFile[1]
Tools → Search	/AcroSrch:Query, /AcroSrch:Indexes, /AcroSrch:Results, /AcroSrch: Assist, /AcroSrch:PrevDoc, /AcroSrch:PrevHit, /AcroSrch:NextHit, /AcroSrch:NextDoc
Window	/ShowHideToolBar, /ShowHideMenuBar, /ShowHideClipboard, /Cascade, /TileHorizontal, /TileVertical, /CloseAll
Help	/HelpUserGuide[1], /HelpTutorial[1], /HelpExchange[1], /HelpScan[1], /HelpCapture[1], /HelpPDFWriter[1], /HelpDistiller[1], /HelpSearch[1], /HelpCatalog[1], /HelpReader[4], /Weblink:Home
Help (Windows) or Apple menu (Mac)	/About

1. Only available in Acrobat Exchange.
2. Unfortunately, this entry is platform dependent – even if you create the button in Exchange. This means that different buttons for the two platforms are required!
3. Only available in Windows or on the Mac with OLE support installed.
4. Only available in Acrobat Reader.

6 Additional Tips for Distilling

Distiller parameters. Distiller's job options can be controlled from within the PostScript code. This provides a means to specify certain options within a PostScript file without having to rely on appropriate menu settings. As an additional plus, this makes it possible to change Distiller settings during processing of a single file. For example, according to the image contents one could deploy different compression schemes for certain images (e.g., gray level images), while the regular Distiller options apply to all other images in the file.

Distiller options can be queried and set using the "currentdistillerparams" and "setdistillerparams" PostScript operators. A complete description of these operators can be found under "Acrobat Distiller Parameters" in the Acrobat documentation.

Distilling multiple PostScript files to a single PDF. Sometimes it is necessary or convenient to distill multiple PostScript files to a single PDF document. For example, the whole document may consist of several chapters in individual files, or you want to include your own pdfmark file. Since fonts are embedded only once, combining multiple files decreases the overall file size. Detailed instructions of how this works can be found in Acrobat Distillers's *Xtras* folder.

Automatically creating named destinations. In many cases named destinations are created by application programs which generate the symbolic name by using the content, e.g. the text in a heading. In order to jump to a specific page of a PDF document via a Web link, it may be useful to assign a symbolic name to each page. Named destinations are covered in more detail in Section 8.6.

By making use of a PostScript Level 2 feature, Distiller may be instructed to automatically create a symbolic name for each page. Phil Smith was the first to implement this idea. Copy the file *namedest.ps* from the accompanying CD-ROM to Distiller's startup directory. This file creates a named destination on each page. The names are "Page1", "Page2", etc. These symbolic names may be used as a fragment identifiers after the "#" character:

```
http://www.ifconnection.de/~tm/manual.pdf#Page41
```

Note that the page numbers refer to physical page numbers (starting with page 1 in the document) and not to whatever page number may be typeset in the footer or on another location on the page.

7 PDF Forms

7.1 Form Features

Forms are an important new feature introduced with Acrobat 3.0 and PDF 1.2. They offer huge potential for interactive applications. Firstly, Acrobat forms emulate the well-known – and not very popular – paper forms containing descriptive text and input fields where the user may enter data. The filled-out form can be printed afterwards. This simplifies using conventional forms but doesn't yet add substantial value. Electronic forms are more interesting if you no longer need to print them out. Instead, the form contents are stored on a disk file or transferred over the intranet or Internet. Web forms gained much popularity by making use of the relevant HTML features. Similarly, Acrobat documents may contain form fields, the contents of which are sent from the Web browser to the Web server. As you would expect from PDF, Acrobat forms offer many more design and layout features than HTML forms.

Since the multitude of Acrobat's forms features cannot be expressed completely in HTML, Adobe developed a new file format for storing and transmitting form contents. This Forms Data Format (FDF) is derived from PDF (but is much simpler), and can be used as an alternative to the common HTML/URL encoding method for sending form contents to the Web server.

Creating PDF forms.   Creating PDF forms is a multilevel process. Obviously, it should begin with thoroughly planning and structuring the data. Next, a user-friendly layout has to be designed. What is the intended use of the form? Will it be filled out on the computer and transmitted digitally, or will it be printed out and sent as paper? Some users may even print the empty form and fill it out with a pen! According to the intended use it may be reasonable to include non-printing fields which only appear on screen but not on paper. In this chapter, I don't want to go into these layout-related issues but instead restrict myself to the technical aspects of form creation.

Figure 7.1 summarizes the steps and options for creating and using PDF forms, and lists the necessary Acrobat and Web software. Designing the form in a graphics or DTP application is first in the process. Currently there is no graphics program which is capable of generating PDF form fields in the original document. For this reason, you have to convert the document to PDF and define the forms fields in Acrobat Exchange manually. Exchange offers many feature for defining graphical and functional properties of PDF forms. However, exact positioning and aligning of the fields in Exchange is

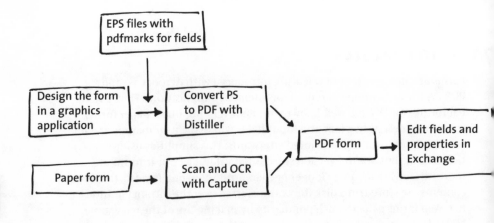

Fig. 7.1.
Creating and using PDF forms

Fòrm creatiòn

a cumbersome procedure. Besides, using two different programs unnecessarily complicates the form design process. As a workaround there are (again!) pdfmark instructions which can define the form fields in the original document. The EPS embedding method (or FrameMaker's PostScript frames) is recommended to facilitate positioning and scaling the fields. After creating dummy EPS files with suitable pdfmarks you place them in the graphics program at the appropriate locations. You can move and scale the fields like regular EPS files. Although not all field properties may be defined via pdfmarks (not all form-related pdfmarks are documented), the pdfmark approach saves many positioning chores in Exchange. A description of the necessary pdfmarks can be found in Section 6.4. All examples in this chapter have been produced with Adobe Illustrator and embedded EPS files with form pdfmarks.

PDF forms.   A PDF form may contain an arbitrary number of fields comprising interactive elements like buttons, lists, and editable text fields. Although a PDF file may contain at most one form, the form fields may span several pages. You may send or process only selected form fields or all fields

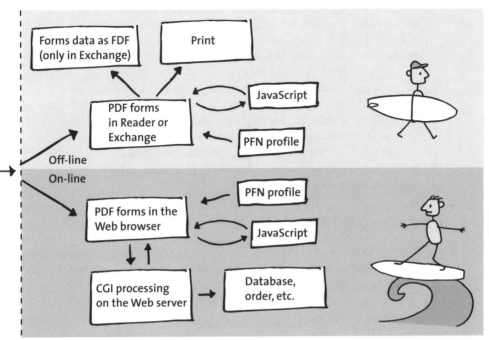

Form usage

in a PDF form. This means that the "one form per file" rule doesn't impose any practical restrictions.

PDF form fields have attributes describing their type, name, value, and appearance. You can specify these attributes using Acrobat Exchange's form tool.

The fields in a form are organized in a hierarchical manner. This hierarchy is defined by the field names. The elements of a field name are simply separated by a period character. The field name

```
business.telephone.voice.number
```

may, for example, relate to an item defined by the hierarchy company – phone – voice extension – number. Although the fields can have arbitrary names, adhering to a standard is recommended for personal data (see Section 7.5).

Availability of form features.   As noted above, Exchange offers extensive possibilities for creating and editing forms. Additionally, form data – i.e., the form contents without the descriptive text – can be exported to a separate file. Form data in such a file may be imported and reused in similar forms.

Here an important restriction of Acrobat Reader must be noted since it doesn't offer any import or export function for form data. This means that users without Exchange can only fill out a form manually, but cannot import existing form data. Although Acrobat Reader cannot save form data in a file, the user may send the data via the Internet. This requires a "send data" push button which has to be implemented by the form designer.

Finally, another restriction relates to Unix versions of Acrobat Reader: These do not include the forms plugin and therefore cannot be used for filling out PDF forms in the browser or Reader.

Note that the free Acrobat Forms plugin (also contained on the CD-ROM accompanying this book) includes a form plugin for Unix versions of Acrobat Reader (see Section 7.6).

7.2 Form Fields

PDF's field types cover the most important features found in most graphical user interfaces. Basically, in a conventional paper form you can only enter text, or choose one or more items from a given list.

Table 7.1. The PDF field types

Name	Description
Check box	Users can select an item by clicking a check box.
Radio button	Group of multiple related check boxes. Only one check box can be selected at a time.
Push button	Buttons are associated with action sequences, such as opening a file or submitting data to a Web server.
List box	The user may choose from a list of several predefined elements. The user can browse the list using scroll bars. The list may contain an arbitrary number of elements.
Combo box	Use the combo box field to create a list of items selectable from a menu. Since all choices appear in a popup menu, the combo box requires less space on the page than a list box.
Text field	Text input on one or more lines

Table 7.1 gives an overview of the field types supported in PDF. The types are presented in more detail on the following pages. Figure 7.2 contains a sample form which uses all field types.

After creating a field with the form tool (or double-clicking an existing field), Acrobat Exchange pops up the field properties dialog box. In addition to name and type of the field, there are three property sheets:

▸ Options for defining the field's functions. The available options depend on the type of the field and are described in more detail below.

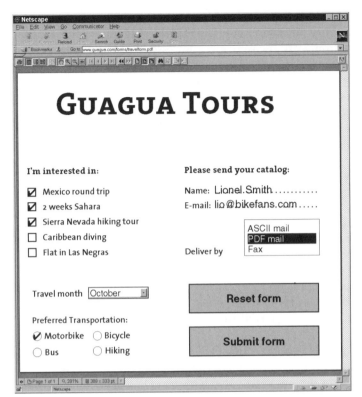

Fig. 7.2.
A PDF form with
all field types

► Appearance of the field. This includes border and background color as well as font name and size. In addition, you can specify whether a field is read-only, hidden, or required, and whether or not it should be printed.
► Actions associated with the field. Actions may be triggered by entering or leaving the field with the mouse, and clicking or releasing the button.

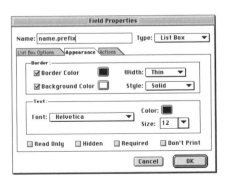

Fig. 7.3.
Field appearance options

Most field types can export a value, i.e., transfer the user's input. The exported values may, for example, contain the text of an input field or the selected choice from a list. The Web server processes the form data by looking at the field names and exported values. When defining a field, the form designer can specify default values which are displayed in the field until the user changes it. Except for push buttons, all field types export some value. For text fields, the exported value is the text typed into the field. The export values of check boxes, radio buttons, list boxes, and combo boxes is specified by the form designer.

Check boxes. Check boxes relate to a Boolean value, i.e., they take one of two possible states. Like a light switch, they toggle between these two states and graphically signal the currently selected state. Check boxes are most of the time implemented as boxes which can be clicked on and off.

☑	Mexico round trip
☑	2 weeks Sahara
☑	Sierra Nevada hiking tour
☐	Caribbean diving
☐	Flat in Las Negras

In the "on" state the box contains a cross or similar symbol. Unlike other field types, it's not possible to set the font name for use in check boxes and the related radio buttons – Exchange always uses the ZapfDingbats font. However, using complicated pdfmark instructions this restriction can be lifted.

Since a check box doesn't contain any text itself, a descriptive caption which explains the field's function must be placed alongside the field.

The check box options specify the character to be displayed in the "selected" state, the export value, and the default value.

Radio buttons. Radio buttons consist of several check boxes which can't be clicked independently, but work as a group. At most one check box of the

● Motorbike	○ Bicycle
○ Bus	○ Hiking

group may be selected at a time – similar to the old car radio buttons from which this field type takes its name. Clicking a box automatically de-selects the previously selected one. Radio buttons therefore guarantee that the user selects at most one of the available options. Whether he has to select a value at all (or leave all buttons unselected) can be specified in the radio button's options.

Exchange doesn't have a tool for grouping the check boxes to be used as radio buttons. The boxes are simply associated by a common name. Check boxes with the same name are a radio button group, regardless of their location on the page or in the document. Each box must export a unique value (otherwise it would be pointless to select a specific value). The options for radio buttons are identical to those for check boxes.

Push buttons. Push buttons are the only type of field which do not export a value. They are only used for triggering actions. Speaking of forms, sending the form contents to a Web server is, of course, the most important action. Most forms take advantage of a "reset" push

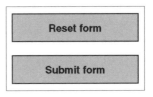

button which resets all fields to their default values. In addition, all actions which may be triggered by links or when opening a page can also be activated via push buttons. This opens the door to many interesting interactive applications.

A button's appearance can be specified in its options dialog box. You can choose among several combinations of text and icon. The button text is typed into the options dialog, the icon is imported from another PDF file. Think twice: push buttons let you change a PDF document's design in Exchange, after creating the file! To make use of this feature, you need a PDF file which contains the desired button design on a separate page. Exchange scales this page to fit into the button, and copies the data to the form file (there is no need to distribute the file from which the button icon was imported along with the form).

In addition, you can specify the button's appearance when it is clicked on. For example, the activated button may change its label or display another icon.

Text fields. Text fields are used for arbitrary text input which resembles the classical use of paper forms. Text fields may contain one or

Name: Lionel.Smith . . . .
E-mail: lio@bikefans.com . . . . .

more lines of text. Optionally, the input may be limited to a certain number of characters.

A text field's options may specify the text alignment in the field and the maximum number of input characters. The password property results in a "*" character being displayed instead of the typed characters. This can be used to protect sensitive data from someone who is peering over your shoulder.

List boxes. List boxes are used for selecting a single value from a set of several available elements. Multiple elements may be visible simultaneously, scroll bars appear if required.

The user may choose among the available elements, but can neither edit nor change list entries.

The list box options contain one or more pairs. Each pair consists of the actual element displayed in the list, and the value to be exported when this element is selected. In addition, a default value may be specified. You can also specify whether the list elements should be sorted alphabetically.

Combo boxes. Combo boxes (or popup menus) extend list boxes. The user can also choose among several list elements, but may optionally type new values and therefore supply new elements. Combo boxes are more space-efficient than list boxes since they normally display the selected element only (unless the menu is popped up).

Combo boxes offer the same options as list boxes. In addition, you can specify whether or not the user is allowed to edit the available elements.

Comparing form features in PDF and HTML. It's not just a matter of chance that Acrobat forms include all HTML form features – the latter surely served as a model when Adobe developed the form function in PDF 1.2. With a view towards conversion of existing HTML forms to PDF forms it's interesting to compare HTML's form tags with Acrobat form features. Table 7.2 lists the corresponding Acrobat functions for all HTML tags (in angle brackets) and their attributes (in the tag's table row).

However, PDF forms do not simply simulate existing HTML options but extend their options in a variety of ways:

► There are no restrictions concerning the field design, for example fonts, color, background images, etc.
► Fields can be printed without restrictions. This is not always the case for HTML forms. On the other hand, PDF form fields may be defined such that they appear only on screen and not on the printed version.
► The Web server can send back data into the form (e.g., an acknowledgment). With HTML forms, the server must generate the complete form code again and retransmit it along with the new contents (more details can be found in Section 7.4).
► Actions related to form fields offer many more field actions than simply sending and resetting the form contents.
► PDF push buttons can change their design when activated. HTML buttons are merely inverted.
► Push buttons and form fields can be spiced up with context sensitive help (see next section).
► Assuming enough bandwidth, multimedia features can be used for user guidance, for example an introductory sound file or a training video.

7.3 Tips on Creating Form Fields

Preparing form fields with pdfmarks in EPS dummies. pdfmark instructions are the most efficient means of generating forms until form features are supported in graphics programs (or other specialized applications). For this reason, I'd like to repeat the reference to Section 6.4. There you will find

Table 7.2. Conversion of HTML 4.0 form tags and their attributes to Acrobat/PDF

HTML	Acrobat/PDF
<FORM>	Not necessary (mere existence of form fields is sufficient)
ACTION	Web server URL is supplied in the submit push button
ENCTYPE	Submit push button defines HTML or FDF as transfer format
METHOD	Transfer method is always POST
ACCEPT-CHARSET	Text fields always use PDFDocEncoding.
General attributes	
ALIGN	Specified by the position on the page
NAME	Field property
SIZE	Specified by the field size or number of characters
READONLY	Text field property "Appearance", "Read Only"
TABINDEX	"Edit", "Fields", "Set Tab Order"
DISABLED	Hiding and showing fields, JavaScript (see Section 7.6)
Events (ON...)	Actions, JavaScript (see Section 7.6)
<INPUT>	Text field, push button, radio button, or check box
TYPE = TEXT	Text field
= PASSWORD	Text field option "Password"
= CHECKBOX	Check box
= FILE	(no equivalent)
= IMAGE	Push button option "Icon..."
= RADIO	Radio button
= SUBMIT	Push button with associated action "Submit Form"
= RESET	Push button with associated action "Reset Form"
= HIDDEN	Appearance "Hidden"
= BUTTON	Push button
CHECKED	Check box option "Default is Checked"
SRC	Select background image in push button options
VALUE	Text field option "Default"
MAXLENGTH	Text field option "Limit of ... characters"
ALT	Alternative text is not required since the layout is always retained.
USEMAP	Image map in Web links (see Section 8.6).
ACCEPT	(Not relevant since file selection is not supported.)
<BUTTON>	Push button
<SELECT>	Combo box or list box
MULTIPLE	–
SIZE	List box: determined by size; Combo box: always 1.
<OPTION>	Values in the list box or combo box options
SELECTED	Default value in the list box or combo box options
VALUE	Export value in the list box or combo box options
<TEXTAREA>	Text field option "Multi-line"
COLS, ROWS	Determined by a text field's size
<LABEL>	Separate label. For push buttons alternatively "Button Options", "Layout". However, pure text labels cannot relay mouse clicks to the corresponding form field like the LABEL tag does.
<FIELDSET> <LEGEND>	Form field grouping by layout, tab order, and hierarchical name structure

examples of pdfmarks which define all six types of form fields. Depending on the field type, this technique requires some additional processing in Exchange. However, this is much less effort than creating the fields from scratch in Exchange.

Duplicating fields. Sometimes it is reasonable to repeat form fields on several pages, for example push buttons for submitting or resetting the form. In Exchange there is a shortcut for duplicating fields on several pages: Select the field to be duplicated with the form tool and choose "Edit", "Fields", "Duplicate...". In the upcoming dialog box you can specify on which pages to duplicate the selected field. The duplicated fields have the same name and properties as the original field. Changing the field's contents affects all duplicate fields. But you can also manipulate the size and position of each field individually.

To place a copy of a form field on the same page, you can drag the field with the mouse while holding the Ctrl (Windows) or Alt key (Mac). Additionally pressing the shift key makes the field move exactly horizontally or vertically.

Taborder. Multiple text fields may be filled more quickly if the user can jump to the next field with the tab key. This requires the fields to be chained in reasonable order. By default, fields are chained in the order of creation. You can change this afterwards using "Edit", "Fields", "Set Tab Order". Tab order is only relevant for text fields.

Push button for jumping to another page. There's an important restriction for the actions associated with a push button. Unlike regular links, you cannot jump to another page but only to the current page – which doesn't make much sense. You can use this feature to change magnification and zoom into a region the author might want the user to examine.

However, using the following detour you can implement jumps to other pages in a roundabout way: Create the push button for the jump on the target (!) page. Select the desired zoom factor because it will become part of the "Go To View" action. Now duplicate the push button to the page(s) where the jump button is to appear (see description above). Finally delete the dummy button on the target page.

Context sensitive help. The "Show-Hide Field" action can be used for implementing context sensitive help with PDF fields. Despite its unwieldy name, this feature is quite user-friendly: When the mouse pointer enters a certain region on the page, a text field appears on a nearby location explaining the respective feature or button (see Figure 7.4). Using context sensitive help you can explain form fields without the user getting confused by too many explanations which are all visible at the same time. Only when the user requires the explanation will it be visible. Since fields may be over-

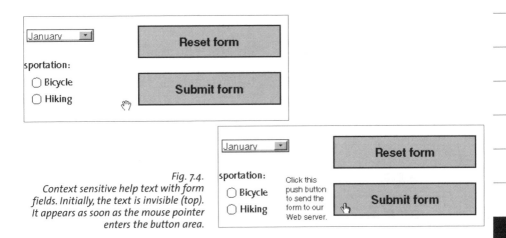

Fig. 7.4.
Context sensitive help text with form
fields. Initially, the text is invisible (top).
It appears as soon as the mouse pointer
enters the button area.

laid (obviously this is only reasonable when only one field is visible at a time), context sensitive help doesn't require much screen estate – several help texts may appear at the same location. The following steps create a textual explanation for a push button:

▸ Use Exchange's form tool to create the field "Order" (this may be a push button or any other type of field). Set the push button's properties as required for your application.

▸ Create a text field for the help text in the desired size and position. Type the help text into the "Default:" field in the options dialog. Also select "Multi-line" if necessary. In the appearance property sheet click "Read only", "Hidden", and "Don't Print". According to taste you can also adjust font name and size. Don't forget to assign a unique name to the field, for example "help text 1".

▸ In the "Order" field's properties, add two actions: Select "Show-Hide field" for the "Mouse Enter" event and select "help text 1" as the field to be shown. In the same dialog box click "Show". Similarly, select "Show-Hide field" for the "Mouse Exit" event too, but click "Hide" and select "help text 1" again.

Important note: Acrobat Exchange 3.0 for the Mac seems to have trouble with field names containing special characters. If a field name contains special characters, the "Show-Hide field" function doesn't find the field – the help text doesn't get displayed. For this reason, don't use special characters in field names. Since field names are not visible to the user, this is an annoyance, but not a severe restriction.

Reusing form fields when layout changes are necessary.   If you spent a lot of effort on generating form fields in a complicated form and then realize that the layout has to be modified or some other changes to the original document are required, you need not recreate all your fields manually. If you want to change the underlying PDF page without losing the form fields, proceed as follows:

- ► Generate the PDF page to be changed with the native application (e.g., your graphics program).
- ► Insert the page into the PDF file containing the form after the page to be replaced.
- ► Select all existing form fields on the old page by using the form tool while holding the shift key, and click "Edit", "Fields", "Duplicate...". Select only the next page (with the inserted new layout) as target for the duplication.
- ► Delete the old form page.

7.4 PDF Forms on the World Wide Web

Using Acrobat forms for printouts which preserve the layout, or locally storing form data, are quite useful features. However, the really interesting thing is integrating Acrobat forms in the World Wide Web. This requires a PDF-aware Web browser on the user's side (see Section 2.1). In addition, the browser must be capable of submitting Acrobat form data. This is the case for Netscape Navigator 3.0 and higher and Microsoft Internet Explorer 3.01 (with Acrobat Reader 3.01) and higher.

To offer PDF forms on the Web you must design a push button for submitting the form data since there is no corresponding menu item or tool. Such a push button in the document corresponds to the users' HTML experience. As an alternative to a submit push button, PDF forms may also use other triggers for sending the form data. For example, leaving the page could automatically submit the field contents to the server (in Exchange: "Document", "Set Page Action..."). Use this method carefully – it isn't familiar to most users, and it must be thoroughly integrated in the form's user interface. Otherwise, the poor user sends the data erroneously, or desperately looks for a submit button. Finally, the PFN standard for field names should be adhered to when creating forms which request personal information from the user (see Section 7.5).

The Forms Data Format (FDF).   Adobe developed a new file format for storing form data (via Exchange's export function) or sending form data over the net. The so-called Forms Data Format (FDF) is a simple text format which is syntactically related to PDF. FDF is fully documented in an appendix of the *Portable Document Format Reference Manual*. FDF only describes the fields of a PDF form, but doesn't contain any layout-related information. FDF files contain the title (/T) and value (/V) of all fields. Additionally, the PDF form's file name may be specified in the FDF file. The following example lists the FDF file for a PDF form with some personal fields:

```
%FDF-1.2
1 0 obj
<<
    /FDF <<
        /Fields [
            << /T (name.first) /V (Thomas) >>
            << /T (name.last) /V (Merz) >>
            << /T (favorite_sports) /V (cycling) >>
        ]
    >>
>>
endobj
trailer
<< /Root 1 0 R >>
%%EOF
```

FDF may also be used for transmitting the form contents from the browser
to the Web server. The form's designer may choose among FDF and HTML
format (in the URL selection box) when defining the "Submit Form" action.
"HTML format" means the usual URL encoding of form data as specified in
Internet RFC 1866. The FDF/HTML decision is based on the required functionality and has consequences on the server side. Basically, we have two
different scenarios, which I want to discuss briefly.

Replacing HTML forms with FDF forms. In the first scenario, existing
HTML forms are to be replaced or amended by PDF forms. In this case,
HTML is preferable as transmission format because all scripts and programs for processing the form data on the server can be reused without
change.

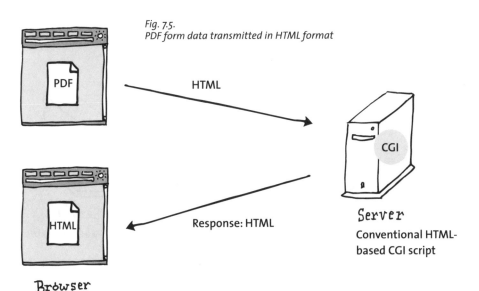

Fig. 7.5.
PDF form data transmitted in HTML format

PDF

HTML

CGI

HTML

Response: HTML

Server
Conventional HTML-
based CGI script

Browser

Most components of the already existing architecture (see Figure 7.5) remain unchanged, only the HTML forms are replaced by their PDF counterparts. In order to make sure that the server's forms processing doesn't break, it is important to choose the same PDF field names as in the HTML forms. The responses which the server may send to acknowledge form data input are still submitted in HTML format to the browser.

FDF based form system. The second scenario is reasonable if there are no legacy CGI scripts, or specific FDF advantages are to be used. An FDF based solution has the big advantage that the server can send his response in FDF too. The browser incorporates this response in the PDF form already displayed on the user's screen. Of course this requires appropriate response fields in the PDF form. The server's answer may contain not only the usual "Thank you!" message but also dynamically generated data according to the field input. For example, the response may contain the nearest business branch (as determined by the user's ZIP code) of the company running the server.

Sending back FDF data allows using PDF's graphical features in the server's response, as opposed to the meager HTML layout. (The next level, dynamic PDF, is covered in Chapter 12). The server's response isn't restricted to using the previously displayed PDF form, but may also request another PDF file from the client machine or the server.

Figure 7.6 illustrates the architecture of an FDF based form system. Note that the URL of a CGI script which sends FDF to the browser must end with

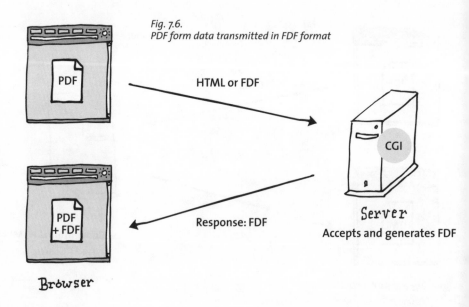

Fig. 7.6.
PDF form data transmitted in FDF format

HTML or FDF

PDF

PDF + FDF

Response: FDF

CGI

Server
Accepts and generates FDF

Browser

the fragment identifier #FDF. Otherwise, the FDF data won't be incorporated into the PDF form.

You can find more information on configuring a Web server for FDF and evaluating or dynamically generating FDF in Chapter 10.

.5 Personal Field Names (PFN)

Since PDF forms are relatively new, they are not yet in wide use on the Internet. However, if many Web servers offer PDF forms, a user may happen to unnecessarily enter his or her personal data (first name, last name, address, etc.) again and again in PDF forms. Since personal data make up a large fraction of the information requested with forms, Adobe have devised a simple scheme which facilitates filling forms repeatedly with the same data.

Detailed information on this mini-standard, dubbed "Personal Field Names", can be found on the Acrobat CD-ROM. The basic idea is quite simple: instead of specifying different names of personal fields in each new form, standardized field names are suggested by PFN. The user creates a file with his or her personal data once, and imports this file into all forms requiring personal information. To cover a broad range of applications, the PFN proposal contains fields detailing names, birthday, home and business address, and many more.

Using PFN compliant forms works as follows: The user uses a form file from the Acrobat CD-ROM to create a so-called profile containing his personal data. The field data are stored as FDF on the user's hard disk. Note that this requires Acrobat Exchange since Reader lacks an export function. However, using the profile later (see below) only requires Acrobat Reader. The profile should be stored with a fixed name in the Acrobat installation directory to make sure the automatic import will work. This file name, also defined in the PFN standard, is *myprof.fdf*.

In the next step, the designer of a PDF form must use the field names in Table 7.3 for all personal fields. However, not all fields from the table must be used. Forms which require less information simply skip unneeded fields. The form should contain some push buttons to facilitate FDF profile import. The first button is labeled "Import FDF profile" and imports the profile *myprof.fdf*. The second button resets all form fields to their default val-

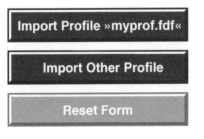

Fig. 7.7.
Recommended buttons for
PFN compliant forms

ue (empty). Additionally a third button may be implemented which allows the user to browse for another FDF profile. Such a button uses "File", "Import", "Form Data..." as its associated action. The buttons are very important since there are no Acrobat menu items available when filling out the PDF form in the Web browser.

Table 7.3. PFN standard field names

Field name	Field name (continued)
name.prefix	business.telephone.fax.extension
name.first	home.address.line1
name.initial	home.address.line2
name.last	home.address.line3
name.suffix	home.address.city
name.nickname	home.address.state
business.title	home.address.zip
business.companyname	home.address.country
business.address.line1	home.telephone.voice.countrycode
business.address.line2	home.telephone.voice.areacode
business.address.line3	home.telephone.voice.number
business.address.city	home.telephone.voice.extension
business.address.state	home.telephone.fax.countrycode
business.address.zip	home.telephone.fax.areacode
business.address.country	home.telephone.fax.number
business.telephone.voice.countrycode	home.telephone.fax.extension
business.telephone.voice.areacode	emailaddress
business.telephone.voice.number	ssn
business.telephone.voice.extension	birthdate.year
business.telephone.fax.countrycode	birthdate.month
business.telephone.fax.areacode	birthdate.day
business.telephone.fax.number	

Adobe recommends placing the PFN logo in the form so that the user can identify PFN compliant forms (see Figure 7.8). You can find a PDF file with the logo on the Acrobat CD-ROM. It's easy to integrate the logo in a PDF form by creating a push button (without any associated action) which uses the logo as icon. Use the following settings in the push button's options property sheet: "Highlight: None" and "Layout: Icon only". Now choose the PFN logo file for "Icon...". Exchange incorporates the logo in the form file.

Differences between Exchange and Reader.   The observant reader will have realized an inconsistency in the PFN concept: the forms are to be filled out with Acrobat Reader which doesn't offer any import function. Indeed,

Fig. 7.8.
The PFN logo

the action "Import Form Data" with a fixed file name works in Exchange as well as in Reader, while the menu item "File", "Import", "Form Data..." only exists in Acrobat Exchange. For this reason the PFN concept also works with Acrobat Reader on the users' side, provided a fixed file name is used for the profile. In this case you have to sacrifice the possibility of importing other FDF profiles than the default *myprof.fdf*.

One problem remains: users need Exchange for creating their profile. Although it only requires several minutes of Exchange access, this may be enough to drive a large site's system administrator crazy.

I can only offer a partial solution to this problem. FDF files are text files with a syntax similar to PDF. The internal structure is much easier than in PDF; in particular, the complicated reference tables, which describe each object's byte offset in the file, are missing. Due to their simple structure, FDF files may be generated or edited with a text editor if you take care of special characters in strings (see Section 6.2). The system administrator creates a dummy profile containing hints instead of real user data. It's best to signal start and end of the variable sections with a special character in order to avoid errors. The following FDF file contains some hints instead of the actual field entries, delimited with exclamation marks. This prevents users from mixing up field name and value:

```
%FDF-1.2
1 0 obj
<<
/FDF << /Fields [ << /T (name) /Kids [
    << /T (name.first)   /V (!Your first name here!) >>
    << /T (name.initial)/V (!Your initial name here!) >>
    << /T (name.last)    /V (!Your last name here!) >>
    << /T (name.nickname)/V (!Your nickname here!) >>
    << /T (name.prefix)  /V (!Your prefix here!) >>
    << /T (name.suffix)  /V (!Your title here!)>> ] >>
...
```

As an alternative to editing an existing FDF file, the user profiles could be generated from the human resources database using a report generator. Yet another possibility is the FDF Toolkit which takes care of the syntactical details of FDF (see Section 10.2).

If every user receives such an FDF dummy along with a description of how to edit the field values, personal profiles for use with PFN compliant forms may be generated without using Acrobat Exchange.

EPS files for PFN form fields.   Finally, I'd like to draw your attention to a set of EPS files in the PFN directory on the Acrobat CD-ROM. These EPS files contain the pdfmark instructions necessary for defining all PFN fields (see also the field examples in Section 6.2). Using these EPS files you can specify the PFN field names in your original document files without risking typos in field names.

7.6 Acrobat Forms

Missing features for PDF forms.   Several form features which are required in many applications are missing from Acrobat 3.0:
- ▶ It's impossible to implement field dependencies.
- ▶ It's impossible to calculate field contents from other fields.
- ▶ User input can only be validated on the server instead of in the client. This is very inefficient.
- ▶ Unix support for forms is missing.

The free Acrobat Forms plugin which you can find on Adobe's Web server or on the accompanying CD-ROM is meant to overcome these shortcomings and to open up new application areas for PDF forms. The main enhancement in the new Acrobat Forms plugin, which replaces the one contained in the standard Acrobat distribution, is the integration of the JavaScript language. There's no doubt that integrating a suitable scripting language is a clever move since this offers a huge potential and enough flexibility for future extensions. Acrobat Forms comes with several other enhancements:
- ▶ Enhanced button features. For example, a different icon may be displayed when the mouse enters the button area.

Fig. 7.9.
Extended field properties
with Acrobat forms:
formatting field contents

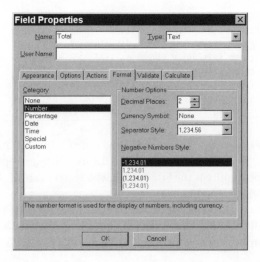

- Field data formatting, e.g., for date, time, and currency values.
- Field validation: user input can be checked for allowed or required length, characters, etc.
- Field calculation: field values may calculated from other fields, e.g., the total sum in an order form.
- Field layout features: a positioning grid and enhanced layout and alignment features make implementing multiple form fields less of a chore.
- Dynamic page templates allow creation of new pages in a PDF form on the fly. For example, an order form could add more pages if required.
- PDF form support for Unix versions of Acrobat.

Acrobat Forms consists of two plugins: The "Maker" plugin for Exchange extends the options for implementing form fields; the free "Filler" plugin is required to use JavaScript-enhanced PDF forms with Acrobat Reader 3.01.

One of the first publicly available examples of JavaScript programming in PDF comes from D. P. Story, math professor at the University of Akron, Ohio. His "Algeboard" game resembles a TV game show board containing algebra questions for the students. JavaScripts attached to form fields and links calculate the current high score according to right or wrong answers. The PDF game is contained on the accompanying CD-ROM and is also available from the following URL (see also Figure 7.11):

`http://www.math.uakron.edu/~dpstory`

Formatting, validating, and calculating form fields. Although the JavaScript binding is very powerful, it requires some programming skills for creating enhanced PDF forms. Three important features, however, are accessible without delving into the details of the JavaScript language. The

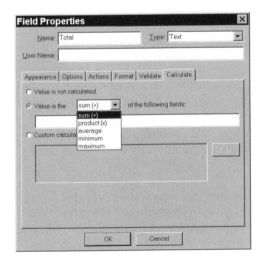

Fig. 7.10.
Extended field options
with Acrobat forms:
Calculating field values

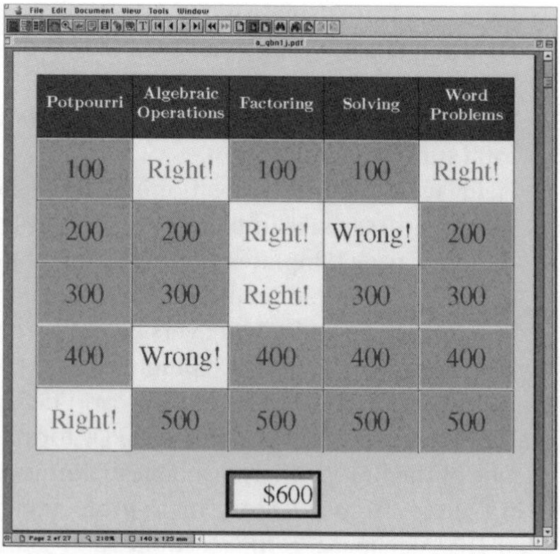

Fig. 7.11.
D. P. Story's Algeboard PDF game
demonstrates the power of JavaScript
programming in PDF documents.

Maker plugin adds three new field property sheets (see Figures 7.9 and 7.10) which can be used for formatting and validating user input, as well as for performing simple calculations based on existing field values.

The formatting features are quite useful for structured data such as currency amounts, time, and date. When the user leaves the field, the input is formatted as specified by the form designer. Several options for fine-tuning the formatting are available, for example, specifying the number of decimal places, choosing the currency symbol, and defining the decimal separator. In addition to the predefined formatting functions, custom formats may be implemented by attaching JavaScript functions to a field. These can be activated for each single keystroke (for more details see next section).

The validate function checks the user's input for plausibility. By default, the form designer can check for numerical intervals ("Value must be greater than ... and less than ..."). Again, custom JavaScripts may be attached for performing arbitrary validity tests, for example dependencies among form fields.

The calculate function performs simple arithmetic with numerical field values. An order form, for example, might calculate the total amount of all products ordered, and display the appropriate VAT, sales tax, or discount percentage. The predefined functions include sum, product, average, minimum, and maximum. Again, this list can be extended with custom JavaScript code.

JavaScript in PDF. Choosing JavaScript as a scripting language for Acrobat has several advantages. JavaScript is a simple yet powerful programming language which is gaining increasing significance for spicing up HTML pages. The language was developed by Netscape and is supported in Netscape

Navigator as well as in Microsoft Internet Explorer (in the Microsoft world it is dubbed JScript). Since Acrobat Forms contains its own JavaScript interpreter, form scripting doesn't require a Web browser environment.

JavaScript extensions for PDF forms are very effective since validation and calculation take place on the client side (i.e., Acrobat Reader, Exchange, or the Web browser), without requiring the data to be sent to the Web server. In the latter case, each field input had to be transferred to the server, resulting in additional network traffic.

JavaScripts may be integrated in PDF files on three different levels:

- On the plugin level JavaScripts exists as separate files with a *.js* file name suffix in Acrobat's plugin folder (on the Mac, in a subfolder called Java-Scripts. Plugin level JavaScript modules are loaded in an unspecified order when Acrobat's JavaScript interpreter starts up. This is useful for functions and variables which might be used on the other levels and should be generally available to all field functions. Acrobat Forms installs JavaScript files in the plugin folder which are required by the form processing engine itself.

- On the document level the form designer may attach JavaScript functions which are executed when opening the PDF file (but after executing the plugin level scripts). Document level scripts can be defined via "Tools", "JavaScript", "Document Scripts...".

- On the field level, JavaScripts can be attached to specific form fields. They are activated by certain events such as clicking the mouse or calculating field values.

JavaScripts on the document and field level are stored within the PDF file and therefore affect PDF file size.

Acrobat-specific JavaScript extensions. Acrobat's JavaScript binding is based on version 1.2 of Netscape's language. Since form processing requires a different runtime environment than using JavaScript in a Web browser – for example, accessing form fields and other parts of a PDF file – Adobe implemented several Acrobat-specific JavaScript extensions. These include additional objects, methods, and events. I'd like to briefly sketch the most important extensions here. More details can be found in the Acrobat Forms documentation. Please also note the example in Section 6.5 for embedding JavaScript code in pdfmark instructions.

The most important object is the field object. JavaScripts may use a field object's properties to access properties of the corresponding form field, such as its name, color, value, default, etc. Using the "App" object a JavaScript can access certain properties of the Acrobat Viewer. For example, full screen mode and toolbar may be activated or deactivated, or an alert box displayed on the screen. The "Doc" object gives access to a PDF file's general document information, the number of pages in the file, the current zoom factor, and other properties. In addition, the "Doc" object includes methods

Fig. 7.12.
Page templates can be used to add pages to a PDF document using Java-Script. The eye symbol to the left of the template name flags whether or not a template page is currently visible.

for navigation in the file. This even includes named destinations as targets (see Section 8.6).

The list of events handled within Acrobat forms is very important since all JavaScript functions are activated by certain events. This includes entering or leaving a field with the mouse, clicking or releasing the mouse button, or typing into a text field or combo box. Leaving a form field triggers the "validate" event which may be used for checking the user input. Next, a "calculate" event is triggered for calculating all field values which depend on the current field (these calculations can, in turn, trigger other events). Finally, a "format" event is generated which activates a field's formatting function.

Dynamic page templates. For database or ordering applications the "fixed layout" property of PDF documents is a disadvantage. For example, to create an order form in PDF requires the number of pages to be fixed, although it is not known how many products will be ordered. The order form will probably need more pages as the form is being filled out.

Using the template feature available with Acrobat Forms it's possible to dynamically add pages to a PDF document. Using "Document", "Page Templates...", arbitrary pages can be assigned a template name and optionally made invisible (making a template page invisible even decreases the file's page count). Having defined one or more templates, a JavaScript can be attached to a push button which adds new pages if the user demands it. The process of creating new pages based on a template is called "spawning". The following JavaScript can be used as a "Mouse Up" action for a push button to add a new page based on the first template page in the document:

```
var Template;
Template = this.getNthTemplate(0);
this.spawnPageFromTemplate(Template);
```

Another way of spawning new pages is an extended version of the FDF Toolkit (see Section 10.1), although I haven't yet tried this method.

Templates are quite a powerful feature for using PDF forms for dynamic applications. Since even page overlays with templates are possible, you can dynamically add form fields and buttons to an existing page.

JavaScript sample form. Obviously, this book doesn't include a JavaScript programming course. The following example is meant to give you a jump-start into JavaScript programming with Acrobat, and to provide a starting point for exploring the new features. Feel free to play with the sample file[1] (which you can find on the accompanying CD-ROM) and customize the JavaScripts contained in the PDF. Remember that you will have to install the Acrobat Forms plugin before you can use the example. For further information check out any recent JavaScript book or online documentation (Netscape supplies the complete language reference as a PDF file on its Web server). Additionally, you will need to read Adobe's documentation on the Acrobat-specific JavaScript extensions. This reference is included with the Acrobat Forms software.

Having looked at the new form features that Acrobat Forms offers, let's try a book order form as an example. The form shown in Figure 7.13 resembles the garden variety of online order forms, but adds some "intelligence" with several JavaScripts. In this form you can enter the ISBN for a book, the quantity, and the price. (Obviously, you don't want to enter the price manually in a real example, but attaching a database is another story which we won't go into here). There are several JavaScripts attached to the form fields:

- ▸ The total price in each row is calculated as the product of quantity and price. This is easily achieved by using the built-in calculation features of Acrobat Forms. Similarly, the values of the subtotal and total fields are calculated from other fields by using simple arithmetic operations in the "calculate" property of the input text field.
- ▸ For the sales tax we use the following JavaScript as a custom calculation script:

```
var subtotal = this.getField("subtotal");
var percentage = 0.075;
event.value =  subtotal.value * percentage;
```

- ▸ All price fields are formatted with two decimal places, the "Price Each" fields additionally get a dollar sign attached. The field formatting is easily defined using the predefined features in the "Format" property sheet.
- ▸ Since the ISBN codes offer plenty of opportunities for JavaScript programming, we will look into them in more detail in the rest of this chapter.

First, you cannot simply make up an arbitrary number and hope that it will work as an ISBN code: the last of the ten digits serves as a check digit for val-

---

1. Needless to say, I generated the form fields including the attached JavaScript routines with pdfmark instructions. The form layout was designed in Adobe Illustrator, pdfmarks were included in EPS files.

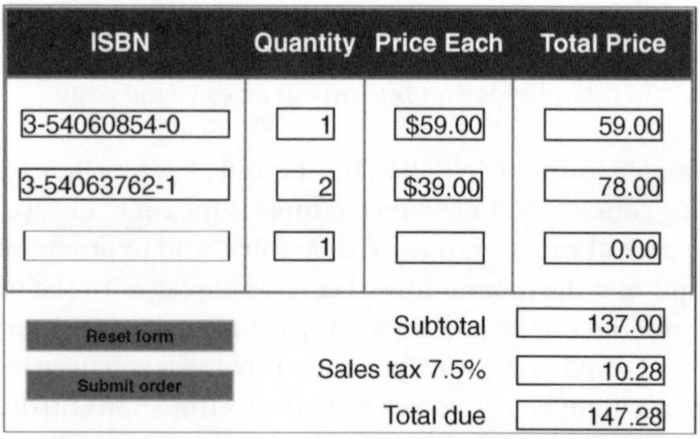

ISBN	Quantity	Price Each	Total Price
3-54060854-0	1	$59.00	59.00
3-54063762-1	2	$39.00	78.00
	1		0.00

Reset form	Subtotal	137.00
Submit order	Sales tax 7.5%	10.28
	Total due	147.28

Fig. 7.13.
The JavaScript-
enhanced book
order form

idating the book number.[1] This is perfectly suited for checking the number for typos. Secondly, we can format the ISBN since the first digits signal the country. By looking at the first digit(s) we can decide whether the country code is one, two, or three digits long, and can format the ISBN code by inserting a hyphen after the country code. Since we will use the ISBN checking and formatting code for several fields, we include the appropriate JavaScript routines on the document level. This saves space in the PDF file and helps keep the actual formatting and checking routines short.

In the first step, we have to validate the user input for the ISBN. Since the last character may be either the letter "X" or a digit, we cannot simply use a standard numeric field. Instead, we define the following JavaScript routine on the document level ("Tools", "JavaScript", "Document Scripts..."). The routine receives an event object as argument:

```
function keystroke_isbn(e) {
    // e.value doesn't yet include the current character
    var len = e.value.length;
    var c = e.change;                  // current character

    // check current character
    if (c < "0" || c > "9") {          // not a digit?
        if (len < 9 || c != "X") {     // special case for last character
            app.beep(0);
            e.rc = false;              // return code
        }
    }
}
```

1. In case you've always been curious: An ISBN book code consists of ten digits in four groups – country code, company code, book code, and a single check digit. The check digit is calculated as follows: Multiply the first digit by ten, the second by nine, and so on up to the ninth, which you multiply by two. Add all the results. The last digit will be the number which is needed to fill this sum to the next multiple of 11. If the check digit is 10, it is replaced by the letter "X". The relationship between the country code and its length (either one, two, or three digits) can be inferred from the format_isbn() routine. Similarly, we could separate company and book code by examining the first digits of the company code. For the sake of simplicity, this is left out in the sample formatting routine.

Using this routine, the custom keystroke script in the "Format" property sheet of the input field is quite terse:

```
if (event.change != "") {
    keystroke_isbn(event);
}
```

Having checked the individual characters, we have to verify that the number indeed makes up a valid ISBN code. Again, we define a JavaScript routine on the document level:

```
function check_isbn(isbn) {
    var sum = 0;
    var i = 0;

    if (isbn.length != 10) {
        app.alert("ISBN doesn't have exactly 10 figures!");
        return false;
    }
    for (i=0; i < 9; i++)
        sum += isbn.charAt(i) * (10-i);

    // dummy multiplication forces integer instead of string handling:
    sum += (isbn.charAt(9) == "X" ? 10 : isbn.charAt(9)) * 1;

    if (sum % 11 != 0) {
        app.alert("Error in ISBN number!");
        return (false);
    } else
        return (true);
}
```

This validation routine is called from a brief segment of JavaScript which is attached to the field as a custom validation script:

```
if (event.value != "") {
    event.rc = check_isbn(event.value);
}
```

If the input doesn't qualify as an ISBN code, an alert box is shown and the user may correct the number. Finally, we apply a little formatting on the ISBN by inserting a hyphen at the appropriate place:

```
function format_isbn(e) {
    var format_string;
    var a = e.value.substring(0, 1);      // first digit
    var b = e.value.substring(0, 2);      // first two digits
    var c = e.value.substring(0, 3);      // first three digits

    if (a >= 0 && a <= 7 && a != 6)
        format_string = "9-99999999-X";   // single-digit country code

    else if ((b >= 80 && b <= 88) || (b >= 90 && b <= 93))
        format_string = "99-9999999-X";   // two digit country code
```

Fig. 7.14.
Attaching custom format and key-stroke JavaScripts to a text field

```
else if (b >= 95 && b <= 99)
    format_string = "999-999999-X";      // three digit country code

else if (c >= 996 && c <= 998)
    format_string = "9999-99999-X";      // four digit country code

else
    format_string = "999999999-X";       // unknown country code

e.value = util.printx(format_string, e.value);
}
```

The actual formatting is done in the utility routine util.printx( ) which is supplied by Acrobat's JavaScript engine. The above script is called with the following code. It is attached to the ISBN input field as a custom format script:

```
if (event.value != "") {
    event.rc = format_isbn(event);
}
```

These samples may have given you an idea of the new possibilities you can explore with Acrobat Forms.

8 PDF in HTML Pages

8.1 Navigator and Internet Explorer

When PDF files are displayed in a Web browser's window, there are two distinct variants:

▸ The Web server sends a PDF file after a specific URL is typed in or called by a link. The Acrobat plugin processes the PDF data, takes control of the browser window, and displays the document in the window. Acrobat's toolbar appears under the browser's toolbar.

▸ Part of an HTML page contains a PDF document (or several PDF documents). The PDF data is not directly embedded in the document, but is called by reference to a separate file (see Figure 8.1). This variant requires the use of special HTML tags.

While there are important differences between the most widespread browsers, Netscape Navigator and Microsoft Internet Explorer, with respect to their architecture and functionality, both are capable of displaying PDF files either as complete pages or as part of an HTML page.

For publishers who wish to integrate PDF in HTML pages, the many detailed differences which become evident when embedding PDFs play a role. On one hand, there is a question regarding the functionality available to

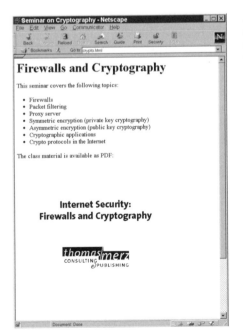

Fig. 8.1.
*Netscape Navigator with a
PDF document embedded
in HTML (in the lower part)*

someone using a particular browser. On the other hand, a publisher must ensure that his Web pages function properly in all browsers and meet their objectives as fully as possible.

I will begin these sections by giving an overview of browser PDF functionality and discussing the differences between browsers. After that, I will go into the HTML tags used for embedding PDF in HTML pages. Further information on browser architecture and the modules for PDF-related extensions can be found in Section 2.1.

Netscape Navigator.   Since version 2.0, Navigator has supported the HTML tag EMBED for embedding multimedia and other data objects which are processed by plugins. This "processing" can be displaying a document on screen, playing a sound or movie file, or starting an interactive element.

Many plugin developers have developed modules to support objects embedded in an HTML page with the EMBED tag.

Another important factor is the JavaScript scripting language which can be used to carry out simple programming tasks using instructions embedded in an HTML page. Despite their similar names, JavaScript does not have much in common with its big brother, the Java programming language, apart from a couple of cosmetic similarities. Because of this, a clear distinction should be made between Java and JavaScript.

Internet Explorer.   As part of its battle to be compatible with Netscape's browsers and at the same time win users over to its products with new functions, Microsoft developed the ActiveX architecture for Internet Explorer (for more on ActiveX, see Section 2.1). For compatibility reasons, Microsoft's browser supports the EMBED tag (introduced by Netscape) to embed PDF and other data types. In addition, Explorer's OBJECT tag offers a generalized interface for integrating any objects into HTML. Apart from ActiveX controls, these objects can be Java applets, plugins, pictures, documents, or scripts.

Apart from JavaScript – the Microsoft version is called JScript and is not totally compatible with the original – Internet Explorer supports "Visual Basic Scripting Edition", or VBScript, a version of Microsoft's own Visual Basic programming language.

At this point another warning about the limitations of ActiveX is appropriate: its architecture is not platform independent but is strongly biased to Microsoft. Internet Explorer 4.0 does support ActiveX on the Mac as well, although there are as yet no Mac ActiveX PDF controls – on the Mac the Acrobat plugin for Netscape Navigator is also used by Internet Explorer.

PDF functionality in Navigator and Internet Explorer.   Both browsers can display PDF files either in the whole window or as part of an HTML page. A glance at the details of the PDF integration, however, shows that this is about the only similarity. How far the differences listed in Table 8.1 affect a

Table 8.1. *Functions for PDF embedding in Netscape Navigator and Internet Explorer together with the Acrobat 3.01 browser plugin*

	Netscape Navigator	Microsoft Internet Explorer
Recognition of the Acrobat plugin with JavaScript/JScript	yes	no
PDF embedding with the EMBED tag	yes	yes
PDF embedding with the OBJECT tag	no	yes
Submission of forms from embedded PDFs	Navigator 3.0 and higher	Internet Explorer 3.01 and higher
Toolbar and window elements displayed for PDF documents embedded in HTML	no	yes (can be turned on or off in document settings)
PDF links and articles also active for PDF embedded in HTML.	no	yes
Automatic download of Acrobat module possible	no	yes, though not recommended
Embedded PDFs scalable using HTML tag attributes	yes	yes, also via PDF document info
Embedded PDFs distorted if size parameters are unsuitable	yes	no
PDF documents can be printed from the browser	yes	yes (print button in Acrobat toolbar or VBScript)
Printing of PDF documents embedded in HTML	no	no
Additional controls for PDF documents embedded in HTML	–	VBScript programming
Highlighting of search results in PDF documents	yes	yes
Saving of PDF files displayed in the browser window	yes	no
Use Acrobat to open PDFs embedded in HTML	yes (right mouse click)	no
Number of PDFs which can be simultaneously embedded on a page	9	6
"Named destinations" in PDF files work correctly	yes	not in a URL, only from PDF links

particular project depend on the exact functions required. Details about the points listed can be found in the following sections.

A particular problem which is caused by a peculiarity of Acrobat Reader or Exchange affects both browsers: Acrobat, even when used in stand-alone mode, can not open more than ten PDF documents at the same time. Attempting to exceed this number causes the software to give an error and ask you to close previously opened documents. This is inconvenient, but is

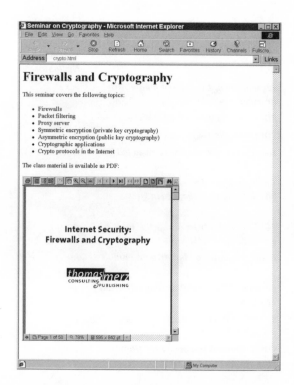

Fig. 8.2.
*Internet Explorer displays the
Acrobat menus and toolbar
for embedded PDFs*

not a great problem. However, within a Web browser, there is a problem in that the documents can not be closed because the menu bar is not visible, and the documents themselves may not be visible at all – either in the browser or in Acrobat! As far as I know, in this case the only answer is to close Acrobat Reader or Exchange and then reload the HTML/PDF page, causing Acrobat to restart.

Adobe makes the "AutoClose" plugin available on its Web site, which closes windows as required and solves the problem when Acrobat is used in stand-alone mode, but unfortunately this does not work in conjunction with Web browsers.

Acrobat controls in the browser.   An important point when PDF documents are embedded in HTML concerns the navigation and other controls needed to use the PDF documents. Because the browser generally regards a PDF document as a closed entity, its navigation controls relate only to whole PDF documents and not to individual PDF pages. Page control, such as zoom, thumbnails, bookmarks etc., can only be controlled via the Acrobat toolbar.

When a PDF document is displayed in the browser window, both Navigator and Internet Explorer display the Acrobat toolbar as well as their own tools so that the user can navigate within the PDF file. The number of tools displayed is limited by the browser's Acrobat plugin. Acrobat 3.01 has added several valuable functions to the tools available in the browser: "Select", "Copy", "Find", and "Find Again" (see also Figure 8.7).

The situation is different for PDF documents embedded in an HTML page: in Navigator they are always displayed without the Acrobat toolbar The designer therefore must offer the user alternative navigation methods, for example links and buttons within the PDF document.

Internet Explorer is much more flexible in this respect. The tool palette and the window controls (at the lower edge of the window) can be turned on or off as desired. This is determined not by the HTML code used to embed the file, but by the PDF file itself. In Acrobat Exchange these settings can be specified by "File", "Document Info", "Open...". Internet Explorer also uses the PDF file's settings for the zoom factor, display with/without thumbnails or with/without bookmarks. These settings can also be specified using pdfmark instructions (see Section 6.4).

Printing embedded PDF files from the browser. When PDF files are printed from the browser, several questions arise: are you going to use the browser print function or Acrobat's? Is only the PDF document to be printed or (in the case of embedded documents) the whole HTML page?

While PDF files which are fully displayed in the browser window can be printed using Netscape Navigator's print function, embedded PDFs (part of an HTML document) can not be printed from Navigator.

Things are different with Internet Explorer: it is not possible to print a PDF document which is displayed completely in the browser window using Explorer's print function, but the user can call Acrobat's print function from the Acrobat menu bar (as long as the menu bar is being displayed).

There are two ways of printing a PDF document from Explorer in addition to the browser's print function or the Acrobat toolbar print button:

▶ A button in the PDF document calls the Acrobat print dialog. This sort of print button is either inserted with the form tool in Exchange as a button to which the "File", "Print..." menu command is allocated, or using pdfmark instructions (see Section 6.4).

▶ VBScript instructions within the HTML page containing an embedded PDF can also be used to print a PDF. The user starts the process by clicking on a button defined in the HTML part of the page. See Section 8.3 for detailed instructions.

Table 8.2 compares the various printing possibilities.

Opening a new browser window using JavaScript. The following short JavaScript application is not restricted to use with Acrobat but is particularly useful in conjunction with PDF files. Using JavaScript, a Web page author can open a new browser window and specify whether or not various window elements, such as navigation bar toolbar, or scrollbars are visible.

Table 8.2. Possible ways of printing PDFs from the browser

	Netscape Navigator	Internet Explorer
Browser print function for PDFs without HTML embedding	yes	yes
Browser print function for embedded PDFs	no	no
Acrobat toolbar print button	no (not visible)	yes (if toolbar is visible)
Acrobat buttons	yes	yes
VBScript programming	no	yes

The following piece of HTML with an embedded JavaScript function defines a button. If the user clicks on it, then the browser opens a new window for the specified PDF file. Unlike a "normal" browser window, the new window does not display the browser's navigation elements which are not required (see Figure 8.3).

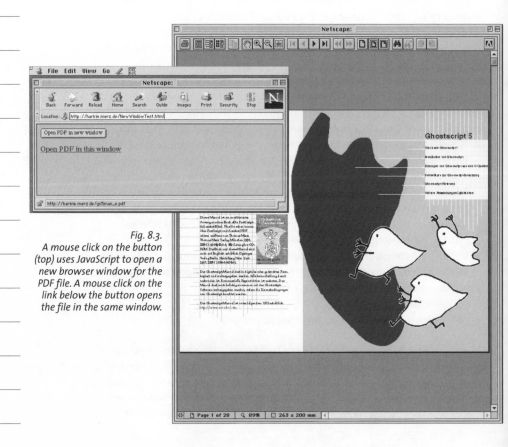

Fig. 8.3.
A mouse click on the button (top) uses JavaScript to open a new browser window for the PDF file. A mouse click on the link below the button opens the file in the same window.

```
<HTML>
<HEAD>
 <SCRIPT language="JavaScript">
<!--
function PDFwindow() {
    window.open("http://www.ifconnection.de/~tm/gs5man_d.pdf","PDF_window",
    "toolbar=0, width=640, height=480, location=0, directories=0," +
    "status=0, menubar=0, scrollbars=1, resizable=yes");
}
// -->
</SCRIPT>

</HEAD>
<BODY>
<FORM>
<INPUT NAME="New Window" TYPE="submit" VALUE="PDF in new window"
onClick="PDFwindow()">
<P><A HREF="http://www.ifconnection.de/~tm/gs5man_d.pdf">PDF in old
window</A></P>
</BODY>
</HTML>
```

So that a user whose browser does not support JavaScript can also get the
file, a conventional link, which opens the file in the same window, is provided under the button. In a full implementation, you should use the usual
JavaScript method to distinguish between the two types of browser and display either a button or a link.

To save searching through JavaScript manuals, here is a summary of the
window.open() command. It is called by:

```
window.open(url, name [, features])
```

The address of the file to be opened in the window is given in "url", and
"name" is the symbolic name of the window. If there is already a window
with this name, the file will be displayed in it. The string "features" gives the
window attributes in comma delimited format. Table 8.3 lists the possible
attributes. With the exception of width and height, each attribute is specified with attribute = yes or attribute = no. Unfortunately, it is not possible
to rely on these attributes being used – some browsers and/or operating
systems simply ignore some attributes.

.2 Embedding PDF in HTML

As mentioned above, both the EMBED and OBJECT HTML tags can be used to
embed PDF files in HTML pages. While EMBED is a nonstandard extension
developed by Netscape, also supported by Microsoft, the OBJECT tag is included in HTML 4.0 and is therefore an "official" component of the markup
language.

Table 8.3. Window property attributes for the JavaScript method window.open( )

Attribute	Meaning
toolbar	Display toolbar?
location	Display browser URL entry field?
directories	Display directory buttons?
status	Display status bar?
menubar	Display menubar?
scrollbars	Display scrollbars?
resizable	Window can be resized?
width	Window width in pixels
height	Window height in pixels

A detailed knowledge of the tags is only needed if you wish to write your own HTML code. If you are using a suitable HTML authoring package (see Section 8.5), you do not need to know details about the tags.

The EMBED tag. The EMBED tag is supported by Netscape Navigator and Microsoft Internet Explorer. It describes, with several attributes which are appended to the tag, the embedded object itself, and geometric properties (mainly width and height) and the distance from the surrounding text. Table 8.4 shows the attributes for the EMBED tag.

Table 8.4. Attributes relevant to PDF embedding for the EMBED tag (Netscape implementation)

Attribute	Meaning
ALIGN=type	Object alignment. Possible values are LEFT, RIGHT, TOP, BOTTOM.
HEIGHT=n[1]	Object height in pixels
HREF=url[2]	URL, if the object is used as a link
HIDDEN=boolean	Specifies whether the object is visible (FALSE) or not (TRUE). If it is TRUE, the WIDTH and HEIGHT attributes are ignored.
HSPACE=n	Horizontal space between the object and adjoining text or images
NAME=name	Name of the object if it is part of form data
PLUGINSPAGE=url	URL for plugin installation instructions. This page is loaded if the plugin is missing.
SRC=url[1]	URL of the object
TYPE=type	MIME type of the object. The browser recognizes from this attribute, without downloading the object, whether or not it can be processed.
VSPACE=n	Vertical space between the object and adjoining text or images
WIDTH=n[1]	Object width in pixels

1. These attributes are generally used when embedding PDF files
2. Does not work in Microsoft Internet Explorer

The following instruction embeds a PDF file on the HTML page:

```
<EMBED SRC="chapter01.pdf" HEIGHT=300 WIDTH=400>
```

The closing tag </EMBED> is not compulsory and is usually left out. It is possible to use percentage values for HEIGHT and WIDTH instead of absolute values in pixels. More tips on scaling embedded PDFs can be found in Section 8.4.

The browser determines the embedded object's MIME type from the data transferred from the server. Errors, such as a missing plugin, can be recognized more quickly if the EMBED tag attribute TYPE contains the object's MIME type, which for PDF is:

```
application/pdf
```

The OBJECT tag. While the EMBED tag is supported by both important browsers, the OBJECT tag only works in Microsoft Internet Explorer with ActiveX support.[1] In the future it is meant to take over the functionality of the IMG, APPLET and EMBED tags, and enable the embedding of images, dynamic data, Java applets and ActiveX controls (OCXs). At present only the integration of ActiveX is implemented. ActiveX modules can be programmed in various languages such as Visual C++, Visual Basic or Delphi. Currently ActiveX only works under Windows and in Internet Explorer 4.0 for the Mac (although there's no Acrobat ActiveX control for the Mac).

The OBJECT tag, compared to the EMBED tag, offers the possibility of downloading and installing missing plugins – ActiveX controls, to be correct – from the server if required. The developer of an HTML page can specify a URL from which the OCX will be loaded if required. This does not make sense in the case of Acrobat Reader as (apart from the file size) it is not sufficient to install the ActiveX control for Acrobat as it is also necessary to install Acrobat Reader. To ensure a proper correlation between the object and the ActiveX module, all OCX modules have a unique identifier, specified with the CLASSID attribute when embedded in HTML code. The CLASSID also describes the corresponding ActiveX control in the Windows registry.

The OBJECT tag also offers, compared to EMBED, another extension: communication between objects. For example, you can write VBScript or JScript scripts for embedded objects or implementing extensions for them. For PDF files it is possible, for example, to define buttons for printing the document (see Section 8.3).

The OBJECT instruction for embedding a PDF file follows this pattern:

```
<OBJECT CLASSID="clsid:CA8A9780-280D-11CF-A24D-444553540000"
    WIDTH=300 HEIGHT=400 ID=PDF1>
    <PARAM NAME="SRC" VALUE="chapter05.pdf">
</OBJECT>
```

---

1. The ScriptActive plugin from NCompass (www.ncompasslabs.com) makes it possible to use ActiveX components in Netscape Navigator too.

The opening OBJECT tag contains information which defines the object more precisely. Additional parameters follow in one or more PARAM tags. The parameters are not evaluated by the browser but are passed to the ActiveX control. The HTML tags up to the closing tag are used if the object can not be displayed because the browser is not properly configured. OBJECT tags can be nested within one another.

The CLASSID attribute for PDFs always has the above value which identifies the Acrobat OCX. If you do not want to type the cryptic class ID, Section 8.5 describes how this is easily done with the Active X Control Pad.

In addition to WIDTH and HEIGHT, the object is also given a symbolic name (ID), which VBScript routines can use to access it (see Section 8.3).

The name of the PDF to be embedded is not given as an OBJECT tag attribute, but is given in the SRC parameter, also used by the Acrobat OCX:

```
<PARAM NAME="SRC" VALUE="chapter05.pdf">
```

Further parameters for use by the OCX module can be specified. However, there are no extra parameters for the Acrobat module.

Table 8.5 lists the OBJECT tag attributes.

Table 8.5. Object tag attributes relevant for PDF embedding (according to HTML 4.0).

Attribute	Meaning
ALIGN=type	Object alignment. Possible types are BASELINE, CENTER, LEFT, MIDDLE, RIGHT, TEXTBOTTOM, TEXTMIDDLE, TEXTTOP. This attribute is deprecated; use style sheets instead.
CLASSID=id	Object implementation type; for ActiveX controls the id has the form clsid:class-identifier. For the Acrobat control it is always "clsid:CA8A9780-280D-11CF-A24D-444553540000".
CODEBASE=url	URL for loading the ActiveX control's code. The URL must point to the same Internet domain as the HTML page.
CODETYPE=type	MIME type of the object to load. For ActiveX controls the MIME type is application/x-oleobject.
HEIGHT=n	Height of the object in pixels, or percentage of total height
ID=name	Arbitrary symbolic name of the object
NAME=url	The object's name as transferred as part of form data
WIDTH=n	Width of the object in pixels, or percentage of total height

PDFs in frames and tables. Much has already been written discussing the pros and cons of frames. Frames allow the HTML developer to divide the browser window into several parts, each of which can serve a different purpose. For example, one frame might contain buttons or a list of contents, giving the user an overview of the site. Another frame might show the contents selected in the navigation frame. This method has the advantage that the context remains clear for the user when navigating within a large Web site, or if sent to another server by a link.

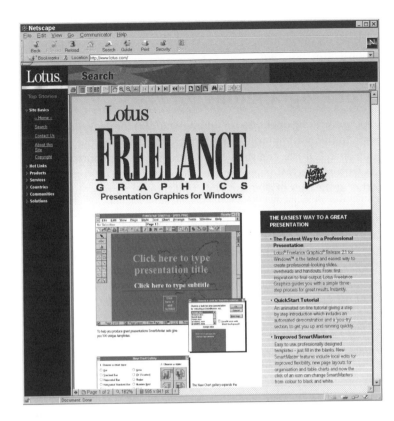

Fig. 8.4.
HTML frames and PDF can be combined effectively

Search queries are another example: The search masks or results of a query are displayed in one frame, while the documents found are displayed in another frame. This makes the process much clearer.

As PDF files can be used as part of a "normal" HTML page (with the help of the Acrobat plugin and the two tags already mentioned), there is nothing to prevent a PDF document from being used within a frame. Disregarding the general disadvantages of frames (for example: bookmarks do not work, complete framesets can not be printed, backward jumps in frames are not included in the history list), there are good opportunities to combine PDF and HTML effectively. One frame could contain HTML navigation controls, while another contains extensively formatted graphical content in PDF format.

Tables often function as an aid to positioning the components of an HTML page and thereby compensate partially for HTML's lack of layout controls (even if that was not their intended purpose). A table cell can contain a PDF file as well as a "normal" HTML element.

If you embed multiple PDFs in frames or tables, be sure to take into account the upper limit on the number of PDF documents which can be displayed simultaneously (see Table 8.11).

8.3 VBScript Programming for PDFs

VBScript programming opens up further possibilities for using PDF files in the browser. In this section I would like to introduce the possible methods for an embedded PDF file, and show how to program a print button for Acrobat files within an HTML page. The second example replaces one PDF file with another at the click of a button. Note that these examples only work in Microsoft Internet Explorer.

The following small examples can naturally only scratch the surface of VBScript programming and should be a catalyst to show how script programming can be used in conjunction with Acrobat. Further information on this theme can be found in VBScript reference literature. If manual VBScript programming is too much for you, then you can read how the task is made easier using a Web page authoring tool called ActiveX Control Pad in Section 8.5.

The following VBScript instructions are available for PDF files embedded in HTML pages:

- Print() calls the Acrobat print function (not the browser's!) to print the PDF file.
- AboutBox() calls a message box with notes about the version of the ActiveX controls for Acrobat. In practice, you can forget about this function.
- The "src" method modifies the object embedding parameter of the same name, hence, a different PDF file is displayed in the same place. This opens interesting possibilities, for example with a single mouse click you can switch to a version of the document in another language.

As an HTML page can contain multiple embedded PDF documents, a clear way is needed of allocating buttons to PDF files. This allocation uses the name specified in the OBJECT tag's ID attribute and must be clear within the page.

The above PDF methods can be triggered in VBScript by many events:

- Opening or closing the window (load/unload). There are not many sensible applications for this – who would want to see a print dialog immediately on opening a page?
- The event can be triggered by a normal HTML button implemented with the INPUT tag. Such buttons can be implemented with a single HTML tag and a few lines of script code.
- Instead of an HTML button, you can use an ActiveX button. The usual form functions such as buttons, input fields, and so on are implemented

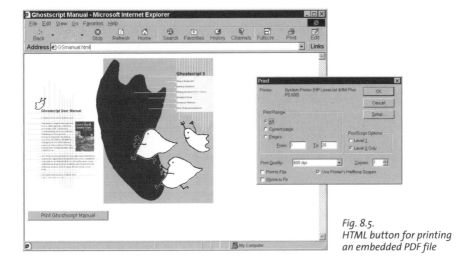

Fig. 8.5.
HTML button for printing
an embedded PDF file

by the "Microsoft Forms 2.0" ActiveX controls which are installed by default in Explorer.

While the objects are defined in the body of the HTML page where they are
to appear, the VBScript usually appears in the header before the BODY tag.

Printing with an HTML button. In the first example I'd like to show how to
define an HTML button which calls a VBScript function. This function then
calls the print method for an embedded PDF file, that is, the print dialog is
displayed. The complete HTML and VBScript code looks like this:

```
<HTML>
<HEAD>
<TITLE>Ghostscript Manual</TITLE>
<SCRIPT LANGUAGE="VBScript">
    <!--
    Sub Printbutton_OnClick
        Manual.print
    End Sub
    '-->
</SCRIPT>
</HEAD>
<BODY>
<OBJECT ID="Manual" WIDTH=622 HEIGHT=472
    CLASSID="CLSID:CA8A9780-280D-11CF-A24D-444553540000">
    <PARAM NAME="SRC" VALUE="gs5man_e.pdf">
</OBJECT>
<BR><BR><BR>
<INPUT TYPE=submit VALUE="Print Ghostscript Manual" NAME="Printbutton">
...more HTML tags and text...
</BODY>
</HTML>
```

The PDF document is embedded under the description "Manual" in the
BODY section, using the OBJECT tag. There then follows the HTML description for a submit button with the legend "Print Ghostscript Manual" and
the internal name "Printbutton". The VBScript routine in the HEADER re-
fers to this name. It is called by clicking on the button (the trigger event is
"OnClick" of "Printbutton") and starts the print routine for "Manual". The
comment symbols <!-- and '--> ensure that browsers which do not support
VBScript do not display the script as text or quit with an error message.
Note that HTML 4.0 mandates using the attribute TYPE (instead of LAN-
GUAGE), which specifies the script language according to its MIME type. For
VBScript this is:

```
text/vbscript
```

If you want to embed multiple PDF documents, each with their own print
button, each PDF and each button must have unique names (ID or NAME attribute). The subroutine specifies which button corresponds to which PDF
file.

Loading another PDF document.   The second example implements a button
which when clicked on replaces the embedded German language PDF document with the corresponding English one, which first has to be downloaded
from the server. To make the example more interesting, it does not use an
HTML button, but instead makes use of an ActiveX control of the type "Microsoft Forms 2.0 Command Button". The button not only loads a new PDF
document, but then changes its own legend and function so that clicking
on it a second time reloads the German version. Please do not say that the
same functionality could be achieved with two simple HTML pages and
suitable links! The VBScript version allows specific parts of a loaded document to be replaced with others. This suggests more complicated applications than in the following simple example. Here is the code:

```
<HTML><HEAD>
<TITLE>Ghostscript Manual</TITLE>
</HEAD>
<BODY>
<OBJECT ID="Manual" WIDTH=622 HEIGHT=472
    CLASSID="CLSID:CA8A9780-280D-11CF-A24D-444553540000">
        <PARAM NAME="SRC" VALUE="gs5man_d.pdf">
</OBJECT>
<BR>
<SCRIPT LANGUAGE="VBScript">
    <!--
    lang="ger"
    Sub translator_Click()
    If lang = "ger" Then
        Manual.src = "gs5man_e.pdf"
        translator.Caption = "Deutsche Ausgabe"
        lang = "eng"
```

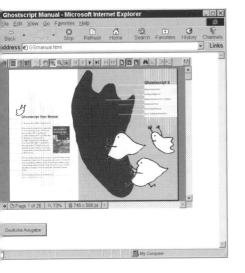

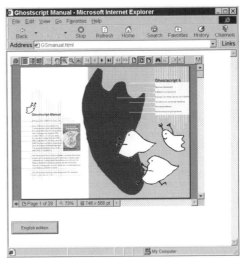

Fig. 8.6.
The VBScript button switches between the English and German editions of a PDF document which is embedded in an HTML page

```
    Else
        Manual.src = "gs5man_d.pdf"
        translator.Caption = "English edition"
        lang = "ger"
    End If
    end sub
    '-->
</SCRIPT>
<OBJECT ID="translator" WIDTH=150 HEIGHT=40
    CLASSID="clsid:D7053240-CE69-11CD-A777-00DD01143C57">
        <PARAM NAME="Caption" VALUE="English edition">
        <PARAM NAME="ParagraphAlign" VALUE="3">
</OBJECT>
...more HTML tags and text...
</BODY></HTML>
```

This time, the PDF object is embedded with the description *Manual*. There then follows the script, which is called by clicking on the "translator" button. Note that the mouse event for ActiveX buttons is called "Click", while the corresponding HTML button is called "OnClick". The "translator" button is itself an embedded object processed by the ActiveX forms module.

The script switches between the German and English versions, depending on the current value of the "lang" variable. The switching is carried out by allocating a new PDF file name to *Manual.src*. An assignment to "translator.caption" changes the button label. Finally, the variable "lang" is reset to the current language.

8.4 Common HTML Code for all Browsers

An important problem when creating Web pages is the overloading with special features and lack of standardization within HTML. The Web's design does not set out minimum requirements for browsers – anything goes, from a text-only mobile phone display to the latest Netscape or Microsoft monster. Creating user-friendly Web pages means designing pages which all browsers can handle properly. Obviously, a text oriented screen can not display graphics or PDF pages. Because of this, as a Web designer you should think of how to make the information accessible to different groups of users. On a company Intranet with a closed group of users who all have the same browser, you can standardize on that browser's feature set. However, for pages published on the Web where any combination of hardware and software may be in use, a little more thought is required.

One solution which is often used is to make more than one version of a Web site available. Two directories for Netscape-compatible and other browsers might be ideally configured for each group, but do require – apart from the work involved in creating and maintaining two sets of pages – extra effort on the part of the user to select the correct branch. In addition, the proud owner of a set-top box for his television might not know which system the built-in browser is compatible with.

Those Web designers who take their job seriously should design their HTML pages so that they can be viewed with a minimum of user intervention on as many different Web browsers as possible.

HTML offers some assistance, for example, displaying alternative text instead of missing graphics. There are also alternative tags for embedded objects. In addition to this, various script languages can distinguish between the browser in use and adapt to its capabilities. In the following sections I would like to introduce some techniques which can be useful in conjunction with PDF. Further hints can be found in books on HTML and the script languages.

Checking for browser plugins with JavaScript. The most important question in conjunction with PDF on the Web is, of course, whether or not the browser can display PDF files. In the case of Web sites which use PDF extensively, the user should be warned early on and given a chance to install Acrobat.

To avoid disappointments – such as after a long download seeing a PDF file as illegible text – it is useful to check for the browser's Acrobat plugin in the HTML. This job is a textbook example for using JavaScript. This language contains objects and methods with which diverse browser functions can be checked. These include the browser's name and version as well as installed plugins and supported MIME types.

To check the browser's PDF functionality it is possible, using JavaScript, to check for the presence of the Acrobat plugin. This idea has its drawbacks:

the "about:plugins" URL, which lists the plugins available in Netscape, returns the value "PDFViewer" with the description "Portable Document Format" on the Mac, but under Windows it returns the plugin name "Adobe Acrobat" with the description "Acrobat"! The plugin name is not yet suitable for the required query.

In its documentation, Netscape suggests opening an extra browser window as a test for the desired MIME type. A corresponding JavaScript routine has the disadvantage (apart from briefly displaying this dummy window) of not working if the plugin is not present.

To achieve a usable JavaScript solution, it is necessary to request a specific MIME type – in our case "application/pdf" – with a method of the "navigator" object. The code looks like this:

```
<HTML><HEAD>
<TITLE>Check for the Acrobat plugin</TITLE></HEAD>
<BODY>
<SCRIPT LANGUAGE="JavaScript">
    <!--
    var mimetype=navigator.mimeTypes["application/pdf"];
    if (mimetype) {
        document.writeln("The Acrobat plugin is installed!<BR>");
        document.writeln("Click here for" +
        "<A HREF=\"docfile.pdf\">Documentation in PDF format</A>.");
    }else{
        document.writeln("Unfortunately, no Acrobat plugin is installed!");
    }
    //-->
</SCRIPT>
...more HTML tags and text...
</BODY></HTML>
```

The comment lines <!-- and //--> again hide the JavaScript code from browsers which can not handle it. In a more complete solution, if the plugin is found, the user would be directed to another document, and if the plugin is missing the user would be given instructions about its installation.

Instead of using the HREF reference in the above example, you could use an EMBED tag to directly embed the PDF file into the HTML page.

The solution shown above works in Netscape Navigator 3.0 and higher. As Microsoft's supposedly JavaScript-compatible JScript in Microsoft Internet Explorer does not support the MIME type query of "navigator" objects, the script does not work in Internet Explorer. I am not aware of any way to make JScript or VBScript check for installed plugins or supported MIME types.

If you do not use such a query, the embedded object's space in Navigator simply remains blank if the PDF plugin is missing. If the EMBED tag contains the TYPE attribute, the user sees a suitable warning and receives guidance on installing the plugin. In Internet Explorer the space also remains empty.

Display alternatives for OBJECT and EMBED tags.   By using a careful combination of the OBJECT, EMBED, NOEMBED, and IMG tags, you can create an HTML sequence which inserts the element into the document, according to the browser's functionality, as an object, embedded file, graphic, or text. The HTML code to this looks like (note, however, that the NOEMBED tag isn't part of any HTML standard):

```
<OBJECT CLASSID="clsid:CA8A9780-280D-11CF-A24D-444553540000"
    WIDTH=423 HEIGHT=333 ID=PDF1>
    <PARAM NAME="SRC" VALUE="intro.pdf">
    <EMBED SRC="intro.pdf" HEIGHT=300 WIDTH=400>
    <NOEMBED>
        <IMG SRC="intro.gif" ALT="Introduction" WIDTH=30 HEIGHT=40>
    </NOEMBED>
</OBJECT>
```

Browsers which do not support the OBJECT function will process the tags between the opening and closing OBJECT tags. If the EMBED function is supported the PDF file is embedded, otherwise the NOEMBED version is used which keeps a GIF picture in reserve via the IMG tag. If this can't be displayed (for example with a text oriented browser) as a last resort there is always the alternate text defined in the ALT tag.

Document settings for the PDF file.   A PDF file can specify how it is to be opened when it is displayed. This includes a preset zoom level, the display of thumbnails or bookmarks as well as the user interface components: the menu bar, toolbar, and window controls. Except for the Acrobat menu bar, which is never visible in the browser, all of these settings are also available in Internet Explorer for PDF files embedded in HTML pages. Netscape Navigator, on the other hand, ignores all these settings, so the different behavior of the two browsers is a potential source of errors.

If it is important that documents are displayed in the same way in Navigator and Explorer, the document settings should be specified in Exchange (or using pdfmarks) to emulate Navigator's behavior, that is without toolbar and window controls. In addition, the size settings have to be carefully observed (see below).

Setting the size.   The WIDTH and HEIGHT attributes of the EMBED and OBJECT tags can contain absolute dimensions in pixels, or a percentage relating to the original size of the document. The simplest way to find out the original size of a PDF file is to set the measurement unit to pixels in Exchange using the menu command "File", "Settings", "General...", and reading the dimensions off the lower part of the window. At 72 dpi (the lowest resolution for current monitors) the number is exactly the same as the number of screen pixels.

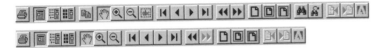

Fig. 8.7. Acrobat 3.01 (top) and 3.0 (bottom) toolbars as displayed in the browser

The question "absolute values or percentages?" has to be answered according to the intended use and content of the document. The important thing is that the PDF document is not distorted in the browser window. This can happen in Navigator if the WIDTH and HEIGHT values have a different relationship to the original page size. Because of this, you should either scale the original sizes proportionally (for example, halve both values) or use percentages.

In Internet Explorer this problem does not arise, as the values are always applied to the whole Acrobat window (within the browser window) and then the PDF file is scaled proportionally within the Acrobat window. If that sounds rather complicated, then a little experimentation will make it clearer.

While the document itself can be scaled freely, there are some items which can not be scaled and must be borne in mind for PDF embedding. If (for Internet Explorer) you choose to display the Acrobat toolbar, do not make the document too narrow or the toolbar will be cut off. The length of the full Acrobat 3.01 toolbar (see Figure 8.7) is at least 577 pixels, on all systems. If the WIDTH value is smaller, then only part of the Acrobat toolbar will be accessible.

Absolute values should also be used for the width of the bookmark window. This can be reduced in size by the user, but if the project is properly planned, this is not necessary. The default width for the bookmark window is 150 pixels. This value has to be taken into account when setting the WIDTH, if the document is to be displayed with visible bookmarks or thumbnails. The width of the bookmark/thumbnail pane is set (under Windows) in the Reader or Exchange INI file:

```
DefaultSplitterPos=150
```

One last remark on scaling embedded PDF documents: if either the WIDTH or HEIGHT is missing, Navigator uses the original value, which usually distorts the document. Internet Explorer, on the other hand, scales the missing value, so that there is no distortion.

8.5 HTML Authoring Tools

Most Web authors have an ambiguous relationship with HTML authoring programs: they do offer (sort of) WYSIWYG ease of use for creating Web pages, but do not support all of the latest tags or do not support them fully. For this reason, many Web publishers combine an easy-to-use HTML authoring program and a less refined but more powerful method of entering HTML tags manually into a text editor. In this section, I would like to describe the ways in which the most important HTML authoring tools support the embedding of PDF files.

Adobe PageMill. It is not particularly surprising that Adobe's program for creating HTML pages and administering Web sites offers full PDF support. PageMill mimics Netscape's plugin interface and because of this can make use of the Acrobat browser plugin. A PDF file can be embedded in an HTML page using the command "File", "Place...", or with Drag & Drop.

When it saves the page, PageMill generates a corresponding EMBED tag. Five variants of the ALIGN attribute take care of alignment. The width and height of the embedded PDF object are displayed in the Inspector window and can also be altered there. Mental arithmetic is usually called for when it comes to scaling: the Mac version of PageMill always embeds the PDF file at a constant size, although the Windows version does at least preserve the page proportions. Unfortunately, it is not possible to embed the PDF document at its original size. The correct values have to be worked out and entered manually in the Inspector (further information on sizing can be found in Section 8.4). It is not possible to use percentage-based sizing in

Fig. 8.8.
Embedding a PDF
document in HTML
using PageMill

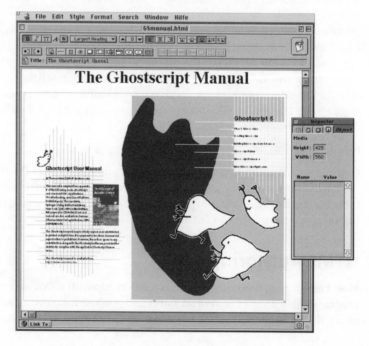

PageMill. Further parameters for the EMBED tag which are not directly supported by PageMill can also be entered in the Inspector window.

Unfortunately the file names of the PDF documents are not visible in Inspector. They are always embedded with relative path names, which means that the directory structure must be the same as on the server. In addition, you must ensure that the saved HTML page and the embedded PDFs are on the same hard disk or partition, otherwise PageMill will create a "file:///..." reference instead of a relative file name. Under Windows, PageMill sometimes puts the file named in the SRC attribute into upper case. If the server runs on a case sensitive platform such as Unix, then the server will not find the PDF files if the case is not changed manually.

HoTMetaL Pro. SoftQuad's powerful HTML authoring tool supports inserting ActiveX controls into HTML for PDF display in Microsoft Internet Explorer. Additionally, you can insert EMBED tags which work in Navigator too.

To place a PDF ActiveX control on an HTML page, choose "Insert", "ActiveX Control", or click the ActiveX symbol in the tool palette. If ActiveX is installed on the system (for example, by having previously installed Internet Explorer), a list of available controls is shown. If Acrobat is also installed, it usually appears at the beginning of the list due to the alphabetical ordering. Setting the file name or URL of the PDF is pretty clumsy: after inserting the ActiveX control, right-click on it and choose "Object Properties...", "Properties". In the "Source URL" field you can now type the file

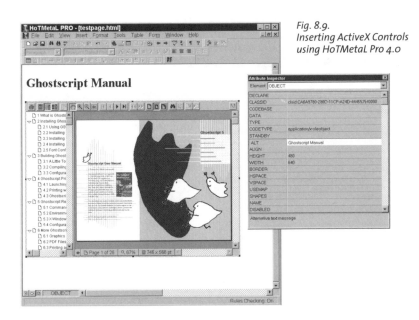

Fig. 8.9.
Inserting ActiveX Controls
using HoTMetaL Pro 4.0

name or complete URL of the PDF document. If the document is locally accessible (i.e., it resides on the disk and need not be retrieved from another server), HoTMetaL displays it in the document window (see Figure 8.9). Another right-click to open the "Attribute Inspector" provides access to the attributes listed in Table 8.5.

To insert a PDF on an HTML page in a Netscape-compatible manner, choose "Insert", "Element...", EMBED. This will insert an embedding placeholder on the page, but HoTMetaL won't be able to display the PDF. Make sure to right-click the inserted object and (in the Attribute Inspector) fill in values for the SRC, WIDTH, and HEIGHT attributes. PDFs embedded this way will work in Internet Explorer as well as in Netscape Navigator.

ActiveX Control Pad. This freely available Microsoft program supports the creation of HTML pages which are to use ActiveX. The ActiveX Control Pad is not a usual HTML authoring program. In particular, it does not have a preview or WYSIWYG mode, but simply makes it easier to create OBJECT tags and VBScript instructions.

You choose the Acrobat control using the menu sequence "Edit", "Insert ActiveX Control" (ActiveX and Acrobat must be installed). The width and height as well as the PDF file name can be specified in the properties panel. After doing this, the ActiveX Control Pad generates a comprehensive OBJECT tag which also contains some internal parameters. As the IDs of the inserted objects are not numbered automatically, if multiple PDFs are embed-

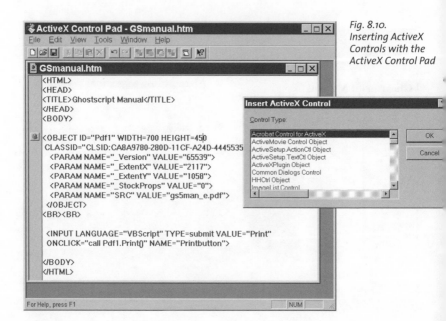

Fig. 8.10.
Inserting ActiveX
Controls with the
ActiveX Control Pad

ded on a page, the ID attributes have to be changed manually to ensure that they can be identified unambiguously.

The second important feature is the "Script Wizard", which simplifies creation of VBScript instructions and allocating them to events. After starting the Wizard with the menu sequence "Tools", "Script Wizard..." it displays an overview of the available events and actions in the upper area (see Section 8.3). For example, if you have already inserted an HTML or ActiveX button into the document, then its name appears in the list on the left ("Printbutton" in Figure 8.11). To embed an HTML button, the corresponding HTML code for the button is typed into the text window, and an ActiveX button is created by an ActiveX control from the standard forms collection installed with Explorer. The methods of the embedded PDF files are available as actions in the list on the right. "Insert Action" combines event and action which causes the Wizard to generate and insert the corresponding VBScript code into the HTML page.

Microsoft FrontPage 98.   FrontPage 98 is a visual authoring system which attempts to integrate all relevant Web techniques. It offers a list of components, supplementary programs and server extensions for transferring Web pages. I do not wish to go into these supplementary modules, but only explain briefly the integration of Acrobat.

As you would expect, FrontPage 98 supports the embedding of ActiveX controls on HTML pages. You can open a dialog box for ActiveX properties in the FrontPage editor with "Insert", "Advanced", "ActiveX control..." (or by clicking on the ActiveX button in the icon bar, see Figure 8.12). If Acrobat is installed on the computer, the corresponding ActiveX control appears in the pick list. Selecting the desired PDF file is done, a little clumsily, via "Properties" and the "src" attribute. Links to PDF files can also be inserted easily using Drag & Drop.

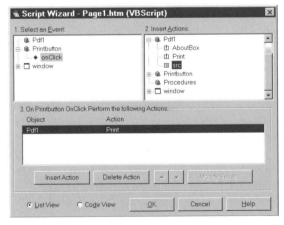

Fig. 8.11.
The Script Wizard of the
ActiveX Control Pad

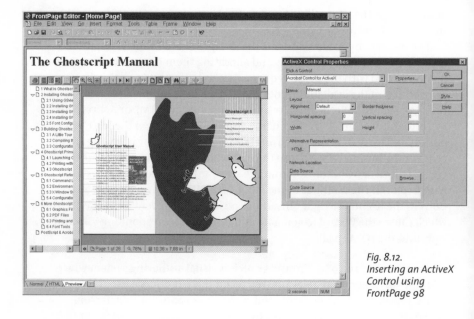

Fig. 8.12.
Inserting an ActiveX
Control using
FrontPage 98

8.6 Navigation

File names.   One of the most important aspects of Acrobat and the World Wide Web is platform independence. As a producer, however, you often come up against the problem of file names, as usually there is more than one platform involved. Imagine that the publisher works on a Mac, the user of the finished CD-ROM uses Windows, and the Web server is running Unix. The same file names should be used on each system so that all links (both PDF and HTML) work properly. Several things are important here:

- ▶ Maximum file name length
- ▶ Case significance. The question is not just whether both upper and lower case are permitted, but also whether or not case is significant: can there be two files which are distinguished only by their names being in upper or lower case?
- ▶ Which characters are permitted in a file name? Even if a system allows the use of any characters in a file name, they will use that system's encoding which might not be correctly recognized on other systems.

Table 8.6 gives an overview of the naming conventions used by the most important file systems.

If a collection of PDF files is to be published on an ISO 9660 format CD-ROM as well as on the Web (ISO 9660 is the least common denominator for CD-ROM formats), then you should use file names complying with the ISO

Table 8.6. Naming conventions of the most important file systems

System	Maximum length	Case significant?	Permitted characters
Macintosh	31	no	all except ":"
MS-DOS	8+3	no	all except \ / : * ? " < > |
Windows 95	256	no	all except \ / : * ? " < > |
Windows NT	256	no	all except \ / : * ? " < > |
Unix	256	yes	all except "/"
ISO 9660 CD-ROM	8+3	no	A-Z, 0-9, _

format to avoid "dead" links caused by renamed files. Another common cause of errors is file names on Unix servers. Here, you have to be careful that file names are not changed during the transfer to the Unix machine. Some FTP clients, for example, force file names on the target computer to upper case only.

How well Acrobat links work depends on the operating system in use. For example, a PDF link refers to the file *chapter1.pdf* (in lower case). Under Windows the link will also work if the file is called *CHAPTER1.PDF*, but this is not the case in Unix – Acrobat Reader will complain about a missing file.

Links. References to other documents and file types are at the core of the World Wide Web. Links in an HTML document which point to a PDF target can be defined using the HTML anchor tag:

```
<A HREF="http://www.ifconnection.de/~tm/gs/gs5manual.pdf">Ghostscript
Manual</A>
```

The Acrobat Weblink plugin handles links in the other direction, from PDF to HTML. Since version 3.0, this has been included as standard with the software. As with a normal PDF link, you use the Acrobat Exchange link tool to create a rectangle with the action type Web link. The URL of the target document has to be entered in the dialog. Alternatively, Web and PDF links can be defined by inserting pdfmarks into the PostScript code (see Section 6.4).

The PDF specification requires URLs in the format specified in Internet RFC 1738 and allows URLs with any protocol type. Exchange's online documentation, on the other hand, states that only the following protocols are allowed: "http", "ftp", and "mailto". I could not confirm this restriction: in my tests the protocols "news", "telnet", and "gopher" also worked (even if they are rarely used in PDF documents).

From the user-friendliness point of view, there is an important difference between HTML links and PDF links. The destination of an HTML link is usually visible (usually at the lower edge of the browser window) before it is clicked on, but as yet no browsers show the destination of Web links from embedded PDFs.

Absolute and relative URLs.   As with HTML it is possible to specify either absolute or relative destinations for links. An absolute URL contains all the components needed to locate the target: that is the protocol name, the server name (and port number if required), directory path, and file name. With a relative path name, some of these details can be left out as they are assumed from where the current document is stored. A base URL can be defined within a PDF file instead of the actual URL by using "File", "Document Info", "Base URL...". Its functions correspond to the HTML BASE tag, that is, it is placed in front of all relative URLs. The base URL only affects Web links, normal links are not affected.

When specifying a base URL, care must be taken that the combination of base URL and Web link gives a permitted URL. To do this, either the base URL must end with the "/" character or the URL of the Web link must start with it.

Using suitable base URLs, it is possible to transfer a whole series of documents to another server without having to change all the links.

Using the same files on CD-ROM and the World Wide Web.   It is extremely important for many users that their PDF files can be used unchanged both on CD-ROM and on the Web. This has been possible since Acrobat 3.0, as relative URLs not only work locally but are also resolved correctly on the server when used on the Web. For this to work properly, it is important to use "normal" PDF links (i.e., those without a server address) and not Weblinks for hyperlinks between PDF files on the same server. Weblinks work on the server, but not on CD-ROM or a hard disk.

Named destinations.   Named destinations are a powerful feature of PDF which allow hyperlinks to a specific location in a PDF file. Functionality and usage correspond to HTML's "fragment identifiers" which allow one to jump to an anchor (a specific point in a document). The following URL links to the location in *manual.html* to which the author has allocated the symbolic name "intro":

```
http://www.ifconnection.de/~tm/manual.html#intro
```

Named destinations allow this functionality for PDF files as well. At the same time, they are one of the greatest mysteries of Acrobat: they are described exhaustively in the PDF specification, but there is no way to access them from Acrobat Exchange! There is no tool for specifying named destinations, neither can existing symbolic names be changed. The only place where named destinations impact on the user interface is in the dialog box for links. If a link points to an existing named destination, then its name appears at the bottom of the dialog box (see Figure 8.13). The name is displayed, but cannot be edited. The destination cannot be changed either.

The observant reader will surely ask why named destinations should be displayed when they can not be created? Since Exchange doesn't offer any user interface for named destination, they have to be created by other means. I am currently aware of the following possibilities for creating named destinations:

- Use pdfmark instructions. This allows the symbolic description and position of a named destination to be defined in the PostScript code. The process of inserting pdfmarks and the necessary instructions are detailed in Sections 6.2 and 6.4.
- As an easy-to-use variation of the pdfmark method, use Phil Smith's PostScript snippet from the accompanying CD-ROM. It creates named destinations for all pages of a PDF file, using symbolic names like "Page1", "Page2", etc. (see Section 6.6 for usage details).
- Use an authoring tool such as FrameMaker which has a user interface for generating named destinations (see Section 5.2 for more details).
- Use the "Name It" Exchange plugin from Merlin Open Systems for directly creating named destinations. This plugin lets you generate named destinations manually, by using existing bookmarks, or for each page in the document. "Name It" simply offers the named destinations user interface which is missing from Acrobat Exchange. More information on Merlin's products can be found at

```
http://www.merlin-os.co.uk
```

How do you use named destinations? In a similar way to HTML, they make it possible to jump straight to a location in a PDF file:

```
http://www.ifconnection.de/~tm/manual.pdf#intro
```

If the file *manual.pdf* contains a named destination called "intro", the corresponding location will be displayed when the above URL is entered into a Web browser. If the specified destination does not exist, then the first page of the PDF file is displayed. However, this doesn't work in all browsers, but is limited to Netscape Navigator. Microsoft Internet Explorer does not support named destinations reliably. In Navigator they can be used everywhere that a URL points to a PDF file:

- direct entry of a URL by the user
- HTML link to a PDF file
- Weblinks within a PDF file
- EMBED tag with a link to a PDF file

The symbolic name and the "#" character are appended to the document URL. The full-blown syntax for a complete "fragment handler" looks like this:

```
http://www.ifconnection.de/~tm/manual.pdf#nameddest=intro
```

The equals sign functions as a separator and therefore can not be used in the fragment description. The identifier "nameddest=" offers potential for extending the fragment notation by entering other "fragment handlers". However, because the preset value is "nameddest" it can also be left out.

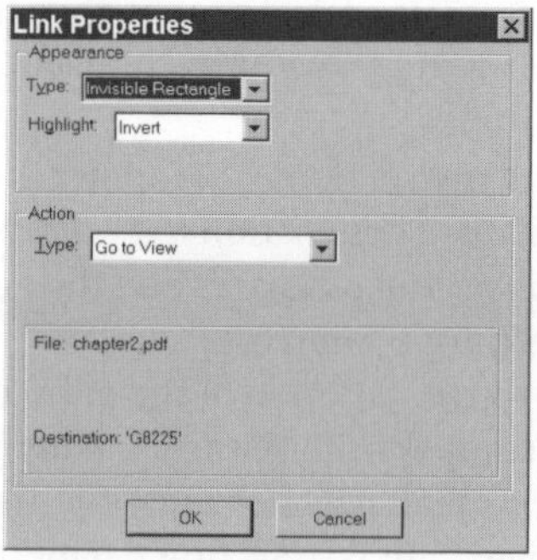

Fig. 8.13.
Named destinations as displayed in the
"Links Properties" dialog box. The symbolic
name "G8225" of the link destination is
shown below the file name chapter2.pdf.

Another way of using named destinations is with a custom JavaScript (see Section 7.6 for more info on JavaScript in Acrobat). Use the following JavaScript line in a JavaScript action of a button to jump to a named destination called "intro":

```
this.gotoNamedDest("intro");
```

The main advantage of named destinations is the ability to define hyperlinks to other PDF files even if the precise destination is not yet known. To do this, define a link to a named destination (which does not have to exist yet) in the source document. As soon as the document containing the target for the link is created, a "named destination" is created for that target. If the number of pages in the destination document changes, the named destination only has to be changed correspondingly. No changes have to be made to the source documents.

Earlier versions of Acrobat had an upper limit for the number of named destinations (which is often exceeded in large documents). This restriction has been lifted in Acrobat 3.0 and higher.

PDF image maps.   Apart from named destinations I would like to introduce one further interesting function for which there is no user interface in Acrobat Exchange. As with graphics in HTML, you can define Weblinks in PDF as an image map, that is, the browser sends the mouse pointer coordinates (in points, relative to the upper left corner of the bounding box) to the server. This allows interesting applications to be implemented. For example, the user can be shown a map of an area. When part of the map is clicked on, the server returns information about the area, for example the nearest company branch or a town plan of the selected town. Instead of geographical data you can of course use diagrams or navigation bars as image maps. The mouse coordinates which the browser sends to the server are processed by a suitable CGI script. Existing scripts for HTML maps can be

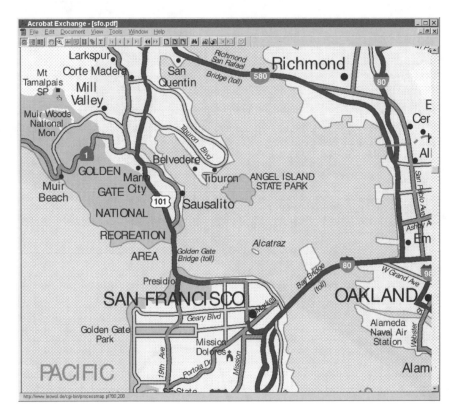

Fig. 8.14.
Image maps can also be configured with PDF files. Acrobat Reader displays the coordinates which the browser will send to the server at the bottom of the window.

used for this, as the coordinates are sent in the same format – they are simply delimited by commas and appended to the URL following a question mark (see Figure 8.14):

```
http://www.ifconnection.de/~tm/cgi-bin/processmap.pl?80,208
```

How do you create such an image map in PDF? It should come as no surprise that there are pdfmark instructions for this as well. The attribute /IsMap of the desired link must have a value of "true". The exact pdfmark instructions and an example can be found in Section 6.5.

9 PDF on the Web Server

9.1 MIME Types and PDF Icons

By its design, the Web isn't restricted to a single file format. Instead, it is extensible and includes mechanisms for integrating new file types. So integrating PDF files into a Web server's data stock seems hardly worth mentioning. However, there are a couple of configuration options which make for smooth PDF integration. First, there's the MIME file classification scheme ("Multipurpose Internet Mail Extensions") along with suitable icons for PDF files. To allow for page-at-time download of PDF files in the browser, the server must support the byterange protocol which is covered in the next section.

This section deals with server configuration options for PDF and FDF (the Forms Data Format, FDF, is covered in Chapter 10). When discussing server features, I'd like to deal with two specific server software packages which – according to the Netcraft survey (http://www.netcraft.com/Survey) from February 1998 – account for the majority of Web servers. These are Apache (46 percent of all servers) and the Microsoft Internet Information Server MIIS (21 percent).

MIME types for PDF files. On the Web and in other areas, the MIME classification scheme aids in distinguishing different types of data. MIME type negotiation is at the core of every HTTP connection and therefore is one of the Web's cornerstones. Two MIME types are officially assigned to Acrobat files:

```
application/pdf        pdf
application/vnd.fdf  ·  fdf
```

The first line describes the MIME type for PDF files and their common file name suffix. This MIME configuration is generally required on the Web server for dealing with PDF files. The second line contains the MIME type for form contents in Forms Data Format (FDF). The FDF MIME type has to be configured on the server only if FDF based form processing is to be implemented.

While the PDF MIME type is preconfigured in most server software packages, this is not the case for FDF.

MIME configuration in Apache. Apache's *mime.types* file contains the list of supported MIME types. The default configuration file in the Apache distribution contains only the PDF line. To configure FDF, you have to manually add the second line shown above.

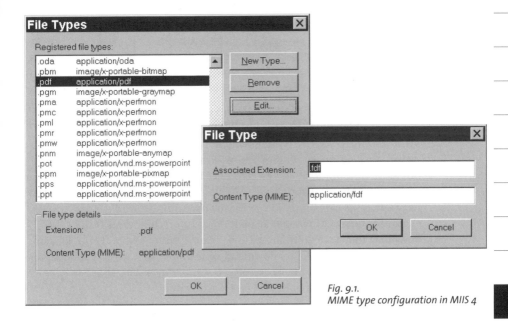

Fig. 9.1.
MIME type configuration in MIIS 4

Apart from the usual MIME type assignment by file name extension, Apache (starting with version 1.3) is able to infer a file's type from its contents. This scheme uses the "magic number" mechanism implemented in the Unix *file* utility. It is implemented in an Apache module called *mime_magic*. This module can be configured via the *conf/magic* file (similarly to */etc/magic* on Unix systems). The appropriate lines for the two Acrobat file types are:

```
0    string    %PDF-    application/pdf
0    string    %FDF-    application/vnd.fdf
```

Like *mime.types*, the default *magic* file already contains an entry for PDF, but not for FDF.

MIME configuration in Microsoft Internet Information Server (MIIS). In MIIS version 4, MIME types are configured in dialog boxes. Again, the default configuration already includes the appropriate PDF entry. To add the FDF MIME type, start the Internet Service Manager (this launches the Management Console). Since the Acrobat MIME types should be used on all virtual Web sites hosted on the machine, right-click the Web server's symbol on the left pane (and not a particular virtual host) and choose "Properties". In the "Computer MIME types" section, click "File Types..." and "New Type...". In this dialog box you can enter the FDF configuration (see Figure 9.1).

Fig. 9.2.
Icons for Acrobat Reader and PDF

Downloading Acrobat Reader.   Unless you're building an intranet for a company which uses only Acrobat based documentation, you should inform visitors to your Web server which file formats are offered, and which viewer applications or plugins are required. For this reason, servers which offer PDF files should include a reference to the Acrobat software, and some usage hints for Acrobat newbies. As detailed in Section 8.2, Microsoft Internet Explorer is capable of automatically installing ActiveX controls. However, due to the size of Acrobat Reader, this is not recommended since the download may take quite some time. Instead, either explicitly put Reader versions on your server for download, or include a link to the Adobe server or an appropriate mirror. Adobe offers several image files which may be used for links to Acrobat Reader (see next section).

PDF icons.   It's much easier for the user if PDF files in server-generated directory listings can be recognized as such instead of being represented by a generic file icon. For this reason, the icon used to represent Acrobat files in the Mac finder or Windows Explorer should also be used on the Web server. Adobe offers GIF files for the PDF icon and the Reader download at the following URL:

```
http://www.adobe.com/prodindex/acrobat/distribute.html
```

As a Webmaster you can install this PDF icon on the server such that it is used for PDF files in directory listings. With the Apache server, icons are configured in the *srm.conf* configuration file. By default, this file contains the following entry:

```
AddIcon /icons/layout.gif .html .shtml .htm .pdf
```

The line assigns a generic "layout file" icon for PDF files. To assign a unique icon to PDF files, you have to delete the *.pdf* from this line and define a new relation for the PDF icons. Additionally, you can take the opportunity and assign the logo to FDF files as well (although FDF files use their own logo at the operating system level, Adobe doesn't offer the respective logo for free):

```
AddIcon /icons/layout.gif .html .shtml .htm
AddIcon /icons/pdficon.gif .fdf .pdf
```

Note that the Apache distribution contains an icon file *pdf.gif*. However, this is not related to the "official" PDF logo and should be ignored to avoid confusion.

In addition to the PDF icon, you can assign a short descriptive string which is used for PDF files in directory listings. Insert the following line in the *conf/srm.conf* configuration file:

```
AddDescription  "PDF document"  .pdf
```

Since Microsoft Internet Information Server doesn't generate icons for directory listings, there's nothing to configure for PDF icons.

Thumbnails for PDF files. While the file icons in a directory listing are primarily useful for signalling a file's type, on HTML pages it's sometimes better to use a miniature image of the first page for links to PDF documents. This requires a thumbnail representation of the page similar to those generated by Acrobat Exchange. But how do you export a document's thumbnails as GIF files for use on HTML pages?

There are several solutions to the problem of converting a PDF page to a low-resolution GIF file. If the page can be opened in Adobe Illustrator (this doesn't always work, see Section 5.7), you simply have to export the page as GIF. Since only a low resolution is required for thumbnails, you can also use a screen shot of the page as it is displayed in Acrobat. Some image conversion tools (e.g., Image Alchemy) also convert PDFs to raster image formats.

The freely available PostScript and PDF interpreter Ghostscript is also able to rasterize PDF files. In addition to the page number, you can also choose the resolution for the output file. The following lengthy command line converts the first page of a PDF file to a 10 dpi PNG raster image file:

```
gs  -dBATCH -q -dNOPAUSE -sDEVICE=png16 -dFirstPage=1 -dLastPage=1 -r10
    -sOutputFile=file.png file.pdf
```

Since the PNG image file format isn't yet widely supported in Web browsers, you have to convert the PNG file to GIF. This can be achieved with most image processing applications and image converters. Since PNG, unlike GIF, isn't subject to patent and licensing issues, and is much more powerful than GIF, it will most likely be the future image file standard on the Internet. PNG images are supported in Netscape Navigator 4.04.

.2 The Byterange Protocol

The byterange protocol already mentioned lifts a restriction which formerly was a severe handicap for Web transactions: the Web browser can only request a whole file from the Web server. Although the browser may close the connection (for example, if the remaining data isn't needed because the user canceled a download), there was no possibility of explicitly requesting a particular section of a file from the server. Such partial downloads are quite useful for transferring the remainder of a file after an interrupt without unnecessarily retransmitting the already downloaded data. This obviously makes more effective use of the available bandwidth. In addition, several applications don't require the complete file to be transmitted. Efficient PDF transfer is one of these. As detailed in Section 2.2, the Acrobat/browser combination explicitly requests individual objects – page descriptions, fonts, graphics, etc. – from the server. This mechanism psychologically speeds up PDF transmission since the user doesn't have to wait for the complete file download to be completed.

The server's and browser's ability to transfer file fragments was first specified in the so-called HTTP byterange or byteserver extension. "Byteserving" is the capability of the server to send arbitrary parts (byte ranges) of a file.

Although currently the byterange concept only supports "byte" as measurement unit, it is extensible and may support other units in the future, for example lines of a text file, or chapters of a (hypothetical) file type "book".

Several conditions must be met in order to make page-at-a-time download work:

- ► The Web server must support the byterange protocol (see below).
- ► The Web browser must send byterange requests. This is the case for Netscape Navigator 2.0 and above, and Microsoft Internet Explorer 3.0 and above.
- ► The PDF files served on the Web must be optimized with Acrobat Exchange (see Section 4.3).

Byterange support on the Web server. In case you're worried about byteserving being an esoteric HTTP extension which is rarely supported in server software – relax. While byteranging started as an extension to HTTP 1.0, the byterange specification is now part of the HTTP 1.1 standard which is implemented in most current server products. Each HTTP 1.1-compatible server supports byteserving. The current versions of the most important Web servers include byteserving support, for example:

- ► Apache 1.2 and above
- ► Microsoft Internet Information Server 3.0 and above
- ► Netscape Enterprise Server 2.0 and FastTrack Server 2.0
- ► OpenMarket Secure WebServer 2.0 and above
- ► O'Reilly and Associates' WebSite
- ► WebStar for Macintosh 2.0 and above

Even if older server software has to be used, page-at-a-time PDF download can be implemented because byteserving need not necessarily be integrated in the server software, but may also be accomplished via the common gateway interface (CGI). The first implementation was the byteserver Perl script which you can find on the accompanying CD-ROM. This CGI script accepts byterange requests from the browser and transfers the requested segments of the file. To use the script, links to PDF files must make a little detour to the script, for example:

```
http://www.ifconnection.de/~tm/cgi-bin/byteserver.pl/manual/chapter1.pdf
```

The script translates the URL section after the script name to a file name on
the server and sends the file fragments requested by the browser. With the
Apache server, you can use the following entry in the *srm.conf* configuration file to avoid changing the links to PDF files:

```
action application/pdf /cgi-bin/byteserve.pl
```

Note that this is only necessary for older server versions since Apache 1.2 is
HTTP 1.1 compliant, and therefore supports byteserving by default. Apart
from the Perl script mentioned above, there are other ways of enabling
byteserving for older server software. For example, an Apache module and
a shared library for older Netscape servers are available.

Checking for byterange support.   You may easily check a certain server for
byterange support by manually issuing an HTTP command in a Telnet session. The HEAD command instructs the server to send meta-information
about a file without transferring the file's actual contents. Simply connect
to the server's HTTP port (80 by default), issue a HEAD command for a file
on the server and press the return key twice:

```
telnet www.ifconnection.de 80
HEAD http://www.ifconnection.de/~tm/file.pdf HTTP/1.0
(press return twice)
```

The server responds with an appropriate header. This header contains the
line "Accept-Ranges: bytes" if byteserver support is available on the server:

```
HTTP/1.1 200 OK
Server: Microsoft-IIS/4.0
Date: Thu, 15 Jan 1998 13:54:14 GMT
Content-Type: application/pdf
Accept-Ranges: bytes
Last-Modified: Sun, 11 Jan 1998 13:30:05 GMT
ETag: "a0a3ba63948bd1:1141"
Content-Length: 526424
```

Analysis of a byterange request.   The byterange protocol has several consequences on the server administration which are detailed in the next section. In this section, I'd like to scrutinize the cause of events when the
browser sends a byterange request to the server. The following example of a
byterange conversation between browser and server may facilitate under-
standing byteserver related issues.

   In our example, the browser requests the file *manual.pdf* from the server
in a usual HTTP request:

```
GET /doc/manual.pdf HTTP/1.0
Referer: http://www.ifconnection.de/~tm/doc/
Connection: Keep-Alive
User-Agent: Mozilla/4.01 [en] (WinNT; I)
```

```
Host: www.ifconnection.de
Accept: image/gif, image/x-xbitmap, image/jpeg, image/pjpeg, */*
Accept-Language: en
Accept-Charset: iso-8859-1,*,utf-8
```

The server responds to this request by sending the common "200 OK" message and transfers the PDF data with MIME type "application/pdf" after sending the HTTP header. In addition, it informs the browser about its byte-serving capability by including the "Accept-Ranges: bytes" header line. However, this line is not mandatory. The browser may request byte ranges out of the blue. If the server doesn't support byteserving, it simply ignores the byterange request and sends the complete file. In our example, the server sends the following response:

```
HTTP/1.1 200 OK
Date: Tue, 13 Jan 1998 14:49:00 GMT
Server: Apache/1.3
Last-Modified: Wed, 30 Jul 1997 17:02:33 GMT
ETag: "1402a-c465-33df73a9"
Content-Length: 50277
Accept-Ranges: bytes
Keep-Alive: timeout=15, max=100
Connection: Keep-Alive
Content-Type: application/pdf

%PDF-1.2
...PDF data...
```

If there is no user intervention while the data is being transmitted, the conversation is completed. However, if the user navigates the PDF file (for example, by following a link or jumping to the end of the file) before it is completely transferred, the browser sends a new request in order to receive the required parts of the file quickly (this requires optimized PDFs). Since at this time the browser already knows that the server supports byteserving, it lists the required byte ranges in the "Range:" header. The browser may combine multiple byterange requests in a single request. HTTP 1.0 is used as protocol since the server may still choose to ignore the range request:

```
GET /doc/manual.pdf HTTP/1.0
Connection: Keep-Alive
User-Agent: Mozilla/4.01 [en] (WinNT; I)
Range: bytes=40817-48442,8192-21520
Host: www.ifconnection.de
Accept: image/gif, image/x-xbitmap, image/jpeg, image/pjpeg, */*
Accept-Language: en
Accept-Charset: iso-8859-1,*,utf-8
```

The server doesn't respond to this request with the usual "200 OK" message, but sends the new "206 Partial Content" reply. This informs the browser that one or more fragments of the file will be sent. The appropriate MIME type is "multipart/byteranges". The server generates a random char-

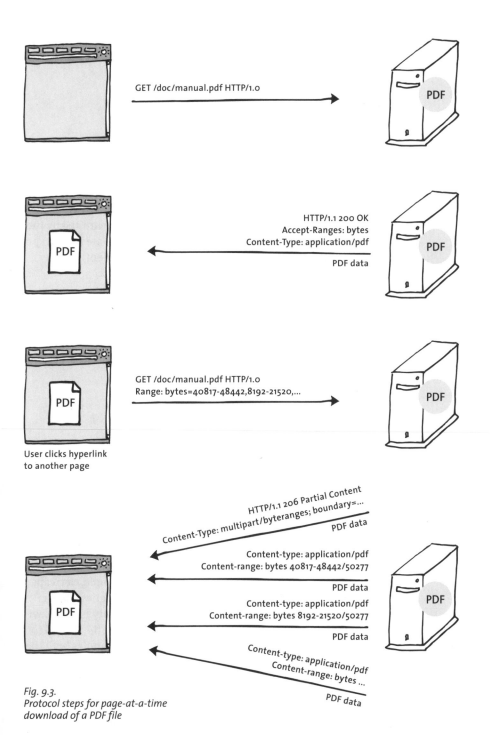

GET /doc/manual.pdf HTTP/1.0

HTTP/1.1 200 OK
Accept-Ranges: bytes
Content-Type: application/pdf

PDF data

GET /doc/manual.pdf HTTP/1.0
Range: bytes=40817-48442,8192-21520,...

User clicks hyperlink
to another page

HTTP/1.1 206 Partial Content
Content-Type: multipart/byteranges; boundary=...

PDF data

Content-type: application/pdf
Content-range: bytes 40817-48442/50277

PDF data

Content-type: application/pdf
Content-range: bytes 8192-21520/50277

PDF data

Content-type: application/pdf
Content-range: bytes ...

PDF data

Fig. 9.3.
Protocol steps for page-at-a-time
download of a PDF file

acter string to mark the end of individual fragments. This characters string is communicated to the browser in the "boundary" parameter. From this point on, both parties use HTTP 1.1:

```
HTTP/1.1 206 Partial Content
Date: Tue, 13 Jan 1998 14:49:00 GMT
Server: Apache/1.3
Last-Modified: Wed, 30 Jul 1997 17:02:33 GMT
ETag: "1402a-c465-33df73a9"
Content-Length: 23077
Keep-Alive: timeout=15, max=100
Connection: Keep-Alive
Content-Type: multipart/byteranges; boundary=33f9b25c773
```

Following this header, the data fragments are transferred, delimited by the boundary string. Each fragment is labeled with the appropriate MIME type "application/pdf" and contains a range description which identifies the segment's position within the file, as well as the total file size:

```
--33f9b25c773
Content-type: application/pdf
Content-range: bytes 40817-48442/50277

24 0 obj
...
...PDF data...
...
--33f9b25c773
Content-type: application/pdf
Content-range: bytes 8192-21520/50277

129 0 obj
...
...PDF data...
...
```

According to available bandwidth, user interaction and contents of the PDF file (fonts, graphics, etc.), this game may be repeated several times.

Since a number of details have changed between the first byterange protocol drafts and the eventual standardization in HTTP 1.1, some clients don't implement the current byterange protocol exactly. For example, Netscape Navigator 2 and 3 and Internet Explorer 3 send the older "Request-Range:" header line instead of "Range:". In order to avoid compatibility issues, Navigator 4 sends both forms (for the sake of simplicity, I deleted the second format from the above protocol). The Apache server correctly handles both the old and the new format of the request. The distinction is important because the old protocol specification mandated "multipart/x-byteranges" as MIME type for individual segments instead of the (now standardized) form "multipart/byteranges". However, due to the fault tolerance built into servers and browsers, both variants work. If Apache receives the older format, it also replies in the older format:

```
Request-Range: bytes=40817-48442,48443-50276,8192-21520
...
Content-Type: multipart/x-byteranges; boundary=33f9b25c773
```

Byte ranges and caching.   Byteserving poses new requirements on the caching mechanisms used to store Web documents in proxy servers or in the browser's cache. Obviously it might result in a disaster if a byte range is taken from a proxy's cache and sent to the browser as a complete document – the proxy doesn't necessarily know about byteserving at all!

For this very reason, partial transfers are labeled with the new response code 206. Older proxies only cache type 200 responses in their cache. Thus, byte serving does not interfere with caching in older proxies. However, HTTP 1.1 has been carefully designed in a way that newer proxy implementations may cache byte ranges. If the time stamps permit, the proxy may even combine multiple byte ranges into a larger segment. This could prevent a complete retransmission of the whole file.

The browser usually doesn't cache byte ranges at all. For example, PDF files retrieved via byteserving don't show up in Netscape Navigator's cache.

Byterange support and Web statistics.   From the above example it should be clear that the browser may possibly send many individual requests for a certain file if the user navigates the document before the transmission is completed. The server logs these requests separately since HTTP – being a stateless protocol – doesn't provide any relationship between the individual byterange requests. For this reason, the server's log may contain many access entries for a file, although only one user requested one single file! Obviously, such erroneously logged "hits" may completely invalidate the server's access statistics. This issue isn't easy to resolve. For example, you could try to combine multiple logged requests for individual byte ranges by checking the access times.

.3 PDF on SSL Servers

Web servers for e-commerce or servers hosting confidential information can be secured with the Secure Socket Layer protocol (SSL). SSL uses digital certificates for user and server identification and sends all data between server and browser in encrypted form. Since SSL is transparent to the application layer, it doesn't affect PDF-related issues such as byteserving. PDF files may be served without any restriction from an SSL site, with or without byteserving.

Dealing with PDF forms on SSL sites, however, is worth a closer look. (Form creation is covered in more detail in Chapter 7, general issues related to form processing on the server in Chapter 10.) While earlier browser versions had some trouble posting form contents to secure sites, SSL form posting works in Netscape Navigator 4 and Microsoft Internet Explorer 4.

However, you can't use the default Acrobat OCX from the Acrobat 3 CD-ROM for use with Internet Explorer, but must install the newer OCX which is contained on the CD-ROM accompanying this book.

Note that secure form processing doesn't only require SSL transmission of the PDF form from the server to the browser (i.e., a URL starting with the "https" protocol identifier). In addition, posting the form contents to the server must use SSL. This means you have to use the "https" protocol identifier in the PDF form's submit button, too. This implies that simply serving PDF forms from a secure server alone isn't enough. Instead, the URLs in the "Submit" buttons have to be adjusted to use SSL for the form submission.

Form Data Processing

.1 FDF and the FDF Toolkit

This chapter builds on the discussion of PDF forms in Chapter 7. In particular, I'd like to point the reader to the treatment of the Forms Data Format (FDF) in Section 7.4. This chapter covers form processing from the server's point of view, or more appropriately, the Webmaster's. Again, we will use the *Guagua* sample form which can be used for ordering travel information. The form is shown in Figure 10.1 with the field names visible. Filling the fields and exporting the field contents (via "File", "Export", "Form Data...") or sending the form to a Web server (with an appropriate PDF push button) yields FDF data similar to the following:

```
%FDF-1.2
1 0 obj
<<
    /FDF << /Fields [
        << /V /On /T (checkbox1) >>
        << /V /On /T (checkbox2) >>
        << /V /On /T (checkbox3) >>
        << /V /Off /T (checkbox4) >>
        << /V /Off /T (checkbox5) >>
        << /V (PDF) /T (deliver) >>
        << /V (lio@bikefans.com) /T (email) >>
        << /V (Click this push button to send the form to our Web server)
           /T (help text) >>
        << /V (10) /T (month) >>
        << /V (Lionel Smith) /T (name) >>
        << /V /motorbike /T (transport) >>
    ]
    /F (guagua.pdf) /ID [ (...binary data...) ] >>
>>
endobj
trailer
<< /Root 1 0 R >>
%%EOF
```

Although FDF is syntactically based on PDF (using objects and many "less than" and "greater than" symbols, an FDF file's structure is much simpler than the unreadable contents of a PDF file. In particular, there is no cross-reference table with file offsets. As can be seen from the above example, an FDF file contains for each form field the title (/T) and the respective value (/V). All strings in FDF use the PDF character set and have to obey the PDF rules for special characters (see Section 6.2 for details). The FDF format is described in Appendix A of the *Portable Document Format Reference Manual*.

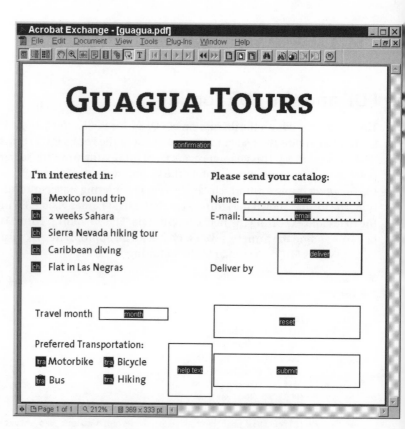

File Edit Document View Tools Plug-Ins Window Help

GUAGUA TOURS

confirmation

I'm interested in:

- [ch] Mexico round trip
- [ch] 2 weeks Sahara
- [ch] Sierra Nevada hiking tour
- [ch] Caribbean diving
- [ch] Flat in Las Negras

Please send your catalog:

Name: [........name........]

E-mail: [........email........]

[deliver]

Deliver by

Travel month [month]

[reset]

Preferred Transportation:

- [tra] Motorbike   [tra] Bicycle
- [tra] Bus   [tra] Hiking

[help text]   [submit]

Page 1 of 1   212%   369 x 333 pt

*Fig. 10.1.
The fields of the
sample form. In
small fields, only
the beginning of
the field name is
visible*

In addition to the field data, an FDF file may also contain the name of the corresponding PDF form in the /F key. However, this key isn't mandatory. If it exists, it contains the name of the PDF forms from which the fields have been exported, or into which they will be imported. In order to keep track of different versions of a PDF file, Acrobat generates a unique identification in addition to the file name. This ID key isn't required – a file name without unique ID string is sufficient.

Finally, there's the /Status key. Although Acrobat never generates this key, it's quite interesting for Web usage. If a server-generated FDF which is sent to the browser contains a /Status entry, the corresponding value is displayed to the user in a separate message window. We will exploit this feature in the examples below.

Comparing the form fields with the sample form in Chapter 7 you will notice a new "confirmation" field below the heading. This is a read-only text field which is invisible at the beginning. When the server's FDF response arrives at the browser, the confirmation field will contain a message from the server. Invisible fields which are populated by the server instead of the user are an easy way of adding contents to an existing PDF file.

A Webmaster who wants to deploy PDF forms has to choose among two formats for transmitting the form contents from the browser to the server. The format used in HTML forms has the MIME type

```
application/x-www-form-urlencoded
```

The newer Forms Data Format (FDF) has the following MIME type:

```
application/vnd.fdf
```

Don't forget to configure the FDF MIME type on the server (see Section 9.1). As detailed in Section 7.4, FDF has advantages over the usual URL encoding. However, the latter is widely supported with a variety of existing scripts and programs for form processing on the server. In this chapter, I'd like to discuss several options for dealing with FDF on the server. This includes collecting form contents from the user, as well as dynamically generating FDF data on the server, for example, for sending response messages back to the user. While the "browser to server" path may use HTML or FDF encoding, the "server to browser" direction must use FDF if the response is to be displayed in a PDF form.

In order to ensure proper FDF transmission from the server to the browser, and to have Acrobat insert the server-generated FDF data into the form, it is crucial to add a "#FDF" suffix to the URL of the script which handles the FDF on the server:

```
http://www.ifconnection.de/~tm/cgi-bin/order.pl#FDF
```

This suffix, along with the FDF MIME type, instructs Acrobat to import the form data into the PDF form which the user filled out, instead of saving the form data to a separate file. (If the FDF data contains an /F key, another form may be loaded into the browser as well.) A URL similar to the one above has to be used in the PDF form's push button in a "Submit Form" action.

There are several possibilities for generating the FDF data:
- ▶ Create an FDF template file (by exporting form fields with Acrobat Exchange) and change the contents with suitable text processing tools. For example, scripting languages like Perl are well suited for this task.
- ▶ A custom program or script may generate the FDF data from scratch. This may be implemented using your favorite programming language or a database report generator.
- ▶ The FDF toolkit simplifies generating FDF data as well as processing the incoming form data, without requiring much programming effort (see the next section).

The FDF toolkit. There's a wealth of freely available scripts, programs, and libraries for processing URL-encoded form data, implemented in most common languages. If the Webmaster decides in favor of FDF form representation, the question of available form-processing tools arises. This issue may seem to be a large handicap for FDF usage. In order to relieve Webmasters and programmers of this issue, Adobe offers the FDF toolkit for free at the following URL:

```
http://beta1.adobe.com/ada/acrosdk
```

This toolkit contains a programming library with functions for FDF data processing. The functions provided by the library include evaluating existing (incoming) FDF data as well as generating outgoing FDF data. The toolkit functions extract field names and values from an FDF file. Additional FDF contents, such as file name or status message, may also be queried. Similar functions are available for assigning new field names and values without the need for tackling FDF's syntactical details.

Reflecting the variety of existing operating system platforms, programming languages, and usage environments, several language bindings are available for the FDF toolkit:

- ▶ A shared library for C or C++ language programming on several common Unix systems is useful for implementing CGI programs.
- ▶ A Windows DLL can be used for developing CGI programs or ISAPI modules for Microsoft Internet Information Server.
- ▶ An in-process ActiveX server component (formerly known as an OLE automation server) can be accessed via Active Server Pages (ASP) and VBScript.
- ▶ A Perl module can be used for accessing the toolkit's function from Perl scripts.
- ▶ A library for PowerPC Macs.

Additional language bindings, such as a Java implementation, will be added in the future.

The sample application. In the following sections I'd like to detail the implementation of CGI and ASP applications for FDF deployment. The scripts and programs presented accept the order information from the *Guagua* form, and send a confirmation to the user (in FDF format, of course). The confirmation instructs Acrobat to display a message pop-up on the client and displays a little status line below the form's heading (see Figure 10.2). "Processing" the form data simply consists of saving the field contents to a text file. Obviously, this kind of form processing is not really useful in a full-blown example. However, it demonstrates dealing with the form's contents and using the FDF toolkit. In a real-world example, you would access a database and store the form contents in appropriate database fields.

All programs and scripts shown can be found on the accompanying CD-ROM, and may be used as a starting point for your own FDF development.

.2 FDF and the CGI Interface

The Common Gateway Interface (CGI).   The Common Gateway Interface is the oldest method for dynamically generating Web content and processing form data. The CGI interface isn't tied to a particular operating system or programming language, and is supported by most server software packages. There are CGI applications written in the C programming language, Perl, Python, shell scripts, Visual Basic programs, and several others.

CGI programs are stand-alone applications which are called by the Web server for each incoming request. Apart from the actual data, CGI programs (often called scripts) must generate their own HTTP header describing the generated data's MIME type. Since CGI applications generally produce HTML output, they are compatible with all kinds of browsers (assuming only commonly accepted HTML constructs are used).

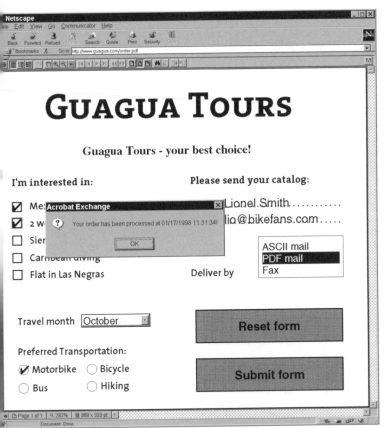

Fig. 10.2.
Confirmation that the form has been received. A write protected field under the heading is filled by the server, and a message window pops up.

C program for FDF processing. A custom C program offers an easy way for implementing FDF handling via CGI. The program listed below runs on a Unix server and needs the include file FdfTk.h with the toolkit declarations (it is part of the toolkit package). It must be linked against the FDF toolkit shared library. The final program is placed in the server's CGI directory and activated via the "Submit Form" push button of the PDF form:

```
/*
 * Demo program for demonstrating the FDF toolkit
 * Process and generate FDF form data
 * (c) Thomas Merz 1998
 */

#include <stdio.h>
#include <stdlib.h>

#include "FdfTk.h"

#define BUFLEN          256
#define DATAFILENAME    "/var/tmp/formdata.txt"

#define CONFIRM         "Guagua Tours - your best choice!"
#define STATUS          "Your order will be processed!"

void do_error(char *message) {
    fprintf(stdout, "Content-type: text/plain\n\n");
    fprintf(stdout, "Form processing error: %s\n", message);
    exit(1);
}

void main(int argc, char** argv) {
    FDFDoc theFDF;
    char name[BUFLEN], value[BUFLEN];
    char *lastfieldname = NULL, *content_length;
    FDFErc err;
    ASInt32 nBytes, datalen;
    FILE *datafile;

    if ((datafile = fopen(DATAFILENAME, "w")) == NULL)
        do_error("Couldn't save form data!");

    FDFInitialize();

    /* Evaluate environment variable for length of stdin data */
    content_length = getenv("CONTENT_LENGTH");
    if (content_length == NULL)
        do_error("Couldn't read form data!");

    datalen = atoi(content_length);

    /* Read FDF data from stdin */
    if (FDFOpen("-", datalen, &theFDF) != FDFErcOK)
```

```
        do_error("Couldn't process FDF data!");

    /* Loop: read all FDF fields and save in a file */
    while (1) {
        err = FDFNextFieldName(theFDF, lastfieldname,
                                 name, BUFLEN-1, &nBytes);
        if (err != FDFErcOK || nBytes == 0)
            break;

        err = FDFGetValue(theFDF, name, value, BUFLEN-1, &nBytes);
        if (err == FDFErcOK && nBytes != 0)
            fprintf(datafile, "%s=%s\n", name, value);

        lastfieldname = name;
    }

    FDFClose(theFDF);
    fclose(datafile);

    /* Generate FDF for the response */
    if (FDFCreate(&theFDF) != FDFErcOK)
        do_error("Couldn't generate response data!");

    /* Fill confirmation and status fields */
    FDFSetValue(theFDF, "confirmation", CONFIRM, true);
    FDFSetStatus(theFDF, STATUS);

    /* Emit FDF MIME type */
    fprintf(stdout, "Content-type: application/vnd.fdf\n\n");

    /* Write FDF to stdout and close */
    FDFSave(theFDF, "-");
    FDFClose(theFDF);

    FDFFinalize();
}
```

The program first initializes the toolkit. According to the CGI specification,
it then extracts the length of the input data stream and hands over the FDF
data from the standard input (note the "-" dummy file name for stdin) to a
toolkit function. Now the program loops through the form fields, using the
FDFGetValue() toolkit function for extracting all field names and values.
The name/value pairs are then written to a text file. Note that the form
handling loop doesn't depend on the particular PDF field names since it
doesn't extract fixed field names, but interprets all fields present in the
form. For this reason, the program fragment isn't limited to the *Guagua*
form but can be used for arbitrary FDF data.

Having processed the incoming data, the program generates an FDF response from the server to the browser. As outlined above, our response contains a confirmation and a status message with a status line. Finally, the
program emits the header line specifying the FDF MIME type and asks the

toolkit to dump the generated FDF (which up to now only exists in the server's memory) to the standard output. The Web server sends this output to the browser.

The necessary function declarations as well as detailed descriptions of all functions and error conditions can be found in the toolkit package.

10.3 FDF and Active Server Pages

Active Server Pages (ASP). ASP is Microsoft's answer to CGI. Like CGI, ASP (formerly codenamed "Denali") is targeted at dynamic Web content generation. As you'd expect, it only works on Windows systems. The ASP technique is integrated into Microsoft Internet Information Server 3.0 and above. Unlike CGI programs, ASP applications aren't executable programs or scripts, but consist of files with an *.asp* suffix which contain text, HTML tags, and scripting instructions. MIIS supports VBScript and JScript as scripting languages by default. Third-party companies will probably supply scripting engines for other languages such as Perl, REXX, Tcl, and Python. Similar to CGI, an ASP application has the advantage that the scripts don't run on the client (which exposes your custom scripts to the curious competition) and can generate HTML code suitable for all kinds of browsers.

ASP includes another well-known technique: ActiveX server components may also be embedded into ASP scripts. The first two examples below cover simple VBScript and JScript applications for generating FDF without the toolkit. The third example demonstrates the integration of the FDF toolkit as an ActiveX server whose methods can be called from within VBScript.

Unfortunately, Active Server Pages suffer from a severe restriction with respect to form data processing: while ASP scripts can nicely access the fields of an HTML form, accessing data with other MIME types doesn't work. This bug also affects the evaluation of FDF data in ASP scripts.

Let's take a quick look at the most important syntactical properties of ASP which are used in the examples, namely the syntax for script instructions and variable output. In order to distinguish between text and HTML tags on the one hand, and scripting code on the other, script instructions are bracketed with the delimiters <% and %>:

```
<% script instructions %>
```

Sending data from a script variable to the browser looks similar:

```
<%= variable %>
```

VBScript for FDF. In the first example, we refrain from processing the incoming form data and simply generate the server's response. This requires a couple of VBScript instructions, along with constant FDF elements:

```
<%@ LANGUAGE = VBScript%>
<% Response.ContentType = "application/vnd.fdf" %>
<% Message = "Guagua Tours - your best choice!" %>%FDF-1.2
1 0 obj
<<
    /FDF <<
        /Fields [ << /T (confirmation) /V (<%= Message %>) >> ]
        /Status (Your order has been processed at <% Response.write(now)%>!)
    >>
>>
endobj
trailer
<<
/Root 1 0 R
>>
%%EOF
```

Basically, this script contains an FDF fragment spiced up with some variables. We include the current time and date in a status message to make the example slightly more interesting. Note that line-end characters in the script don't matter, since the script interpreter ignores them. However, line breaks in FDF strings are part of the respective message which is generally not intended. Also, the "%FDF-1.2" header line is deliberately placed at the end of the line, since otherwise the script engine would generate a blank line at the beginning of the output.

The "Response" object includes a method for setting the appropriate MIME type of the response data. The "write" method can be used to send variable contents to the output data stream.

JScript for FDF.   The VBScript shown above could be modified to a JScript program which can also be run as an Active Server Page. To bring some variation to the examples, our JScript version will use a function which is defined in the header of the ASP file. Since JScript instructions inside SCRIPT tags could also be run on the browser, we force evaluation on the server with the RUNAT attribute. The remainder of the script (the last line) simply calls the function which is responsible for setting the correct MIME type and generating the FDF data:

```
<SCRIPT LANGUAGE=JSCRIPT RUNAT=Server>
function Write_FDF () {
    Response.ContentType = "application/vnd.fdf";
    Message = "Guagua Tours - your best choice!";
    Response.write('%FDF-1.2\r1 0 obj\r<< /FDF <<');
    Response.write('/Fields [ << /T (confirmation) /V (');
    Response.write(Message);
    Response.write(') >> ]\r/Status (Your order has been processed at ');
    now = new Date();
    Response.write(now.toLocaleString());
    Response.write('!)>> >>\rendobj\rtrailer\r');
    Response.write('<< /Root 1 0 R >>\r%%EOF');
```

```
}
</SCRIPT>
<% Call Write_FDF %>
```

The line end character "\r" results in a line break at several places in the generated FDF.

ActiveX server component for FDF.   The Dynamic Link Library (DLL) contained in the FDF toolkit can also be installed as an ActiveX server component for use with ASP. To achieve this, you have to copy the files *FdfAcX.dll* and *FdfTk.dll* from the toolkit to the ASP component directory and register the FDF library:

```
cd \WINNT\system32\inetsrv\ASP\Cmpnts
regsvr32 FdfAcX.dll
```

After these preliminaries, the FDF toolkit functions can be called from VB-Script programs on Active Server Pages. As already noted, a bug in MIIS 3 and 4 prevents evaluating incoming FDF data. This means that the Get functions of the toolkit cannot be used. We will adapt our example accordingly and assume that the PDF form's contents are sent to the server HTML encoded (instead of FDF encoded). The script for evaluating and saving the incoming data looks as follows:

```
<%@ LANGUAGE = VBScript%>
<%
' Store form field contents on file
' Form data arrive in HTML format!

    Set fs = CreateObject("Scripting.FileSystemObject")
    Set a = fs.CreateTextFile("c:\tmp\formdata.txt", True)
    a.WriteLine("Name = " + Request.Form("name"))
    a.WriteLine("Email = " + Request.Form("email"))
    a.WriteLine("Deliver = " + Request.Form("deliver"))
    a.WriteLine("Month = " + Request.Form("month"))
    a.WriteLine("Transport = " + Request.Form("transport"))
    a.WriteLine("checkbox1 = " + Request.Form("checkbox1"))
    a.WriteLine("checkbox2 = " + Request.Form("checkbox2"))
    a.WriteLine("checkbox3 = " + Request.Form("checkbox3"))
    a.WriteLine("checkbox4 = " + Request.Form("checkbox4"))
    a.WriteLine("checkbox5 = " + Request.Form("checkbox5"))
    a.Close

' Create an instance of the FDF toolkit
    Set FdfTk = Server.CreateObject("FdfApp.FdfApp")

' Define FDF as response type. The URL of the script must end in
' #FDF or the response won't work!
    Response.ContentType = "application/vnd.fdf"

' Generate confirmation fields for the form and send to the browser
    Set theFdf = FdfTk.FDFCreate
```

```
    theFdf.FDFSetValue "confirmation",
        "Guagua Tours - your best choice!", False
    theFdf.FDFSetStatus "The requested material will be sent to you!"
    Response.BinaryWrite theFdf.FDFSaveToBuf
    theFdf.FDFClose
%>
```

The script creates a text file on disk and stores the form contents on the file. The value of each field is stored along with the field name. Next, an instance of the FDF toolkit is created (i.e., the DLL is loaded), and the MIME type for the FDF data is defined using the "Response" object. With the help of several toolkit functions, the script populates the confirmation and status fields of the FDF file, and finally sends the FDF to the browser.

.4 Software for PDF Forms

Having dealt with the basics of custom programming for FDF processing applications, I'd like to present several shrink-wrapped solutions. Although PDF forms are relatively new, there are some programs which support FDF form data processing on the server.

HAHTsite.   The HAHTsite Application Server for Windows allows easy deployment of Web-based enterprise applications. The Enterprise Solution Module (ESM) adds dynamic HTML and FDF generation features to the Web server. A very interesting feature is its ability to link PDF form fields to a database via ODBC.

In order to make use of the form features, a PDF form has to be created in Acrobat Exchange. Then the Acrobat Form Wizard is launched. The Wizard opens an OLE connection to Acrobat Exchange to interpret the field names in the PDF. In the next step, the mapping between PDF field names and data base fields is defined (see Figure 10.3). Push buttons and other field types may have several actions assigned, including database transactions

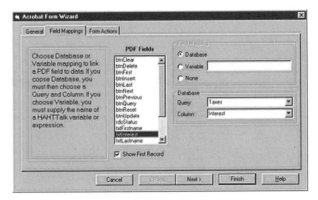

Fig. 10.3.
HAHTsite

and custom procedure calls. Apart from predefined database actions, this allows custom calculations. The wizard generates script code which can be manually adapted.

You can find more information on HAHTsite on the company's Web site:

http://www.haht.com

N/D Form. N/D Form for Windows 95 and NT from Nikao Solutions is a Foxpro application for linking PDF forms to a database. The product allows processing the contents of PDF forms without CGI programming, as well as populating PDF fields with values from a database.

As usual, the PDF forms are defined in Acrobat Exchange. Using special naming conventions for the fields, the type of the corresponding database field can be determined. For example, if a text field's name ends in "#c/10", the corresponding database field is an array of 10 characters. N/D Form supports text, number, date, and Boolean database field types. Acrobat notes can be incorporated into the database as memo fields.

To support the assignment of different databases to multiple forms, a hidden field named "Form Title" may contain the name of the corresponding database. Hidden fields are perfectly suited for communicating user-invisible information to the server or the evaluation software.

Having assigned form fields and database fields to each other, PDF or FDF files can be processed in batch mode. This makes it easy to process large numbers of forms automatically.

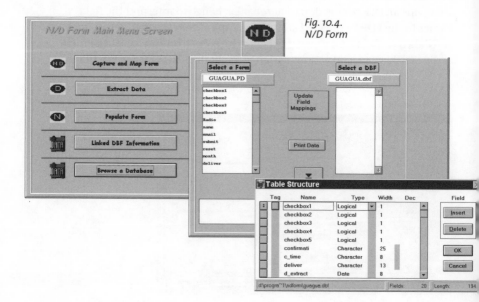

Fig. 10.4.
N/D Form

Note that Nikao Solutions is among the first companies to make use of the JavaScript features available in Acrobat Forms (see Section 7.6). More information on N/D Form can be found on the company's Web server:

```
http://www.asah.com
```

WebObjects.   WebObjects is the product name of a large Web development system from Apple Enterprise, a company formerly known as NeXT Software. WebObjects is available for Windows NT, Solaris, and NEXTSTEP, and supports dynamic generation of Web pages. To this end, most popular Web techniques are supported: scripting with JavaScript, programming with Objective-C, C, or C++, ActiveX, VRML, and database connectors.

Starting with version 3.1, WebObjects supports PDF integration and dynamic PDF generation. This feature makes use of PDF's form function and FDF.

The base product, called WebObjects Pro, contains several development tools for creating a graphical user interface and dynamically generating HTML. The large edition, called WebObjects Enterprise, adds the Enterprise Object Framework for database connectivity. Apple announced that parts of WebObjects will be included in the new Rhapsody operating system. More information on WebObjects can be found at

```
http://www.apple.com/webobjects
```

1 Full Text Retrieval and Search Engines

1.1 Motivation

Every Web surfer knows that you only tackle the unstructured information flooding in the World Wide Web with the help of search engines. There are millions of Web pages on thousands of servers. Some page somewhere surely contains the needed information – but which one is it? Web search engines read a high percentage of all available pages, and use the contents to build a database of words, a so-called full text index. Using this index, particular terms can be located quickly. Depending on the indexing and query software, complex queries – such as queries involving Boolean operators (and, or, not) for combining multiple terms – may be used.

Acrobat Catalog offers similar functionality for collections of PDF files. Catalog indexes an arbitrary number of PDF files and generates an index which consists of a .pdx file and several supplementary files and directories. This index can be distributed along with the PDF files on CD-ROM, and facilitates searching for information in large document collections. Generally, an Acrobat index isn't suited for Web usage since the query within the Search plugin for Acrobat takes place on the client. This means the index has to be available locally and not on the server. Downloading the index files, however, isn't practical due to their size.

Increasing use of PDF files brought the requirement to use the index feature for PDF files on the Web server too. Basically, the producers of indexing software have two possibilities: they can either expand the list of file formats handled by their index program (which usually covers HTML, plain text, and common text processing formats such as Word) to include PDF, or they can devise a way to incorporate an index created with Acrobat Catalog on the Web server. Verity chose the second option and supports Acrobat index files on the Web server. This shouldn't be much of a surprise, since Adobe licensed the index and search engine used in Acrobat from Verity.

Incorporating a PDF index on the Web server may be accomplished by server-specific extension mechanisms (which usually tie the Webmaster to a particular software company), or may be based on standard mechanisms such as CGI or ISAPI. Obviously, a standards-based solution is preferable if you want to keep the door to other vendors open.

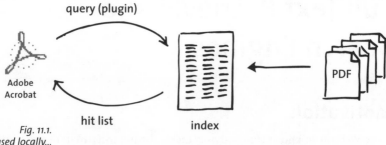

query (plugin)

Adobe
Acrobat

hit list   index

Fig. 11.1.
Index files used locally...

Full text retrieval on the Web server takes place in several steps:

► Indexing software must read all documents from the collection (sometimes also referred to as the corpus) and generate the index from their
  contents. The index is stored on the server along with the document
  files.
► The user types his query into a query form displayed in the browser.
  Usually, the query form is written in HTML.
► Another component on the server accepts the query and uses the index
  to find all files which match the query. A hit list containing the names of
  all matching files and probably other useful information (e.g., file size or
  meta-information) is returned to the browser. This component may be
  implemented as a CGI application or incorporated into the server software.
► The user loads the required documents or refines the query to narrow
  down the hit list.

Fig. 11.2.
...and on the Web

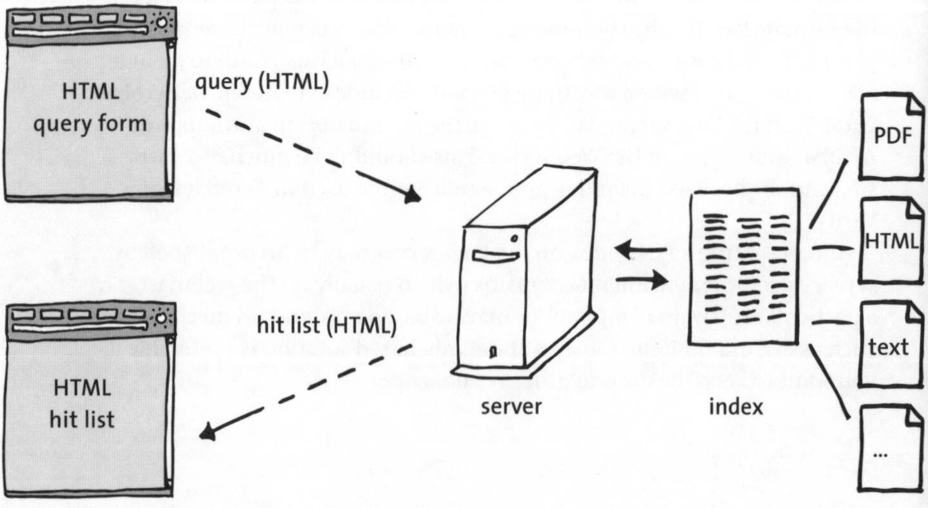

HTML
query form

query (HTML)

PDF

HTML

hit list (HTML)

text

HTML
hit list

server   index

...

Long documents may be easier to use if highlighting is employed: the query terms in the target documents are displayed in a highlight color or reverse video in order to emphasize the query terms within the page.

Indexing software for PDF on the Web. With the increasing deployment of PDF on the Web, most vendors of text retrieval software made their products PDF aware in order to index and search Acrobat documents. Currently a variety of products is available:

- ► Microsoft Index Server and the PDF IFilter from Adobe. This combination will be examined in more detail in the next section.
- ► TopicSearch and Search97 by Verity. The advantage of this solution is that Verity builds the core software used in Acrobat Catalog and Search and can therefore use Acrobat index files on the Web server without any change. Introduced in 1996, the SearchPDF software has been freely available for some time. Meanwhile, it has been replaced by the commercial product Search97. The Verity solution can be implemented on several operating systems and with many server software packages due to its support of the CGI interface (www.verity.com).
- ► Netscape Compass Server (www.netscape.com)
- ► MediaSphere/W3 by Cascade (w3.cascadenet.com)
- ► RetrievalWare from Excalibur Technologies Corporation (www.excalib. com)
- ► Fulcrum SearchServer (www.fulcrum.com)
- ► Livelink Search from Open Text Corporation (www.opentext.com)
- ► Personal Library Software PLWeb (www.pls.com)
- ► Muscat FX search engine from Muscat Limited (www.muscat.co.uk)

1.2 Microsoft Index Server and PDF IFilter

In this section will cover full text retrieval on the Web server in more detail using the freely available Index Server from Microsoft as an example. Although this indexing software is limited to the Windows platform and Microsoft's Web server, it nicely demonstrates the separate tasks related to PDF indexing and searching. In addition, this solution allows use of PDF's document info fields in the search query as well as in the hit list.

Architecture of Microsoft Index Server. MS Index Server 2.0 is part of the freely available Windows NT Option Pack which also contains Internet Information Server 4.0. The Option Pack and more details can be found at

```
http://www.microsoft.com/ntserver
```

The Index Server indexes the text contained in the documents on the server and deals with general document properties which can also be queried. By default, Index Server supports HTML, plain text, and Office 97 document

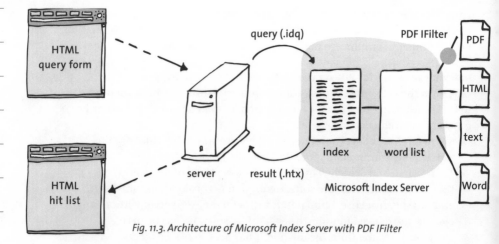

Fig. 11.3. Architecture of Microsoft Index Server with PDF IFilter

formats. Due to its modular architecture, Index Server can be extended with specialized content filters called IFilter modules. The IFilter interface is based on OLE and ActiveX and allows indexing of other file formats. Indexing takes place in three steps:

- ▸ The filter DLL extracts the text from a given file. The association defining the appropriate filter for a specific document type is stored in the Windows registry.
- ▸ A word breaking module analyzes the text and generates a word list. Since breaking text flows into separate words depends on the language used, several modules – one for each supported language – are available.
- ▸ Insignificant words, also called stop words, which should be ignored in the query, are removed from the word list (the list of stop words is also called the "noise file"). The larger the stop list, the smaller the index.

The Index Server has two tasks: first it indexes the document corpus on the server and generates the index, then it deals with incoming queries and tries to satisfy them from the generated index.

PDF IFilter. Adobe implemented a PDF module according to the IFilter specification which can be plugged into Microsoft Internet Information Server 3.0 and above and Index Server 1.0 and above. The PDF IFilter is available from the following URL:

http://www.adobe.com/prodindex/acrobat/ifilter.html

In this section I will describe the implementation of PDF-related features with the Windows NT Option Pack containing Internet Information Server 4.0 and Index Server 2.0, and PDF IFilter 1.1.

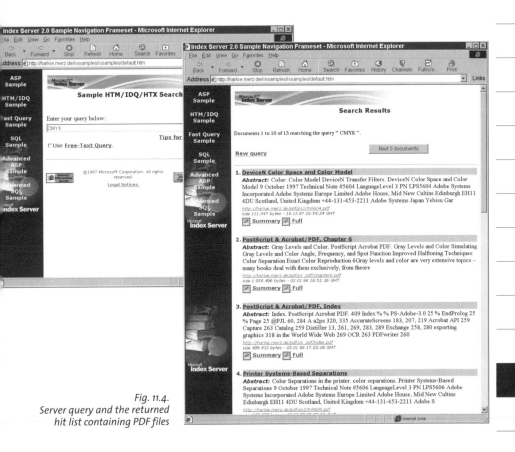

Fig. 11.4.
Server query and the returned
hit list containing PDF files

Unfortunately, Index Server 2.0 contains a severe bug which prevents indexing PDF files. For the following examples, I used a crude hack to resolve the issue.[1] However, since the problem is very severe, I expect it to be fixed soon. Note that the above combination does not work in the default configuration.

The PDF IFilter basically consists of a single DLL which creates several registry entries when installed. This DLL extracts text from PDF files and passes it on to the Index Server according to the IFilter specification. With this filter, PDF files may be indexed on the server along with HTML and Office97 documents. In addition to the file's text contents, PDF IFilter 1.1 is capable of extracting general document information which can be used for very effective queries. However, custom document info fields currently can't be used for queries because the IFilter specification doesn't allow

---

1. The basic problem is that Index Server 2.0 tries to find registry entries for .pfd (!) files instead of .pdf. Obviously, the PDF IFilter creates registry entries for .pdf files. The short-term solution was to patch the file query.dll which specifies the wrong file name suffix.

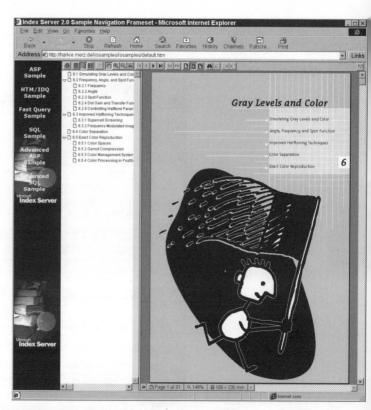

Fig. 11.5.
A PDF matching the query
is displayed in the browser

communicating this kind of information to the Index Server. Using the
four standard document info fields in index queries is covered in more detail below.

Ideally, the search terms are highlighted in the displayed documents
matching the query. Unfortunately, this isn't currently possible for PDF
files. The only work-around is to use Acrobat's "Find" tool to locate the
search terms within the returned file.

If you click the "Summary" or "Full" links on the hit list page, you will realize that these features don't work for PDF files. However, you can customize the result page template to avoid displaying these links at all. If you click
the PDF's file name, the document will be displayed in a frame within the
browser window (see Figure 11.5).

Note that the results page displays the document title info field instead
of the file name if the PDF contains this field. Since a descriptive title is
much more user-friendly than the mere file name (and the file name is displayed in the link anyway), this is another reason for properly setting document info fields.

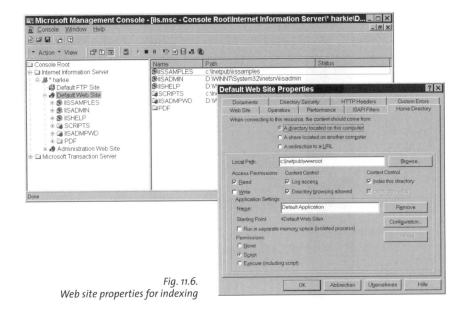

Fig. 11.6.
Web site properties for indexing

Other limitations of the software combination outlined in this section relate to the PDF's language and character set. Currently, the PDF IFilter only supports English language PDFs. This means that the word breaking algorithm may produce strange results for PDFs containing other languages. Abstracts created for PDF files generated on the Mac may contain strange characters since the character set isn't always correctly translated to the Windows encoding. Kanji PDFs can't be indexed at all. Finally, PDF files encrypted with Acrobat's security feature also can't be dealt with in the indexing process (see Section 4.4 for more details).

You should reserve plenty of disk space for the index. The index files need approximately one third of the disk space required for the document corpus.

Note that the following description only covers PDF related issues. It assumes that the Index Server is already installed and running, and that you are already familiar with the basic setup (see the Index Server documentation for more information).

Basic software setup. Let's take a brief look at the installation and setup steps necessary for implementing PDF indexing on your Web server:

- ▶ Install the Windows NT Option Pack with Microsoft Internet Information Server 4.0 and Index Server 2.0.
- ▶ Install PDF IFilter.
- ▶ Launch the Internet Service Manager (in a Management Console window) and right-click the name of your Web site or a particular directory

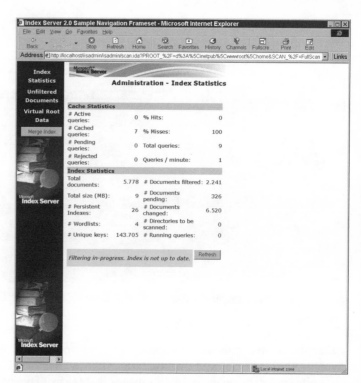

Fig. 11.7.
*Statistics page of the
index Server*

to display the properties sheet. In the "Home Directory" or "Directory" tab, make sure that "Index this directory" is checked.

► According to the size of the corpus, it may take quite a while until the complete index is generated. You can check the current status of index generation with the statistics page ("Index Server Manager (HTML)" in the Option Pack's start menu).

► As a first check, and in order to find out how many PDFs have been indexed, go to the supplied "Index Server Sample Query Form" (also to be found in the start menu) and issue the following query:

```
#filename *.pdf
```

This query asks for all PDF files, without specifying any particular content. If everything is OK, the result page will contain the number of PDFs indexed (unless this number is larger than 300, the default limit for the hit list's length).

► Copy the sample query files to your Web site's directory and customize them according to your needs. In the examples, I have used the sample pages without changing the layout and logos.

Querying the server. An index query is similar to a database query via ODBC. The Webmaster installs a simple HTML form where the user enters the text to be searched for. The form's contents are submitted to the server and processed by an *.idq* (internet data query) file. This file contains several definitions establishing a framework for the query:

```
[Query]
CiColumns=filename,size,rank,characterization,vpath,DocTitle,write
CiFlags=DEEP
CiRestriction=%CiRestriction%
CiMaxRecordsInResultSet=300
CiMaxRecordsPerPage=%CiMaxRecordsPerPage%
CiScope=%CiScope%
CiTemplate=/scripts/samples/search/%TemplateName%.htx
CiSort=%CiSort%
CiForceUseCi=true
```

Using the .idq definition and the search term, the Index Server looks for files which match the query. The server then generates abstracts, called characterizations in Microsoft lingo. Another supplementary file called *.htx* (HTML extension) is used to combine these abstracts, the files' URLs, and some additional information such as file size into an HTML page. The *.htx* file contains HTML code and several variables which specify the results to be returned from the Index Server. The HTML generated from this template is transferred to the user who can choose among the documents contained in the hit list.

Using document info fields in hit lists and queries. When your basic PDF indexing is working, you can implement document info fields. Perform the following steps in order to make the default PDF info fields title, author, subject, and keywords work in the Index Server/PDF IFilter combination:

- ▸ Although the PDF IFilter extracts the PDF info fields, with the exception of the document title, they aren't by default stored in the Index Server's property cache. But caching is necessary for retrieving the meta-information in a query. Launch the Index Server Manager and locate the entries "DocKeywords", "DocAuthor", and "DocSubject" in the properties list. Right-click on each entry and adjust the settings, using "DocTitle" as a model (see Figure 11.8).

- ▸ The *query.idq* file describes which fields are to be supplied for constructing the hit list. Add the respective entries to the "CiColumns" line:

  ```
  CiColumns=filename,size,rank,characterization,vpath,DocTitle,
  DocSubject,DocAuthor,DocKeywords,write
  ```

- ▸ If you want the info fields to appear in the hit list, add four lines after the abstract definition in *query.htx* (note that the following is only an excerpt of the file):

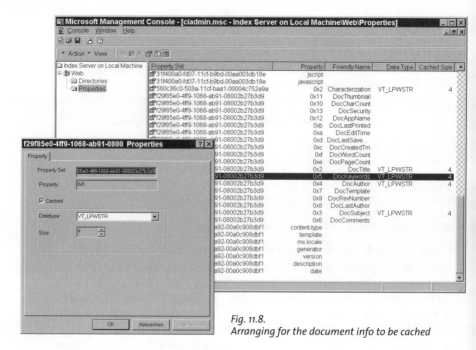

Fig. 11.8.
Arranging for the document info to be cached

```
<td><b><i>Abstract: </i></b><%characterization%></td></tr>
<tr><td></td><td><b><i>Title: </i></b><%DocTitle%></td></tr>
<tr><td></td><td><b><i>Subject: </i></b><%DocSubject%></td></tr>
<tr><td></td><td><b><i>Author: </i></b><%DocAuthor%></td></tr>
<tr><td></td><td><b><i>Keywords: </i></b><%DocKeywords%></td></tr>
```

▶ Since the "Summary" and "Full" fields don't work anyway for PDFs, you
  may as well completely delete them from the .htx template.

After these adjustments the document info fields will appear in the sum-
maries on the results page (see Figure 11.9). They are displayed below the abstract which is generated by the server.

To query for document info fields use the "@" or "#" syntax (for exact
matches or regular expressions, respectively) along with special parameters
designating the info fields. A few query examples involving the four default
info fields:

```
@DocTitle Chapter 3
#DocAuthor Thomas Merz
@DocSubject Color
@DocKeywords Color management
```

As noted above, custom info fields currently can't be indexed or searched
for. For more information on the query syntax, refer to the Microsoft documentation.

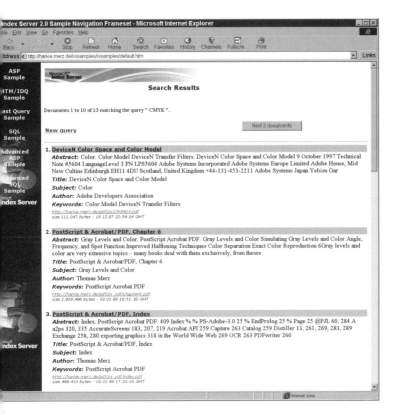

Fig. 11.9.
The customized hit list containing document info fields

11.3 The Highlight File Format

In order to let Acrobat highlight the query terms in the document, the server must not only transfer the names of the matching file, but also the location of the matches within the file. Adobe defined the "Highlight File Format" to achieve this goal. This file format is based on the Extensible Markup Language (XML) which we already encountered in Chapter 1. Currently, the Highlight File Format is only rarely supported in PDF-savvy search engines. For example, the Cascade, Muscat, and Verity products do support it, whereas Microsoft Index Server, Netscape Compass, and others don't.

The highlighting file is transferred from the server alongside the PDF file in which hits are to be highlighted. To associate the correct highlight file to a PDF, its URL is appended to the URL of the PDF document:

```
http://www.server.com/manual.pdf#xml=http://www.server.com/manual.txt
```

In this example, *manual.txt* is the highlight file describing the matches within the PDF file *manual.pdf*. The highlight file looks as follows:

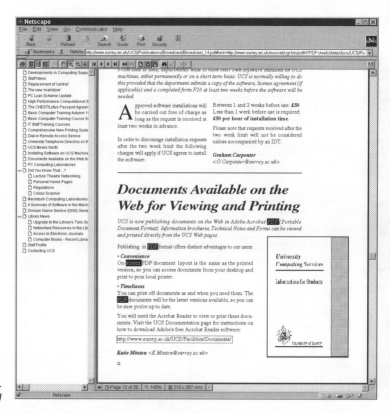

Fig. 11.10.
XML highlighting

```
<XML>
    <Body units=words color=#FF0000 mode=active version=2>
        <Highlight>
            <loc pg=0 pos=0 len=5>
            <loc pg=3 pos=4 len=1>
        </Highlight>
    </Body>
</XML>
```

This file describes the matches which are to be highlighted in red color (#FF0000). The first match starts at the first word on page 1 and consists of five words, and the second match starts at the fifth word on page 4 of the document (pages and words are counted from zero).

2 Dynamic PDF

2.1 Dynamic Web Pages

The single most important trend in Web server development is dynamic content generation. Prefabricated Web pages on the server can't satisfy all requirements for Internet and intranet applications. The restrictions imposed by static Web pages become evident in several situations:

- ▸ Constantly changing information should be presented to the user in the most current version.
- ▸ The contents of large databases would use too much disk space if stored as HTML pages.
- ▸ Answers to queries defined by user input (e.g., in a form) can't be stored ahead of time.

As an example, imagine a stock exchange service on the Web: what is stock data good for if it's not up to date? Who wants to book a last-minute trip from a server which presents week-old offers? Many important Web applications are based on information stored in a database. Only when a query is issued are the database contents converted to HTML and sent to the browser. The data volume problem is illustrated by Web search engines: how would you store the answer to all possible queries on the server?

HTML pages are easily generated automatically due to their simple structure. Even a short script with access to the data can deliver dynamic HTML. Several techniques and interfaces have been developed to incorporate external data sources in the Web server.

Most server software supports the Common Gateway Interface (CGI) as a platform and server independent standard. CGI defines a simple and general interface for plugging programs into the server. These programs may dynamically generate HTML or other data types. CGI applications can be implemented as shell, Perl, Python or other scripts, or written in languages such as C or C++. Due to their universal nature, CGI scripts can be used with almost any operating system and server software. However, for the very same reason, they usually can't take advantage of a given platform's specific advantages.

In addition to the unified CGI interface, there are a number of extension techniques defined by the vendors of Web server software. For example, Apache implements a special module interface; Microsoft uses Active Server Pages (ASP) and ISAPI (Internet Server Application Programming Interface) for scripting and programming server extensions for Microsoft Internet Information Server (MIIS); Netscape has a similar interface called NSAPI.

The considerations on static and dynamic data apply not only to HTML but also to PDF. Compared to HTML, PDF's structure is much more complex. For this reason, PDF files can't be generated with a set of simple scripts. Currently, almost all PDF applications are of a static nature, which is surely suitable for large or durable documents. However, for some kinds of applications PDF could draw from its superiority over HTML if it were only possible to generate PDF dynamically.

Let's consider the advantages of dynamic PDF by looking at some examples:

- A real estate server sends addresses of the houses offered on the server. The address list isn't formatted in HTML but in PDF for easy use as envelope labels.
- A stock exchange server generates stock price curves as PDF. The user may zoom into the graphic and therefore can choose between a long-time overview or daily variations. Currently, GIF files are used for this kind of application which means that zooming and exact detail are not available.
- Records from a database can be requested as PDF, which means they are easily archived (contrary to HTML pages containing many images). A real-life example for this kind of application will be presented later in this chapter.

12.2 Dynamic PDF Generation

Generating PDF on the server with Acrobat software.   Why shouldn't it be possible to use the common techniques for PDF generation – Distiller and PDF Writer – also for dynamic generation on the Web server? Aside from PDF Writer's platform dependence, a printer driver simply doesn't offer enough automation features and flexibility for use on a Web server. Even if one could technically work around this restriction with scripting and other control features, launching a separate application (e.g., Microsoft Word) and calling the print routine is certainly not feasible for a server with hundreds of hits per second.

Similar restrictions apply to Acrobat Distiller, although this software is available on several Unix systems (which are often used as server platforms). Distiller's performance isn't sufficient for dynamic PDF. In order to distribute information from a database, you would have to ask a report generator to generate PostScript data, convert it to PDF with Distiller, and send the output to the browser via CGI. Although this course of events could be easily automated, it isn't suited to a heavy-duty Web server since generating PostScript and converting to PDF are quite compute-intensive. Since Web deployment generally doesn't require the complete PostScript functionality, Distiller is rather an overkill for this kind of application. In addi-

Database

Report
Generator

Acrobat
Distiller

CGI script

PS

PDF

Server

PDF

Browser

Fig. 12.1.
Architecture of a Web
server with dynamic PDF
via Acrobat Distiller

tion, since Distiller is unable to produce optimized PDFs, it would be impossible to take advantage of page-at-a-time download.

FDF for dynamic data.   PDF forms offer some limited scope for dynamically changing PDF if used appropriately. As detailed in Chapter 10, the server can send FDF data to the browser which imports it into an existing PDF form. This doesn't only apply to simple confirmation messages in an order form. You could also provide data fields in the form which are to be filled with the results of a database query. In this case, the question of dynamic PDF is reduced to dynamic FDF. This format is much easier to generate, as we saw in Chapter 10 where several solutions were presented. Although existing text fields in a PDF can be populated with server-generated contents, the choice of fonts and other formatting is very poor compared to the wealth of graphics features available in general PDF files.

However, the form solution to the dynamic PDF problem has the disadvantage that the document layout is completely fixed and cannot be modified. If there is much variation in the length of the returned database records, it is difficult to produce PDF forms with the appropriate number of pages. Although adding pages to PDF forms has recently been made possible with the new Acrobat Forms plugin and JavaScript (see Section 7.6), it's not perfectly suited to our problem since the document contents outside of form fields can't be changed dynamically. Nevertheless, for applications with small amounts of data, forms might be a feasible solution. FDF can easily be generated with a report generator or script, with most of the FDF-generating work delegated to the FDF toolkit.

The PDF-PL Perl library. The first attempt at dynamically generating PDF can be found at the following URL:

http://www.ep.cs.nott.ac.uk/pdf-pl

PDF-PL is a library of Perl scripts for generating PDF. Using this library, a Perl programmer can generate PDF files without Acrobat software. The choice of Perl for implementing the library reflects the wide deployment of this powerful scripting language on Web servers, especially as CGI scripts.

PDF-PL offers functions for text output (using the base fonts) and for drawing lines and curves. This allows implementation of quite useful applications. However, larger applications are generally written in languages such as C or C++ for performance reasons. As another disadvantage, PDF-PL doesn't have functions for embedding raster images.

12.3 The PDFlib C Library

The PDFlib C programming library, which can be found on the accompanying CD-ROM, resulted from my own experiments with dynamic PDF. It allows PDF to be generated directly (without PostScript involved) for professional use on the Web server. The following goals have influenced PDFlib development:

- Although the feature set doesn't match that of PostScript, it is sufficient for common dynamic applications.
- Due to its speed and PDF-related features, it is suited for use on a Web server.
- ANSI C implementation without any platform-specific features makes it easy to port the library to several operating systems.
- The modular architecture of the library allows integration of other existing programming libraries.

The PDFlib C library can be thought of as similar to PDF Writer. Unlike this printer driver, however, the library is platform independent and isn't called via the platform-specific printer interface, but via a general application programming interface (API) which is the same on all operating systems.

PDFlib in itself doesn't constitute a useful application program, but only works as a backend module in programs for retrieving, processing, and formatting the data. After performing these steps, the program hands over the data to the library via the PDFlib API. The library generates PDF output according to the functions called by the main program. While the application programmer is responsible for issuing database queries, processing the data records, etc., PDFlib frees him or her from the nontrivial subtleties of

PDF and generates Acrobat-compatible output. The API covers the following areas:

- ► Text output in arbitrary font and size
- ► Metrics calculations for text (necessary for left-, center-, or right-aligning text)
- ► Embedding PostScript fonts
- ► Graphics functions for lines, curves, circles, rectangles, etc.
- ► Embedding raster images in the common file formats TIFF, GIF, and JPEG. If possible, compressed image data is incorporated in compressed format in the PDF output.
- ► Hypertext features, for example, bookmarks
- ► Additional PDF features which are not directly accessible in Acrobat, such as page transition effects
- ► Document info fields

Using these features, PDFlib can be used for generating complex PDF documents of arbitrary size. Detailed documentation on the PDFlib API can be found in the *PDFlib Programming Manual* which is also contained on the CD-ROM.

PDFlib is constantly being enhanced in order to add more features and lift existing restrictions. For example, currently output compression is only supported for already compressed image files. Another restriction relates to optimized PDFs which PDFlib is unable to generate. This means that page-at-time download currently isn't available.

PDFlib applications. Although the main focus for PDFlib development was Web usage, other applications are possible. For example, a PDFlib-powered report generator may answer a database query with PDF files. The PDFlib functions for raster images allow implementation of converters for TIFF,

Fig. 12.2.
How PDFLib works

GIF, or JPEG files. The PDFlib package contains an image converter for these formats, which can also be used in batch mode for conversion of large numbers of images. However, using the image converter currently suffers from its incomplete support of compression.

Embedding PDFlib applications on the Web server.   In our context, embedding PDFlib applications on the Web server is relevant. In this section, I'd like to give some hints on using PDFlib programs via CGI. This is only meant as an example, since the PDFlib implementation also allows other scenarios. Generating a DLL for the Microsoft ISAPI interface, or creating a module for the Apache server is similarly feasible.

   The CGI rules may be implemented inside the PDFlib application. This means that the program is responsible for processing CGI variables and emitting HTTP headers. Alternatively, a little shell or Perl script may be used as a wrapper for calling PDFlib applications. The following example will use a wrapper script.

PDFclock: a PDFlib example.   Although the following example doesn't make any sense in the real world, it nicely demonstrates using PDFlib and interacting with the relevant components and interfaces. To present a dynamic example without delving into database programming, we exploit the most dynamic of all data sources – the current time. The PDFclock demo application contained in the PDFlib distribution draws an analog clock

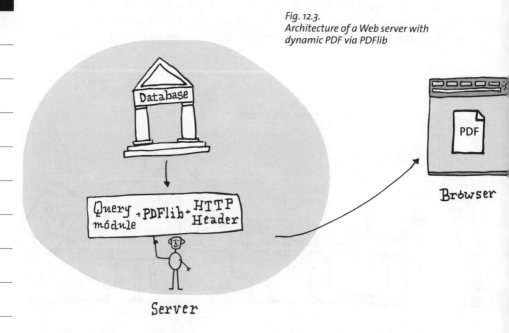

Fig. 12.3.
Architecture of a Web server with
dynamic PDF via PDFlib

showing the current time, and uses PDFlib to represent the clock in PDF format. The resulting PDF file will be sent to the Web browser via CGI (see Figure 12.4). The sample implementation uses the Apache server on a Unix system, but the technique isn't restricted to this environment.

The scenario is as follows: The user accesses a URL to the following script:

```
#!/bin/sh
TMP=/var/tmp/clock.$$.pdf
PATH=/usr/local/bin:$PATH

echo Content-type: application/pdf
echo

PDFclock -o $TMP
cat $TMP
rm $TMP
exit 0
```

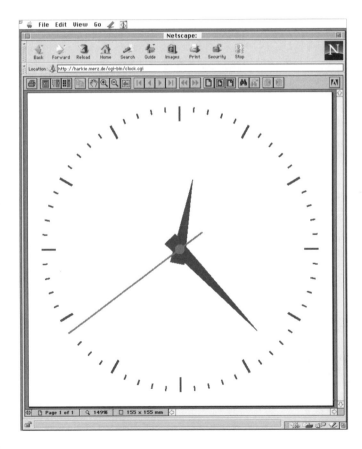

Fig. 12.4.
PDFclock – a trivial
example of a PDFlib
application

This script launches the PDFclock program for generating a temporary PDF file, and transfers the PDF output along with a suitable HTTP header with the PDF MIME type to the browser. Note that some details necessary for a real application are missing from this miniature script (for example, error handling and signal catching).

The one-page clock representation might as well stem from a static PDF file on the server. The dynamic nature of the example is illustrated by pressing the browser's reload button. This makes the browser load a new PDF from the same URL with the then-current time (on the server). This game can be repeated, and eventually be used for measuring the total transfer time by looking at the second hand's advance. Using server push, the game may even be promoted to a little animation: Each second the server sends a new PDF with the clock. A desktop clock programmed in this manner is probably the silliest application on the World Wide Web!

To give you an idea of programming with the PDFlib API, I included the heart of the PDFclock program below:

```
info              = PDF_get_info();
info->Title       = "PDF Clock";
info->Creator     = "PDFclock";

p = PDF_open(pdffile, info);

PDF_begin_page(p, 2 * (RADIUS + MARGIN), 2 * (RADIUS + MARGIN));

PDF_set_transition(p, trans_wipe);
PDF_set_duration(p, 0.5);

PDF_translate(p, RADIUS + MARGIN, RADIUS + MARGIN);
PDF_setrgbcolor(p, 0, 0, 255);
PDF_save(p);

/* minute strokes */
PDF_setlinewidth(p, 2.0);
for (alpha = 0; alpha < 360; alpha += 6)
{
    PDF_rotate(p, 6.0);
    PDF_moveto(p, RADIUS, 0.0);
    PDF_lineto(p, RADIUS-MARGIN/3, 0.0);
    PDF_stroke(p);
}

PDF_restore(p);
PDF_save(p);

/* 5 minute strokes */
PDF_setlinewidth(p, 3.0);
for (alpha = 0; alpha < 360; alpha += 30)
{
    PDF_rotate(p, 30.0);
```

```
        PDF_moveto(p, RADIUS, 0.0);
        PDF_lineto(p, RADIUS-MARGIN, 0.0);
        PDF_stroke(p);
}

time(&timer);
ltime = *localtime(&timer);

/* draw hour hand */
PDF_save(p);
PDF_rotate(p, (float)(-((ltime.tm_min/60.0) + ltime.tm_hour - 3.0) * 30.0));
PDF_moveto(p, -RADIUS/10, -RADIUS/20);
PDF_lineto(p, RADIUS/2, 0.0);
PDF_lineto(p, -RADIUS/10, RADIUS/20);
PDF_closepath(p);
PDF_fill(p);
PDF_restore(p);

/* draw minute hand */
PDF_save(p);
PDF_rotate(p, (float) (-((ltime.tm_sec/60.0) + ltime.tm_min - 15.0) * 6.0));
PDF_moveto(p, -RADIUS/10, -RADIUS/20);
PDF_lineto(p, RADIUS * 0.8, 0.0);
PDF_lineto(p, -RADIUS/10, RADIUS/20);
PDF_closepath(p);
PDF_fill(p);
PDF_restore(p);

/* draw second hand */
PDF_setrgbcolor(p, 255, 0, 0);
PDF_setlinewidth(p, 2);
PDF_save(p);
PDF_rotate(p, (float) -((ltime.tm_sec - 15.0) * 6.0));
PDF_moveto(p, -RADIUS/5, 0.0);
PDF_lineto(p, RADIUS, 0.0);
PDF_stroke(p);
PDF_restore(p);

/* draw little circle at center */
PDF_circle(p, 0, 0, RADIUS/30);
PDF_fill(p);

PDF_restore(p);
PDF_end_page(p);
PDF_close(p);
```

A commercial PDFlib application.   After the clock example, which demonstrates the principles of PDFlib programming, let's take a look at a commercial PDFlib application, which is one of the first implementations of dynamic PDF on the Web. The server is hosted by a German direct marketing company which sells address and company data on the Web. The PDFlib-

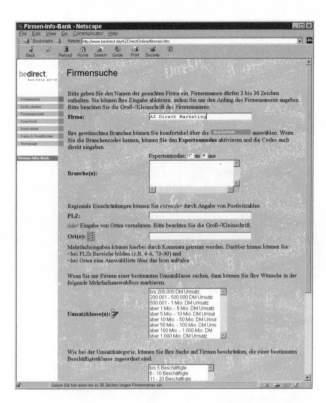

Fig. 12.5.
A user queries a database
via an HTML form...

based software for the server has been developed by the German software company debis Systemhaus GEI.

Unfortunately the database and PDF reports aren't freely available but require registering with the company and paying a base fee. (The database contents are in German anyway.)

The Web server works as an interface between user and database. A query can be issued in an HTML form (see Figure 12.5). Like a Web search engine, the server replies with a hit list. The user chooses the relevant entries from the list in order to request more detailed information on the selected company. The respective company record is queried from the database and made available for download. The reports generated from the database can be downloaded in HTML or PDF format. The PDF output is generated with a PDFlib application running on a Solaris server. The generated PDFs are available for FTP in a designated download area, or may be viewed inline in the browser (see Figure 12.6). Since FTP is used instead of HTTP as the transfer protocol, page-at-a-time download isn't possible (currently PDFlib output isn't optimized anyway).

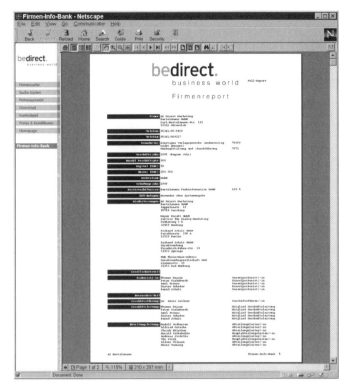

Fig. 12.6.
...and receives PDF data
created on the fly

Licensing conditions. Although the PDFlib C library is available on the CD-ROM and on the Web, this doesn't mean it is in the public domain. The package is subject to the "Aladdin Free Public License" which can be found in the file *LICENSE* in the PDFlib distribution. In a nutshell, the licensing conditions are as follows:

▸ You may copy and redistribute PDFlib if no payment is involved.
▸ You may use PDFlib to develop software for personal use or which is made available to the public under the PDFlib license too.
▸ PDFlib based software mustn't be sold without prior permission.
▸ Commercial software containing PDFlib requires a commercial license.

Please send licensing requests for commercial PDFlib deployment to the author (the address can be found on page iv of this book). Current PDFlib versions can be found on the Web at

    http://www.ifconnection.de/~tm

A Contents of the CD-ROM

Format of the CD-ROM.   The accompanying CD-ROM is a hybrid CD recorded in both Mac and ISO 9660 format.

Acrobat Reader 3.01.   The *acrobat* directory contains installation files for the English language versions of Acrobat Reader 3.01 (with the search module) for the following operating systems and platforms:
- Windows 16 and 32 bit
- Macintosh
- OS/2 Warp
- Various flavors of Unix: IBM AIX, SGI IRIX, Sun Solaris, SunOS, HP-UX, Linux, Digital Unix

Acrobat Forms.   The *forms* directory contains the Acrobat Forms plugins (Maker and Filler) for the platforms listed above (except OS/2 Warp). The Maker plugin requires Acrobat Exchange, the Filler plugin Acrobat Reader.

Byteserver Perl script.   The *bserver* directory contains a Perl script for the byterange protocol for use on older Web servers via the CGI interface (see Section 9.2). The versions for MS-DOS and Unix differ only in the line-end characters.

PDFlib.   The *pdflib* directory contains the C source code for the program library PDFlib described in Chapter 12, and some demo programs. The package is available in two formats: a Windows ZIP file, and a Unix tar archive compressed with gzip. More information on using the library can be found in the manual which is included as a PDF file in the same directory. How to generate the library from the C code is described in the *readme* file.

html2ps.   The *html2ps* directory contains a Perl script by Jan Kärrmann for converting HTML files to PDF via PostScript (see Section 2.4). The package consists of a tar archive compressed with gzip. More information on using the script can be found in the manual in the same directory.

Form processing programs and scripts.   The *scripts* directory contains the sample program for FDF processing from Chapter 10:
- The subdirectory *cgi* contains the C program *order.c* and a corresponding *makefile* for use with the FDF toolkit and the CGI interface.
- The subdirectory *asp* contains three scripts for use with the FDF toolkit and Active Server Pages: *order.vb* for VBScript, *order.js* for JScript, and *order.ax* as ActiveX server component.

PDF files. The *pdf* directory contains several PDF files:

- The file *primer.pdf* containing Chapter 6 of this book to allow copy-and-paste with respect to the pdfmark examples.
- The file *menu.pdf* with all Acrobat menu functions as PDF clickable buttons (see Section 6.5).
- *guagua.pdf* with the sample fields discussed in Section 7.2.
- *algebra.pdf* with D. P. Story's Algebra quiz as a JavaScript enhanced PDF form.
- *isbn.pdf* with several JavaScript samples (see Section 7.6).

Auxiliary PostScript file for named destinations. The *ps* directory contains the PostScript file *namedest.ps* by Phil Smith, which specifies named destinations for every page of a PDF file.

Copy *namedest.ps* into Distiller's *startup* directory. When PostScript files are converted to PDF a named destination is created for each page, after the pattern "Page1" etc. Further hints on using named destinations can be found in Section 8.6.

GIF icons for Acrobat Reader and PDF. The *icons* directory contains the logos for PDF files and for downloading Acrobat Reader described in Section 9.1.

Acrobat control for Microsoft Internet Explorer. The *ocx* directory contains a version of the Acrobat ActiveX control (OCX) for Microsoft Internet Explorer which is newer than the one contained on the Acrobat 3.01 CD-ROM (see Section 2.1 for details).

B PDF-related Web Resources

The Web site for this book with samples, additional material, and updates can be found at

```
http://www.ifconnection.de/~tm
```

Naturally, Adobe's Web site is a great place to regularly scan for news and updates:

```
http://www.adobe.com/prodindex/acrobat
```

Emerge, a PDF service house and reseller, collects lots of useful Acrobat-related resources on their Web site. Among much other stuff, you can find free Acrobat plugins on their site. They also host several PDF-related mailing lists:

```
http://www.pdfzone.com
```

PDF has its own newsgroup where many questions concerning Acrobat and PDF are discussed:

```
news://comp.text.pdf
```

Glyphica, a California-based production consultancy company, hosts the PurePDF site which offers a wealth of interesting material on Acrobat and PDF:

```
http://www.purepdf.com
```

Ghostscript, the well-known PostScript and PDF interpreter, displays and prints PDF files, and works as a free Distiller substitute. Ghostscript's home page can be found at

```
http://www.cs.wisc.edu/~ghost
```

Index

About the Author

Thomas Merz works as a software developer and technology consultant and is the owner of a small publishing house in Munich, Germany. He became aware of PostScript for the first time in 1985 during a lecture on computer graphics while studying mathematics and computer science. Since then he has not been able to escape from the subject: employed at a software company for several years, he developed drivers and converters. Personal relations awakened his interest in fonts and typography ("Typography is the mathematics among the arts"). Translating and typesetting computer books – specializing in computer graphics, Internet, and cryptography – gave him ample opportunity to get the user's perspective on DTP. Since 1993 his use of PostScript and digital books have led almost inevitably to an intensive involvement with Adobe Acrobat. The Internet did the rest – as a long-term Web addict, this author could not resist the excitement offered by the combination of Acrobat and the World Wide Web.

Thomas Merz published the *TerminalBuch PostScript* in 1991, and *PostScript & Acrobat/PDF: Applications, Troubleshooting, and Cross-Platform Publishing* in 1996. In addition, he is a regular contributor to various German computer magazines.

As well as consulting in the areas of publishing, the Internet, and cryptography, Thomas Merz teaches at the University of Augsburg, and also offers user and developer seminars on PostScript and Acrobat.

Colophon

Layout and illustrations.   The layout and illustrations for this book were designed by Alessio Leonardi (Leonardi.Wollein, Berlin). Hand drawn sketches were scanned, traced, and processed to finished form using Macromedia FreeHand and Adobe Photoshop. Screen shots were taken on Macintosh and Windows computers and modified with Adobe Photoshop. The picture on the inside front cover was created with alpha device, a custom program for converting images to text files, with the characters of the text corresponding to the brightness of the respective pixels.

Archetipetti.   The figures found on the cover and in many of the illustrations are called Archetipetti and were also designed by Alessio Leonardi. The upper class of the Archetipetti gang have assembled in several PostScript fonts, which also include matching symbols (for example Letterine Archetipetti One). Some of these fonts are available from FontShop in Berlin.

Fonts.   The basic font used in this book is TheAntiqua, which is not yet commercially available. Like all fonts used in this book it is part of the FF Thesis font family, designed by the dutch typographer Luc(as) de Groot who works in Berlin. Thesis is said to be the most extensive digitized font family: the basic variations TheSans, TheSerif, and TheMix each include 48 fonts, carefully matched to each other. In addition to the text face TheAntiqua, there is also a monospaced variant, which we use in examples and listings. The picture on the inside front cover consists of TheSans Mono Condensed-ExtraBold at 2.5 points. Finally there are also Typewriter and Correspondence variants.

We wish to thank Luc(as) de Groot and FontShop Berlin/FSI for their friendly support with the use of fonts.

Page layout and imagesetting.   This book was laid out and typeset using Adobe FrameMaker 5.5 for Macintosh. The PostScript output was converted to PDF for imagesetting.

Printing: Saladruck, Berlin
Binding: Buchbinderei Lüderitz & Bauer, Berlin

6170 158

CHECK FOR 1co PARTS